Minefields in Their Hearts

Minefields in Their Hearts

The Mental Health of Children in War
and Communal Violence

**Edited by Roberta J. Apfel, M.D., M.P.H.
and Bennett Simon, M.D.**

Yale University Press   New Haven and London

This book is a project of Children in War and Communal Violence:
International Working Group, an affiliate of the International
Association of Child and Adolescent Psychiatry and Allied Professions.

Excerpts from Yitzhak Katzenelson, "The First Ones," in *Song of the
Murdered Jewish People,* trans. N. Rosenbloom, reprinted with permission
of Hakibbutz Hameuchad Publishing House, Tel Aviv, and Ghetto
Fighters' House (Beit Lohamei Haghettaot), Kibbutz Ghetto Fighters,
Israel.

Designed by Sonia L. Scanlon.
Set in Bembo type by Keystone Typesetting, Inc.,
Orwigsburg, Pennsylvania.
Printed in the United States of America by BookCrafters,
Inc., Chelsea, Michigan.

Library of Congress Cataloging-in-Publication Data
Minefields in their hearts : the mental health of children in war and
    communal violence / edited by Roberta J. Apfel and Bennett Simon.
        p.   cm.
    Includes bibliographical references and index.
    ISBN 0-300-06570-1 (alk. paper)
    1. Children and war.   2. Children and violence.   3. Children—
Mental health.   4. Psychic trauma in children.   I. Apfel, Roberta J.,
1938–   .   II. Simon, Bennet, 1933–   .
HQ784.W3M54   1996   96-10976
305.23—dc20   CIP

A catalogue record for this book is available from the British Library.

The paper in this book meets the guidelines for permanence
and durability of the Committee on Production Guidelines
for Book Longevity of the Council on Library Resources.

10 9 8 7 6 5 4 3 2 1

Contents

To our children and our children's children

Acknowledgments

We started out our study of children and violence expecting to learn a great deal about human aggression. We did not know how much we would learn about altruism, empathy, hope, and long-term persistence in working with children in very difficult circumstances. The contributors to this book are among those from whom we learned about these life-affirming qualities, and it is to them that we owe an enormous debt, not only for their contributions to this book but also for their contributions to caring for and about children with a deep humanitarian passion combined with keen intelligence. This has been for us a great gift.

Many people contributed directly and indirectly to this project, from our earliest efforts in working on the issues of children in war through the published book. Special thanks to Judith Kestenberg and Norman Garmezy, who provided models for emulation and conceptual frameworks with which to begin the work. The 1988 Physicians for Human Rights group (which included Bennett Simon) that investigated the medical consequences of the Intifada—Jack Geiger, Jennifer Leaning, and Leon Shapiro—also provided incentive and inspiration.

We thank the Children in War and Communal Violence: International Working Group, especially Donald Cohen, James Garbarino, and the other members of the group who have contributed to the book. Tesfay Aradon and M. Brinton Lykes helped in many ways. Several foundations, including the Irving Harris Foundation, have generously supported the activities of the working group. They have also played a role in the genesis of this book, as well as in facilitating bibliography on children in war.

The institutions with which we are affiliated in Boston have been important for this work. At the Cambridge Hospital, we appreciate the backing of the chairpersons—Myron Belfer, Robert Dorwart, and Malkah Notman—and of John Mack. We thank Holly Aldrich, Mary Harvey, Judith Herman, Janet Yassen, and others in the Victims of Violence Program and the Community Crisis Response Team, as well as colleagues and students whose curiosity about our work helped us move forward. We thank our colleagues at the Boston Psychoanalytic Society and Institute, who welcomed presentations of our material, hosted meetings, and generously helped support the Slovene Foundation's work with Bosnian refugee children. Diana Nugent and her staff have supported us with generous hospitality and spirit. Doris Shay and Maurice Vanderpol have been steady supporters, and we are deeply grateful to them for introducing us to another colleague and friend, Marion Pritchard. James Herzog has also set an example with his long-term work on children and the Holocaust. Evoleen Rexford and James and Ida Mann were there from the beginning.

The Massachusetts Psychiatric Society Newsletter and Eileen Kahan provided us with the opportunity to report back regularly during our sabbatical year in Israel (1989–90).

Family, friends, and colleagues here in the United States to whom we owe special thanks include Eugene Brody, Amy Kass, and Elliott Mishler and Vicki Steinitz (who, with M. Brinton Lykes and Tesfay Aradon, gave substantial help on our chapter of the book). Pauline Stitt, Sally Mack, and John and Suellyn Woodall set an example of steady commitment. Hannah Kranzberg, Margot and Lowell Rubin, and Stanley and Marion Simon generously helped support early stages of the work. Joy Ungerleider Mayerson, Jeanne Springer, and A. Joshua Sherman were steady sources of encouragement and ideas. Marie Zinkevich provided an example of empathy and optimism in her work with people in situations of great physical and mental distress. Sherry Grossman and Roberta Isberg helped us in interviewing young children in the Boston area. Noah Springer, at age eight, helped us to launch our interview studies of children during the Persian Gulf War and to continue our interaction with students in Boston. Jeffrey Rubin and Shoshana Sokoloff assisted with the conference on children in war, as did Sarah Shay, who contributed artistically.

Colleagues and friends around the world whose work has especially informed our thinking include Hubertus Adam, Silvia Amati, Helga Braun, Julia Braun, Gertrud Hardtmann, Anica Kos, Maria Pelento, Peter Riedesser, Gillian Straker, Ursula Walters, and Vamik Volkan.

Foundations that gave crucial support in the early stages include Conanima, Dorot, and Margate.

We are deeply grateful to the numerous people here and abroad who volunteered to be formally interviewed about or to informally discuss their experiences as children in war and persecution, as well as to our patients, from whom we have also learned a great deal about trauma and resiliency. Julia Braun, Arn Chorn, Frieda Grayzel, Ester and Karoly Kelemen, Nicholas Kouretas, Maria Lymberis, Judit Mezaros, Samia Mora, Maria Orvid and her colleagues in Poland, Dennis Skiotis, Nettie and Maurice Vanderpol, and several Harvard students from Southeast Asia and from the Balkans are among those who shared their experiences with us. In particular we have learned much from those who suffered from persecution and violence as children or young adults and who later became mental health professionals.

In our visits to Israel, including our sabbatical year, we encountered and worked with many to whom we are deeply appreciative. Professor Albert Solnit set an example as a Freud Professor by combining clinical skills, research, scholarship, and activism in many humanitarian endeavors. Eric Cohen, in 1989–90 the dean of the faculty of social sciences of the Hebrew University in Jerusalem, endorsed and supported our conference on children in war, and the staff of the

Freud Center there made the conference possible. Atara Kaplan gave us the marvelous opportunity to work with trainees in the department of psychiatry at Hadassah Hospital. Lisa Cooper assisted us in preparing our teaching videotape from the children in war conference, an idea suggested by Sarah Kass.

Diana Abdel-Nour, Suhaila Abu-Ghosh, Malka and Kloni Haas, Abla Nasir, Bracha Rosenberg, and Georgette Shamshoun made possible our work with the groups of Israeli and Palestinian children and their families whom we have followed in our interview study. To the children themselves—now teenagers— much thanks. Rachel Durlacher, Judy Erez, and Beth and Bill Knittle arranged our meetings with classes of high school children in Israel and Jordan.

Thanks to Moshe Abramowitz, Cairo Arafat, the Abu-Zaid family— Mohammed, Wafa, Beissan, and Rajwa, Moustafa Barghouti, Rami Bar-Giora, Rina Bar-Lev Elieli, Dan Bar-On, Yoram Bilu, Judy Blanc, Rachel Blass, Nomi Chazan, Yechezkiel Cohn, Alice and Robert Cooper and Lisa Cooper, Chaim Dasberg, Shmuel Ehrlich, Rivka Eiferman, Eyad El-Serraj, Sidra and Yaron Ezrachi, Yolanda Gampel and Galit Gampel, Galia Golan-Gild and Doron Gild, Charles and Judy Greenbaum, Cornelius Gropp, the Gutkowski family— Silvio, Hilda, Ana, and Natalia, the Haberman-Browns family—Shmuel, Bonna, Tiferet, Uriel, Bezalel, Amitai and Adir Chai, Jocelyn Hattab, Judith Issroff, Moslih Kanaaneh and Marit Netland, Levi Kelman and Congregation Kol Haneshama, Ilany Kogan, Lilli Kopecky, Tami Kron, Sue and Ilan Kutz, Nathaniel Laor, Eitan Lewow, Itamar Luria, Shafiq Mashala, Rina and Raphael Moses, Rana Nashashibi, Abla Nasir, Yuval Neria, Ruth and Natan Nevo, Anne Nixon, Anne Marie Oliver and Paul Steinberg, Phyllis Palgi, Tirza Sandbank, Yehoyakim Stein, Phillip and Leah Veerman, Anne and Martin Wangh, Anita and Eugene Weiner, Micki and Hanoch Yerushalmi, Beth Yuval, and Ruth Zafrir.

Special thanks to the Children of War Group, especially Judith Thompson, Arn Chorn, Miriam and Jonathan Bentwich, and Sana Al-Okbi.

In that mixture of labor of love and pure labor that goes into writing a book, we received substantial assistance and encouragement from Stacey Liberty, Louise Neiterman, Helene Ragone, and Rochelle Tayag.

Steven Swanson's report on the children of Rwanda and his concern for the "minefields in the hearts" provided the inspiration for the title of the book, and Celia Savitz helped craft it further.

At Yale University Press, Gladys Topkis gave her full support and energy to this book from the beginning. Heidi Downey skillfully and tactfully helped to make the book an organic whole, and she and Gladys Topkis made it a privilege and a learning experience to be edited. Janyce Beck shepherded the work from start to finish, and Nancy Herington prepared the index.

Our children provide a continuous source of inspiration, challenge, growth, hope for the future, and love: Amy Simon, Celia Savitz, Jonathan Simon, Karin and Michael Savitz, and Molly Savitz.

Roberta J. Apfel and Bennett Simon

CHAPTER ONE

Introduction

ROBERTA J. APFEL AND BENNETT SIMON

"Interview me first! I am a child of war," exclaimed a Palestinian teacher. We were visiting her classroom in wartime to interview her eight-year-old pupils. Half in jest, this competent adult revealed that wars have marked her life significantly. The child of war lives within her and is agitated anew when she observes the struggles of the children in her charge and worries about herself and her own children.

We have learned about such minefields in the heart of the child—and in the heart of the grown child—from interviews with Israeli and Palestinian children and their teachers, from our clinical work, from interviews with people who were children during the Holocaust, and from autobiographies and biographies of adults who were children during other situations of war or communal violence. From colleagues who have worked extensively and intensively with children we have also learned that it is possible to help reduce the impact of these explosive forces.

In this book we and other mental health professionals speak of children wounded by war, persecution, and communal violence. The wounds are caused by direct bodily injury, by witnessing violence done to others, and by separation from loved ones. The loss of a childhood and of the opportunity to be nourished in a secure environment are overarching deprivations. Their effects may be felt into the next generations.

We have also come to realize that children have unexpected resources and resiliency that may emerge during and after violent trauma. Children may grow up strong at the broken places, with qualities that permit them not only to survive but also to flower. Trauma produces "salutogenic," or health-promoting, forces (Antonovsky, 1987) as well as "pathogenic," or destructive, ones. We believe that psychologically informed interventions, from individual psychotherapy to communal programs, can shift the balance between the pathogenic and the salutogenic forces by taking advantage of this resilience.

Through the wisdom of the clinicians and researchers who have contributed to this book, we have learned that work with children living in situations of war and communal violence, or with adults who lived through these situations as children, is profoundly political. A commitment to helping such children inevitably means a commitment to try to change the conditions that allow the violence. Our vision is that psychologically informed interventions ultimately empower the children by enlarging their self-understanding to include the moral, political, social, and economic contexts of their lives. This is a broader and more active definition of psychological work than is used by many of our colleagues. Psychotherapists trained in individual work are geared to the child's self-understanding and are often uneasy about promoting action, especially in controversial political arenas. Even our statement that there are powerful health- and growth-promoting resources within the traumatized child has political overtones. Although it may be taken to justify not worrying too much about the consequences of violence to children, we intend it to encourage those who work with traumatized children to understand what growth resources lie within the children and the adults working with them. Claiming political neutrality is not a nonpartisan act, for silence may signal acquiescence to or even collusion with those who perpetrate the violence.[1] As psychoanalysts, we take "therapeutic neutrality" to mean a nonjudgmental stance vis-à-vis the conflicted feelings within each patient. It is crucial to realize that maintaining such neutrality in the clinical setting does not preclude taking a stance about what has happened to the person who is the patient. Indeed, clinicians working in violent situations need to break new ground and to innovate beyond the comforts provided by the guidelines of their training. These issues are addressed throughout this book, most notably in the next chapter, by Gillian Straker, on ethical issues.

Working with children affected by the violence of international or civil warfare or by violence in the streets demands long-term commitment, and long-term commitment requires the conviction that such work will help prevent further suffering and violence. Awareness of the amazing resiliency of children themselves as well as of the resourcefulness and dedication of those who work with them can help everyone to maintain the morale for persisting over the long haul.

We did not begin working in the area of children and violence until fairly recently; indeed, most of our professional time and effort is not spent on direct work with children. We both have backgrounds in clinical psychiatry and psychoanalysis, and one of us also has a background in public health—specifically, in maternal and child health. Through clinical work, political work, and medical human rights investigations we became aware of the profound psychological consequences that violence has for children. Our interest and commitment crystallized during a sabbatical year in Israel, where we worked with both Israelis and Palestinians and organized an international conference on children in war, held in Jerusalem in June 1990. Since then we have affiliated with others who share our

1. This view is most clearly articulated in the posthumously published work of Ignacio Martín-Baró (1994), one of six Jesuits slain in 1989 in El Salvador. See Eth, 1992, for an argument that takes some issue with the position espoused by Martín-Baró and others.

interests, many of whom have dedicated years to working with children affected by violence. With Donald Cohen and James Garbarino we formed Children in War and Communal Violence: International Working Group,[2] an organization of mental health professionals that has supported the writing and editing of this book, and a number of whose members have contributed chapters. This affiliation has been gratifying and sustaining, and it has confirmed our belief in the value of exchanging knowledge and experience.

A few mental health professionals are in the field full time, working in war zones; others are involved in research, teaching, and part-time clinical and programmatic activities. There is room for a great range of contributions, enough to meet the interests, temperaments, skills, stage of life, and moral and political commitments of all mental health professionals seeking to enter the field. We hope that the information presented here will persuade others to take an active stance in work with such children by showing that there is a great deal of accumulated and effective knowledge and skill on which to draw and a variety of needs to be met.

Among those committed to working with children traumatized by violence are some who themselves suffered as children under war or communal violence. We represent another group. As children during World War II, we were fortunate enough to live in the United States, at a safe remove from the violence. Even so, the war surrounded and colored our lives. Our parents were directly involved in the war effort. We followed the war in newsreels and on the radio, vicariously experiencing the excitement and dread of air raids and anxiously wondering when the war would come closer and disrupt our lives still further.[3] As Jews, we had special anxieties about the fate of our distant relatives in Europe and of the Jewish people. Yet we did not lose anyone close to us or have the trajectory of our lives broken. The war was far away "over there," and it was not until years later that we appreciated how terrifying those years must have been for those who experienced the violence more closely. We were aware of but not overwhelmed by the negative emotions and memories that make talking about and working on war so conflicted for many survivors of violence and persecution.

Our hope is that this book will have emotional resonance both for those mental health professionals sensitized to the suffering of children through their own experiences in childhood and for those with remote and indirect experience. In particular, chapter 3, by James Garbarino and Kathleen Kostelny, on child development; chapter 9, by Dan Bar-On, on the intergenerational transmission of trauma; and chapter 10, by Yael Danieli, on care of the caretakers, address the contemporary experiences of the caregivers in relation to trauma in their own early development.

2. Organized soon after the Gulf War, the working committee is affiliated with the International Association of Child and Adolescent Psychiatry and Allied Professions.

3. See Tuttle, 1992, for a description of the impact of World War II on American children.

Definitions

We have spoken thus far in general terms about children, violence, trauma, resiliency, healthy and unhealthy development, and therapeutic interventions. Each of these terms is subject to controversy, and each carries a host of overtones and reverberations, necessitating some definition.

Child

At what age does a child stop being a child and become something else? In this book we are adopting the somewhat arbitrary age limit of about eighteen; after that age, we speak of youth, and then of young adulthood. Each author more or less follows this convention but specifies the age range discussed in her or his contribution.

But the definition of *child* is problematic in two ways. First, one must understand the historical, social, and political contexts in which a definition of childhood is developed. For example, the United Nations Convention on the Rights of the Child adopted age fifteen as the lower limit for military service. Considerable political and legal controversy attended this choice, with the Scandinavian countries and the Organization of African Unity pushing for age eighteen, other countries for age twelve, and the United States, for complex reasons, holding out for age fifteen. Differing conceptions of what constitutes a family and of what role children play in the family also shape ideas on when childhood ceases, influencing such attitudes as those toward child labor.

The definition of childhood is problematic also because of the psychological point mentioned at the beginning of this chapter: the child lives on inside the adult. That child may be a source of energy, vitality, and hope or, conversely, of lethargy, apathy, and despair. A great deal of therapeutic work with adults traumatized by childhood violence involves a reawakening of childhood—often a tumultuous and painful reawakening. Concomitantly, there may be a revival of the childhood of the helping person that in turn influences how that therapist hears and responds to the adult seeking help. Parenting, of course, involves a continuous dialogue between the chronological child and the child within the parent. "It is never too late to have a happy childhood," proclaims an American bumper sticker. The slogan is overoptimistic, but it does convey the truth that one's childhood is forever being reshaped as the individual develops and revisits that childhood. In broad definition, then, childhood is a phenomenon manifesting itself throughout the life cycle and is also an intergenerational phenomenon.

War and Communal Violence

In this book we deal with situations of frank warfare—between nations or between factions within nations—and with violence in communities where every child has witnessed or expects to witness violence and has been or expects to be violated. We use the term *communal violence* for the latter category rather than *urban violence,* because communal violence is not confined to cities. Further, at least in the United States, urban violence has come to connote violence generated among poor people of color. It has become yet another term that tends to obscure, to distance us from some plain and painful facts.[4]

As for war, there is a spectrum of types affecting children: at one extreme are situations in which children are the incidental victims of armed warfare. The wars in Lebanon, a complex mixture of civil warfare and warfare with Israel, have not been characterized by systematic assaults on children, but thousands of surviving Lebanese children nevertheless have been maimed, orphaned, dislocated, disillusioned. At the other extreme are situations in which an aggressor specifically tries to maim, kill, and spiritually destroy the enemy's children. Clear examples of terror and destruction aimed at children include the Nazi persecution and extermination of Jewish children; the Khmer Rouge's use of children as slaves and its torture and murder of countless Cambodian children; and the Argentinian military government's "dirty war" against the children of "Leftists." There is evidence that children, in trying to make sense of the violent world around them, perceive the different motivations for the violence they suffer, and their psychological responses reflect that awareness. However, there is not always a distinction between children as incidental victims of armed conflict and as objects of genocide. The Turkish persecution of the Armenians may not have been genocidal at the outset, but it became so over time. Further, military strategies often involve attacking civilian populations, cutting off supplies of food, water, and medicines and thus causing death and disease among young children. Guerrilla warfare and counterinsurgency in Central America and Africa have often involved such activities by one or another of the antagonists. There are also instances of actions and inactions that eventuate in the victimization of children. In the United States, for example, legislators have been reluctant to ban assault weapons from the streets, and the funding and staffing of social services and schools are grossly inadequate to the needs of children.[5]

In the interests of producing a book of manageable length we have had to neglect some important topics. Some omissions were dictated by the wide availability of many excellent books; for example, our authors do not deal with intrafamilial violence.[6] In our chapter prefaces we identify areas that are not covered and suggest some existing resources. We also have not addressed how

4. We realize that the term *communal violence* also has shortcomings; it may imply that the community alone is responsible for the level of violence rather than being subject to forces beyond its control.

5. A 1969 paper by Evoleen Rexford describes the "discrepancies between word and act, inconsistencies between wish and performance, contradictions between aim and investment in accomplishment of that aim" in relation to child services. That description, tragically, is still accurate.

6. See the *Bibliography on the Psychological and Psychosocial Aspects of Children in War and Situations of Violence,* available in print or on computer disk from the editors.

children who have not been directly subjected to violence deal with their awareness of extensive violence in their neighborhoods and in the world at large.
Adults, including mental health professionals and educators, are frequently unsure of how best to talk with children about their fears and concerns regarding
violence. This problem warrants detailed treatment in its own right; we hope that
the material in this book will stimulate others to fill the gap.

The nature of the problems of war and communal violence shifts over time
and with locale. History never repeats itself exactly. A problem pressing at one
moment all too easily is eclipsed by a newer problem of greater magnitude or
immediacy—thus Rwanda quickly displaces Bosnia from the headlines. The
problems of street children, despite their long antecedents, have only recently
(and grudgingly) been recognized (see Amnesty International, 1990, 1992, on
Guatemala and Brazil). We hope that this book yields general principles that can
be applied even though times, locales, and situations change.

Trauma

Several contributors address the problem of formulating a useful definition
of trauma, especially William Arroyo and Spencer Eth in chapter 4, on traumatic
stress reactions, and Mona Macksoud, J. Lawrence Aber, and Ilene Cohn, in
chapter 12, on the impact of war on children. In American psychiatric usage,
trauma tends to be defined as the effects of external events impinging on the
individual—events that are beyond the usual expectation of what life should be.
Whether the trauma is acute (resulting from a car accident, a murder, a fire, a
rape) or chronic (for example, some forms of child abuse), this definition posits a
world of reasonable stability and sanity in which such events and patterns of
behavior are distinctly unusual and deemed abnormal. To the children described
in this book, however, the world is predictably violent and cruel (the second
definition of trauma). Both definitions fill a need for an ideal standard and a need
to acknowledge a painful reality. It is essential to keep both in mind.[7]

Normal and Abnormal Development

Parallel to the need for two definitions of trauma is the need for a bifocal
view of development. One view defines norms of development as a universal
standard—an ideal for the dignity, well-being, and unfolding of the full potential
of the child. The other acknowledges that most children in the world suffer from
poverty, malnutrition, and violence, living in situations vastly different from
those in which our Western norms of child development have been formulated.

7. We note that the older definition of *trauma* (used especially in psychoanalysis) to characterize such events as the birth of a sibling has almost disappeared. It is no longer thinkable to
use the same word to denote the child's experience of the birth of a sibling and the murder of a
sibling.

Being "normal" and developing as best one can—let alone surviving—may require social, cognitive, and emotional skills that are as yet unarticulated and barely understood in our conventional psychological schemas. But the two perspectives on development can be seen as complementary, and that complementarity is implicit in much of this book. For example, Michael Greene's chapter on devising programs for inner-city youth in violent situations (chapter 7) draws on a deep knowledge of development under great adversity but is informed by a knowledge of the more ordinary developmental tasks of teenagers. His findings on how to work effectively with troubled youth in turn contribute to a view of what might enrich the moral and spiritual lives of youth living in more affluent and secure circumstances.

Of course, specifics of context and culture influence both the form and the content of development. After decades of investigation into what is universal in development and what is culture-specific, we still do not have clear answers. We are especially likely to invoke our own biases when it comes to value issues. The role of corporal punishment in child rearing is a pressing example; in the United States today, schools and social service agencies often encounter refugee children from groups with ideas about beating children that are very different from those of many Americans. Joseph Westermeyer and Karen Wahmanholm (chapter 5) provide more examples.

We also need to know much more about how community status affects the development of individual children. Again, there are important differences between children who have been resettled in a country where they expect to stay and those whose settlement is temporary. Also important is a knowledge of the spiritual and cultural integrity of the refugee child's community. During some thirty years of war and persecution by the Ethiopians, Eritreans, even those in exile, maintained a strong sense of cultural integrity and an impressive dedication to the welfare of their children (Aradom, 1994). Other cultures and groups have been so devastated and demoralized by warfare and persecution that their children are at great risk of being cut off from their roots and subjected to an even more anarchic development. A few Native American groups, nearly extinguished, have struggled with this issue (see Fineman, 1995).

Age and stage of development shape how a child responds to such trauma as separation from or loss of a loved one. Children from age two to eight, for example, are likely to ascribe the terrible things that happen to them or to their loved ones to their own "badness." Similarly, the capacities for recouping and regrouping, for buffering and transcending, are largely age- and stage-dependent. An eight-year-old separated from his parents has much more powerful imaginative resources for recalling (and indeed creating) images of loving, nurturing parents than does a two-year-old. The desperate situations in Rwanda and elsewhere have produced numerous heart-wrenching photographs of children aged two or under trying to rouse a dying or already dead mother. The preverbal child's capacities to process the loss, to sense the futility of attempting to awaken the mother, to grasp death and its finality are considerably less developed than those of an older child. Conversely, the two-year-old may have recuperative capacities that would allow him or her to respond to a new and devoted caretaker more quickly than would the eight-year-old.

War, persecution, and exposure to chronic violence dramatically increase the burdens of child rearing and typically reduce parents' capacity to protect a child from harm and humiliation. A crucial premise of development is that children need the constancy, caring, and love of adults not merely to survive but to flourish. We know something of what development is like when parents are unable to provide this nurture or when parents or other relatives are absent or dead. We need to know more about what kinds of parental and adult presence, and what kinds of institutional settings, enhance or diminish a child's chances for successful development.

Fantasy and imaginative play are a vital part of ordinary child development, helping the child progress from stage to stage. War and violence typically constrict the child's ability to use play and fantasy for progression, because in such circumstances play is entrained in day-to-day mastery of the ongoing trauma. The inability to imagine a future is a common consequence of severe trauma—children in violent situations may be repetitively and compulsively playing funeral games and simultaneously envisioning no future for themselves except death at an early age. When reality is too grim, the ordinary and necessary free flow between imagination and reality cannot take place.

The issue of sex differences in development is addressed only briefly in this book, although they are crucial to understanding the multiple impacts of violence, especially chronic violence. Eleven-year-old Israeli girls on a kibbutz describe their fears of going out at night to empty the trash because the dump is near the kibbutz fence, which literally and symbolically helps to protect them from infiltrators and terrorists. The boys are allegedly not afraid because, as one girl explains: "Both boys and girls will go into the army, but girls become teachers in the army and boys fight in the front lines. They're brave." Twelve-year-old Palestinian girls describe their feeling of being constricted by the increasing influence of Islamic fundamentalism. For example, they are not allowed to dress as their adolescent tastes dictate; they are threatened with physical violence and public humiliation if they wear shorts in public in hot summer, or if they wear slacks instead of dresses. Rape is perpetrated against teenage girls in war zones, in refugee situations, and in violent communities. In refugee camps, rape can be a significant factor in suicide among teenage girls (Mollica, Fish-Murray et al., n.d.).

Numerous studies of gangs in American cities and portrayals in such movies as *Boyz N the Hood* illustrate the marked differences in roles assigned to boys and girls (Spergel, 1995). Sex differences are often greatly magnified by the stresses of armed conflict and persecution. War may also reduce the role and status differential between boys and girls as they work together in a common effort, but usually the differential is quickly restored when the crisis is past (see Tuttle, 1992).

Though there are certain developmental probabilities for how children will

construe the meanings of traumatic events, there are so many individual variations that it is difficult to predict how a particular child will experience a particular situation. Again, war and violence introduce still more elements of unpre-
dictability. The outcomes of some serious studies—be they retrospective (few
enough) or prospective (even fewer)—have surprised the investigators. For example, a major prospective study of Greek children imprisoned as infants with their
mothers during the civil war started out as an investigation of the effects of early
trauma on subsequent development, including the capacity to rear children, but
ended up demonstrating the protective factors that allowed most of these children to do reasonably well in later life (Dalianis, 1994).

Resiliency

Some children who have lived through unspeakable horrors and unimaginable traumas have turned out to be healthy, vibrant, contributing adults. Studies
of resilient children and the "invulnerable child" are important to our understanding of child development, and there is substantial research literature on these
phenomena. The salient implication of these studies is that it might be possible to
foster resiliency. Below we outline the factors recognized as contributing to
resiliency.[8] In the next section we define appropriate interventions.

Resourcefulness. This ability enables one to make something out of nothing,
to use imaginative skills in garnering or creating resources—both concrete material resources and the psychic resources needed for survival. This includes the
ability to extract some amount of human warmth and loving kindness in the
direst of circumstances, even from one's enemies or persecutors.

Ability to attract and use adult support. This skill in turn leads to an early sense of
one's own power and competence. This also entails using adults as a "polestar"
(Sheehy, 1991); resilient children have a knack for turning to adults other than
parents for guidance and resources they cannot find in their own families. It is not
merely that resilient children can get adults to care about them and for them; they
also somehow promote a reciprocity in their exchanges with adults, so that the
adults also feel that they are deriving something from the relationship. It is a way
of continually interacting so as to generate new emotional supplies for all concerned.

Curiosity and intellectual mastery. Becoming knowledgeable about the crises
around one increases the chances of survival, gives one a "commodity" (that is,
knowledge) that can be traded with others, and provides a sense of activity rather
than passivity. Exercising this skill may mean bearing the anxiety and pain of

8. This list is based on our review of the literature, principally works of Garmezy and
Rutter (for example, Haggerty, Sherrod, Garmezy, and Rutter, 1994); E. J. Anthony and B. J.
Cohler (for example, 1987); Dalianis (1994); Dugan and Coles (1989); our interviews with
survivors and reading of their autobiographies and biographies; clinical work; and discussions
with clinicians with extensive experience treating survivors. Some of the literature is well summarized for nonprofessionals in Sheehy, 1986.

looking and finding out rather than the temporary psychic relief afforded by avoidance and denial.

Compassion—but with detachment. This means that a child can feel compassion for a caretaker who is sick, disturbed, or out of control but still know that he or she must keep a safe distance.

Ability to conceptualize. Conceptualizing is comprehending an experience not only as a personal travail but as a phenomenon affecting others as well. Such understanding diminishes feelings of isolation, failure and defectiveness and may also contribute to the development of empathy. At times we hear survivors conceptualizing their suffering in relation to the suffering of others and exclaiming, "I didn't have it so bad. You should talk to so-and-so, who really went through terrible times."

Conviction of one's right to survive. This conviction is associated with an urge to survive, even amid unbearable external situations. A more elaborated form of the right to survive is the notion of "survival merit" (Sheehy, 1991), the feeling that one has been permitted to survive for some special purpose, such as to help others. Survival merit can counter the impact of survivor guilt.

Ability to remember and invoke images of good and sustaining figures. These images usually are parental figures. They might be critical and demanding or warm, loving, and encouraging. It appears that the critical voice of the parent is important for maintaining certain ideals and standards as well as for keeping in touch with some sense of the security that comes with belief in a "normal" moral order. Also important is the ability to remember, imagine, and be in touch with sustaining family stories and community legends. For example, Le Ly Hayslip, a Vietnamese woman, records how the legend of a distant ancestor, a woman warrior pregnant in battle, sustained her when she herself was pregnant during the Vietnam War.

Ability to be in touch with a variety of affects, not denying or suppressing major affects as they arise. At the same time, one has some ability to defer or to defend against overwhelming anxiety or depression when emergency resources are needed. This may mean compartmentalizing the pain and postponing the affect until it is safe to experience it. A flexible array of defenses includes the ability to evoke mild amounts of denial when necessary for psychic sanity and survival, but not so much as to impair reality testing.

A goal to live for. Victor Frankl wrote on survival in the death camps: "Give me a why [to live], and I will find the how." The sustaining goal may be to see one's parents again or to "get your little brother to Palestine, no matter what!" Again, there is a delicate balance: autobiographical accounts suggest that failure to achieve the goal can lead to terrible self-reproach and suicidal despair.

A vision of the possibility and desirability of the restoration of a civilized moral order. Even in the worst of situations, a child may take great risks to help someone else in order to feel and implement a sense of decency. A Lebanese Catholic boy whose brother was killed in a Syrian shelling and who himself was seriously injured asked a nun—who had taught him that Christ said to love one's enemies—whether he now had to start hating the Syrians, in contravention of her teaching (Rosenblatt, 1983). A child may harbor fantasies of revenge at moments when a persecutor is especially cruel and sadistic but has the freedom not to have to act on those wishes even when revenge is possible. A need to act in order to restore the moral order may take precedence over the need to get even.

The need and ability to help others. This is accompanied by the unspoken assumption that somehow giving benefits the giver as well as the recipient. A "learned helpfulness," in contrast with a "learned helplessness," is a powerful mode of survival (Seligman, 1975). This skill often draws on identification with parents who themselves have demonstrated the effectiveness of altruistic acts.

An affective repertory. Such a repertory includes the ability to laugh, even in the most trying circumstances, and to delay crying until a safer time. This capacity can be learned from older children and adults. Cambodian children who survived the Pol Pot terror reported how dangerous it was to cry and how crying was disallowed (Apfel and Simon, 1990; Sheehy, 1991). Yet they were able to laugh, and their laughter provided emotional release of tension and also a group acknowledgment of something ludicrous in the surroundings. In this regard, affective constancy in parents is particularly important for very young children. Under fire, it is the affect of the mother that determines the affective response of the infant in arms, or of the young child. But how is the parent supposed to remain calm during a bombing?

Consider this anecdote from Anna Freud's wartime diaries (1973, 426–427):

> [Jack, 2½ years old,] cried whenever a plane drew near, rushed to the nearest adult, and called out: "Airplane is hurting me!" He was taught to look out for the planes, to recognize them in the distance, to follow their course, etc., until his fear of planes gave way to an active interest in them. [Two weeks later]
>
> He was most interested in watching a number of pigs in a pigsty and ran to his nurse to tell her that all the pigs were "in the shelter." A few minutes later, when an airplane was heard overhead, he ran to the sty and shouted into it: "Airplanes not hurting you!" and then informed the nurse that "the piggies are frightened." He had by then exchanged his role of being frightened himself for that of protector and comforter for the pigs, to which he ascribed his former anxiety.

Altruism toward others. Altruistic behavior by the parents communicates to a child not just calm but a certain competence and a sense that "you may be helpless to stop a bomb from falling, but you are not helpless to deal with its human consequences." Detailed studies of mothers under fire in Beirut (Bryce, 1989) have shown that children instructed to use the interval between shellings to bring food to an invalid relative did much better (that is, were not symptomatic clinically) than those who occupied the time watching television. Maternal competence and altruism were strongly associated with children's being relatively symptom-free under conditions of severe stress and danger, as well as in the quieter intervals.

Consider the following vignette, also from Anna Freud (p. 8):

"Our big girls, 6 and 9 years old, when we take them for a walk and pass by damaged houses, make expert casual remarks: 'Incendiary bomb' . . . ; 'high explosive.'" The same two girls spoke about the time when they still lived with their parents in a badly bombed area: "Every evening when the first bombs came down, Daddy would grab his coat and run out to help and Mummy would always call after him: 'Don't forget that we have two spare beds—bring in people if you find them homeless.'" Children whose parents behave in this way naturally show no sign of fear themselves. The father of the 6-year-old girl said: "You would have to drop a bomb down her back before she would take notice!"

Interventions

What constitutes a psychologically informed and resiliency-promoting intervention for children in situations of war and communal violence? Our guideline is: those interventions that allow the child first to survive, then to experience a measure of well-being, and then to flourish. Intervention, for the purposes of this book, covers a range of practices, from "school in a box" (shipping containers that have the basic supplies for a schoolroom of fifty children—paper, pencils, scissors, blackboard, some basic texts, and teacher support materials) to expressive therapies involving art and drama to intensive psychotherapy. Each of the contributors has experience with one or more types of intervention. There is no single or right psychological intervention; what is possible and practical is at least as important as what is ideal in determining an intervention in a situation of violence. The goal is to keep the child alive and as secure as possible with the best possible adult supervision, to allow the mind and imagination to rework traumatic experiences and to further develop, and to allow for strengthening peer relationships.

As clinical psychiatrists and psychoanalysts, we customarily work with adults—patients who come for help (or are brought in for it) far from the scene of and long after their traumatic experience. In work with children of war, however, our interventions take place with people who are not designated by us or by themselves as patients, and they occur (optimally) close to the time and scene of the event that is disrupting their lives.[9] The survivor, child or adult, has often

9. We use the term *patient* to refer to the person the professional is helping, despite some preference for the term *clients*. The latter term does not really remove the issue of differences in power and position between the helper and the one helped. Etymologically, *patient* is one who suffers, and *client* is one who is dependent on a more powerful person. In using *patient* we are

endured what we cannot imagine with extraordinary emotional strength. Survivors understandably may resent being designated patients. Most survivors are not sick, and attempts to categorize them can recapitulate oppressive situations in which they were classified, numbered, and (literally) stamped as inferior, subhuman creatures. To the extent that a survivor acknowledges emotional difficulty, he or she is likely to view that difficulty as secondary to the violent experience. Our interventions need to respect the experience of surviving basically intact something horrific. Indeed, most survivors do not ask for psychological help, because mental and emotional well-being typically are low priorities after a violent encounter, and intervention by a mental health professional can seem stigmatizing and frivolous.

The important question of who determines how and to whom services and resources are distributed is beyond the scope of this book. We instead focus on interventions that are relatively feasible, use available resources creatively, and collaborate with the survivor in a comeback and progression.

Though interventions can vary greatly, there are some commonalities among the effective ones described in this book: (1) genuine and nonjudgmental caring for the child survivors; (2) respect for the child, whatever his or her age and stage, and for the strengths of the survivor while providing for his or her needs; (3) recognition of the complexity of the child's experience and nonpartisan empathy with the child's struggle; (4) willingness to try nontraditional approaches derived from the particular culture, child, or situation; (5) willingness to try another intervention when something is not working, using as indicators the child's response and the input of local resources; (6) attentiveness to the caregivers' needs so as to minimize burnout; (7) encouragement of acts that help build or restore community—especially acts of altruism and helpfulness; (8) development of approaches that progressively empower and encourage initiative for the individual child or group of children; (9) awareness of the political dimensions of violence, so that one can help the child form an age-appropriate understanding of the larger political and social context.

Many modalities of intervention will be described throughout this book. Few involve actually meeting with the child as a patient in a therapy setting (in chapter 6 Steven Marans and his colleagues describe an exception that will be familiar to most mental health professionals). All are informed by the basic values of psychoanalysis, however: open-ended listening, bearing painful affects, and doing what is in the best interests of those in our care. For very young children, the main intervention can be arranging close and consistent adult attention, someone to meet the basic needs for love, conversation, safety, and nurturance. For preschool and school-age children who have suffered the unspeakable (see Lykes, 1994), modalities include nonverbal expressive therapies. Psychologists

---

not invoking a stereotyped medical model of working with traumatized people but are choosing a term that says there is a suffering person and a person trying to help that sufferer.

have collaborated with actors, mimes, dancers, and graphic artists to provide ways for children to tell without talking. For unaccompanied refugee children from places where the infrastructure has been badly damaged, the main intervention may be one that provides for a sense of community and an opportunity to resume, however modestly, the trajectory of emotional and cognitive development, to learn new skills, and to live in a morally ordered environment. Thus, resumption of schooling can be the optimal intervention for such children. In Rwanda, this means U.N.-supplied schools in a box.

Similarly, interventions are needed later in the life cycle of those afflicted by violence as children, such as the child warrior or young soldier who has both committed and experienced violence; the sexually abused refugee woman who is now a wife and mother and is rearing her own children; the concentration camp survivor in old age; descendants of Nazis meeting descendants of Holocaust survivors (chapter 9 by Dan Bar-On). Each of these people may need several different interventions, flexibly and imaginatively applied, simultaneously or sequentially. For any given community, what can be accomplished will change as the infrastructure is slowly rebuilt. For any given child, the best intervention will shift as the child grows and heals.

Plan of the Book

The following chapters cover the questions we have posed here, and the authors address them with detailed examples and the stamp of experience. Each chapter has an editorial introduction that contextualizes the general applications of the material in the chapter.

In chapter 2, "Ethical Issues in Working with Children in War Zones," Gillian Straker draws primarily on her long experience in South Africa, where she worked with black township youth. She presents dilemmas that arise in extreme but not necessarily rare situations, and she develops some general principles of wide applicability.

Chapter 3, "What Do We Need to Know to Understand Children in War and Communal Violence?" by James Garbarino and Kathleen Kostelny, is based on the authors' experience with children in violence-ridden areas of Chicago and in many areas of the world where there is or has recently been armed combat or oppression. They present their framework for understanding the ways that violence affects child development, a framework that draws on psychoanalytic (primarily Eriksonian), cognitive, and spiritual-philosophical perspectives.

Chapter 4, "Post-Traumatic Stress Disorder and Other Stress Reactions," by William Arroyo and Spencer Eth, also draws on the authors' clinical and research experience with traumatized children in presenting an approach to both assessment and formulation of treatment.

In chapter 5, "Refugee Children," Joseph Westermeyer and Karen Wahmanholm base their arguments on their clinical and programmatic work with refugee children in Minneapolis. The chapter, heavily clinical in its focus, provides a framework for sorting out the multiple problems stemming from the different routes by which children become refugees. The authors provide important guidelines for choosing modalities of treatment and intervention.

Chapter 6, "Child Development and Adaptation to Catastrophic Circumstances," by Steven Marans, Miriam Berkman, and Donald Cohen, is based primarily on the authors' experiences with the Child Development–Community Policing Program in New Haven, Connecticut, and on Cohen's experience as a member of the National Commission for the Child. They present examples of several types of programmatic and individual psychotherapeutic interventions and discuss how they dovetail.

In chapter 7, "Youth and Violence: Trends, Principles, and Programmatic Interventions," Michael B. Greene addresses issues that affect adolescents in particular, drawing heavily on his experiences in the Deputy Mayor's Office in New York City, coordinating violence prevention programs. He offers a way to conceptualize the strengths and adaptive resources of teenagers, who can be both victims and perpetrators of violence, and to use teenagers' strengths in community programs aimed at both short-term and long-term violence prevention.

In chapter 8, "Mobilizing Communities to Meet the Psychosocial Needs of Children in War and Refugee Crises," Neil Boothby continues the theme of the previous chapter, showing how programmatic interventions can build on the realities and strengths of particular communities and countries. Boothby has worked primarily in Mozambique, and his contribution draws on his experience there and as a consultant elsewhere in Africa, Southeast Asia, and other strife-torn areas.

Chapter 9, "Attempting to Overcome the Intergenerational Transmission of Trauma" is informed by the experiences of the author, Dan Bar-On, in studying descendants of Nazis and of Holocaust survivors. The insights generated in those studies helped shape the "case study" reported in detail—a series of structured meetings between representatives of the two groups. These encounters in turn shed further light both on the pathways of destructive transmission of trauma and on the possibilities for creative transformation.

Chapter 10, "Who Takes Care of the Caretakers? The Emotional Consequences of Working with Children Traumatized by War and Communal Violence," is by Yael Danieli. She extends the theme of transmission of trauma to the encounter between helper and victim, drawing heavily on her experience studying therapists who work with victims of war and persecution and on her construction of practical programs to help those therapists cope in their work.

Chapter 11, "Practical Approaches to Research with Children in Violent Settings," by Peter S. Jensen, serves as a guide to the complex effort of gathering usable data on children in situations of violence. Jensen draws on his experience in military settings in the United States as well as on his work in assessing the extent and impact of violence on children in the Washington, D.C., area.

In chapter 12, "Assessing the Impact of War on Children," Mona Macksoud, J. Lawrence Aber, and Ilene Cohn distill their collective experience in simultaneously working out a theoretical framework for assessment and performing the actual assessments leading to interventions. They present a detailed picture of their work with the children of Kuwait in the wake of the Persian Gulf War as an instantiation of their ways of conceptualizing and working.

Our hope is that this book will be useful for other mental health workers, the people they try to help, and those they teach and train. We offer it as a contribution to dialogue among mental health workers and those in related helping fields and as a way to help reach the hearts and minds of children afflicted by war, persecution, and communal violence.

REFERENCES

Amnesty International. 1990. *Guatemala: Extrajudicial executions and human rights violences against street children.* New York: Amnesty International.
———. 1992. *Brazil: Extrajudicial execution of street children in Sergipe.* London: Amnesty International.
Anthony, E. J., and Cohler, B. J., eds. 1987. *The invulnerable child.* New York: Guilford.
Antonovsky, A. 1987. *Unraveling the mystery of health: How people manage stress and stay well.* San Francisco: Jossey-Bass.
Apfel, R. J., and Simon, B. 1990. *Not allowed to cry.* Video (excerpts from conference "Children in War"). Jerusalem.
Aradom, T. 1994. Personal communication.
Bryce, J. 1989. Life experiences, response styles and mental health among mothers and children in Beirut, Lebanon. *Social Science and Medicine* 28:685–695.
Dalianis, A. 1994. *Children in turmoil during the Greek Civil War, 1946–1949: Today's adults: Follow-up of Greek children imprisoned with their mothers during the Civil War.* Stockholm: Karolinska University.
Dugan, T. F., and Coles, R., eds. 1989. *The child in our times: Studies in the development of resiliency.* New York: Brunner/Mazel.
Eth, S. 1992. Ethical challenges in the treatment of traumatized refugees. *Journal of Traumatic Stress* 5:103–110.
Fineman, J. 1995. Loss, aggression, and violence: Two groups of traumatized children. In T. Cohen, M. Etezady, and B. Pacella, eds., *The vulnerable child.* Madison, Conn.: International Universities Press.
Freud, A. 1973. *The writings of Anna Freud.* Vol. 3: *Infants without families: Reports on the Hampstead Nurseries, 1939–1945.* New York: International Universities Press.
Haggerty, R. J., Sherrod, L. R., Garmezy, N., and Rutter, M. 1994. *Stress, risk and resilience in children and adolescents: Processes, mechanisms and interventions.* Cambridge, Eng.: Cambridge University Press.
Lykes, M. B. 1994. Terror, silencing, and children: International multidisciplinary collaboration with Guatemalan Maya communities. *Social Science and Medicine* 38:543–552.
Martín-Baró, I. 1994. *Writings for a liberation psychology.* Edited by A. Aron and S. Corne. Cambridge, Mass.: Harvard University Press.

Mollica, R. F., Fish-Murray, C. C., et al. N.d. *Repatriation and disability: A community study of health, mental health, and social functioning of the Khmer residents of Site Two.* Vol. 2: *Khmer Children,* 12 to 13 years of age. Cambridge, Mass.: Harvard Program in Refugee Trauma, Harvard School of Public Health.

Rexford, E. N. 1969. Children, child psychiatry, and our brave new world. *Archives of General Psychiatry* 20:25–37.

Rosenblatt, R. 1983. *Children of war.* New York: Doubleday Anchor.

Seligman, M. 1975. *Helplessness: On depression, development, and death.* New York: Knopf.

Sheehy, G. 1986. *Spirit of survival.* New York: William Morrow.

Spergel, I. A. 1995. *The youth gang problem.* New York: Oxford University Press.

Tuttle, W. M. 1993. *Daddy's gone to war: The Second World War in the lives of America's children.* New York: Oxford University Press.

CHAPTER TWO

Ethical Issues in Working with Children in War Zones

GILLIAN STRAKER

We begin with a chapter on ethical issues because ethical strains are inevitable for anyone working with children in contested situations. Because the work is so emotionally demanding, and because it requires an unusually active stance, many mental health professionals try to avoid it. Ethical personal dilemmas can discourage professionals from psychotherapeutic work with children and youths who are suffering the effects of their external circumstances. By addressing these dilemmas immediately and directly we hope to help reduce anxiety about working with such young people.

When we met Gillian Straker, in Jerusalem, the situation in South Africa was characterized both by terrible violence and oppression and by the presence of a large number of well-trained mental health professionals and professional organizations, many with formal codes of ethics. Straker writes from her base in South Africa, but her lessons apply to situations of communal violence, ethnic war, and government violence against some of its people. She forces us to examine the ethical and value practices of our work, asking to whom our allegiance is due and what constitutes the "best interest of the child" in the different settings and cultural systems in which we are attempting to intervene.

The issue of children, war, and communal violence evokes strong emotions. But if policies are to be formulated and decisions made that are truly in children's best interests, it is important to temper passion with reflection and outrage with reason. Working with children in violent contexts inevitably challenges the value assumptions on which we base clinical work. To understand these challenges and their accompanying emotions it is perhaps best to begin with case studies that show the dilemmas commonly encountered by those working with children in war zones.

A Case Study of a Child Activist

The following situation was reported by a therapist working against apartheid at the height of South Africa's civil conflict. She requested a consultation with me following a session with a student activist, a fourteen-year-old boy who sought help because he was suffering a variety of psychological symptoms after having been detained (detainees are arrested and held for a period of days or months without trial). Toward the end of his session he began to reveal a plan to bomb a police station. He indicated a need to discuss this plan further in his next session.

When the therapist consulted with me, she was agitated. She felt ethically challenged on several levels: she was aware that the plan may have been an adolescent fantasy and that the boy's mentioning it to her had transference implications. However, the possibility that this was a real plan of action had to be considered.

The first moral dilemma of which my colleague spoke was that between her patient's right to autonomy and the related issue of confidentiality versus others' right to life. In times of peace, under a government whose legitimacy is recognized, as is currently the case in South Africa, I would have referred my colleague to the precedents set in similar cases, in which resolution was reached by following the maxim "Protective privilege ends where public peril begins" (Karasu, 1991). This principle was formulated in the resolution of the now-famous Tarasoff case, in which a patient disclosed to his therapist that he intended to kill his girlfriend. The therapist notified the police of the patient's intention but not the victim or her relatives. The patient did kill the woman, and her relatives sued the therapist. The court found that the therapist's actions had not been sufficiently protective of the public, and it ruled that therapists must warn both the authorities and the potential victims when patients threaten dangerous actions (Karasu, 1991).

In line with the Tarasoff decision, therapists are bound to disclose confidential information to all relevant parties when there is possible public peril. The question then becomes how to assess the nature of this peril. The factors to be weighed include the clarity of the threat, the actuality and severity of the danger, the identifiability of the potential victims, and the imminence of the danger (Gross et al., 1987). But both the Tarasoff decision and the principles to guide one's decisions described by Gross et al. presuppose a context in which the public interest is best served by the prevention of violence and the violence in question is of a private rather than collective nature.

In the case presented here, however, the violence in question was of a political nature and was supported by large numbers of South Africans who had committed themselves officially to the notion of armed struggle. Disclosure of the youth's plans to the authorities would have implications far beyond those normally attached to violating a patient's privacy, for it could lead to his detention and torture. If the therapist disclosed this information she would be contravening not only the principle of autonomy but also the principle of nonmaleficence, which holds that no harm should befall a patient because of a therapist's action. Furthermore, disclosure of this information might have delayed the achievement of social justice—depending on how one construes the notion of justice—for a large sector of the population.

Nondisclosure of this information, however, would leave the therapist a potential accomplice to a plot in which human lives could be lost and an accessory to what the formal government would define as a crime. Thus, nondisclosure would contravene the principle of self-interest, at least at a legal level, although this was not a particular concern for this therapist, who indicated that by working with political activists in the first place she had defined her self-interest as outside the legal system.

What did concern her, as a committed pacifist, was that nondisclosure might make her an unwitting accomplice in the taking of human lives, which she would find impossible to reconcile with her values and her self-image. Disclosure would therefore leave her in contravention of the principle of self-interest.

I found myself unable to resolve this therapist's dilemma by turning to the principles outlined in the South African psychologists' code of ethics. The actions prescribed by one principle contradicted those prescribed by another. Furthermore, deciding whether one was in contravention of any particular principle depended on how one defined such concepts as public interest, self-interest, and justice.

In light of my dilemmas concerning these issues, I suggested to my colleague that the case be discussed at our fortnightly support meeting for therapists. At these meetings a small group of therapists aligned with the antiapartheid movement met to provide peer supervision, discuss policy issues regarding the provision of treatment in particular circumstances, and share experiences and feelings evoked by working therapeutically with those persecuted by apartheid.

In the meantime I suggested to my colleague that she tell the youth about her difficulties in accepting his intended course of action, indicating to him that, while she felt it might be fruitful to explore his thoughts and feelings about his intended plan, she did not think it would be useful to discuss the plan itself. By thus limiting the information to which she had access, she could limit the information she could potentially disclose. Furthermore, by directing the patient's attention to an exploration of thoughts, feelings, and meanings she could reestablish a therapeutic agenda.

By becoming self-disclosing this therapist was also following the advice of Lifton (1976) that the therapeutic relationship in this context needs to incorporate greater equality and collaboration than are customary in conventional therapy. He stresses the ethical importance for the therapist to be open to learning from the patient, who has had experiences the therapist has not. In the case presented here the therapist's disclosure of her own conflicts about the planned action opened a space for her to learn more about the boy's frame of reference but also allowed him to explore his own doubts about the action. Thus the therapist's self-disclosure promoted autonomy in the sense of greater choice for both of them. The fact that this led the youth to abandon his plan has other ethical implications, assuming of course that he was discussing a reality rather than a fantasy. To understand these implications, we may imagine this scenario in a different context.

A Hypothetical Case Study

A fourteen-year-old boy involved in the French Resistance consults a doctor sympathetic to the movement and complains of recurring headaches. It is clear to the doctor that the headaches are related to the stress of the boy's involvement in the movement.

Should the doctor encourage the exploration of the boy's conflicts, acknowledging the possibility that this may lead the boy to leave the movement or at least limit what he is prepared to do for it? Or should she help him to strengthen his defenses so that he may continue on his path, even if it involves continued stress? In other words, should the doctor encourage the boy to put himself in danger and possibly contribute greatly to the common good, or should she promote the boy's insight, giving him a freer choice, and perhaps lead him out of the movement? The answer depends on the relative value that the doctor places on the ethical principle of autonomy versus interdependence, and on her concept of childhood. It is of course possible that the boy, even with greater insight, will choose to remain committed and that both the principle of autonomy and the promotion of the greater good will be actualized—but there is no guarantee of this.

What is at stake is not only the autonomy of the activist but also that of the therapist. Can a therapist allied to a liberation movement exercise autonomy when treating a member of this movement and discourage the patient from following the official policy of the movement, including, for example, involving an adolescent in acts of extreme violence? Where does the therapist's first responsibility lie: with the liberation movement (which in South Africa, as in the case of the French Resistance, was representative of the broader society), with the individual, with the individual's parents, or with the United Nations, whose conventions dictate that individuals under age fifteen not be involved in war?

These questions pertain not only to child activists. Questions concerning what is indeed in the best interests of the child, when these interests should be given priority, and who should represent them apply equally to children in war who are not activists, as the following case study illustrates.

A Case Study of an Unaccompanied Child Refugee

Clara was thirteen when her village in Mozambique was attacked. During her flight from the village she was separated from her companions; she eventually found her way to Zimbabwe with a group of refugees from a different part of Mozambique.

On her arrival in the refugee camp she remained with a family to which she had attached herself during the journey and which had agreed to foster her, even though she was from a different ethnic group. Like many children thus placed, she formed strong attachments to the family, a situation that can be problematic, particularly for younger children, if the biological family is later located.

After Clara had spent about a year with this family, a man in the camp expressed an interest in her and approached her foster family with a marriage proposal. The suitor was from the same ethnic group as the foster family—a group with whom intermarriage would have been unacceptable in Clara's biological family. Nevertheless, Clara indicated that she would accept him. She was under the legal age of marriage in the host country, but that fact would not prevent the traditional marriage the family intended.

This situation raises a number of complex questions. First there is the issue of the girl's consent. Should it be accepted as legitimate, in view of the possibility that it may have been subtly coerced? In a culture that accepts arranged marriages, was it necessary to seek her consent at all? If so, was she old enough to give informed consent?

If it was not necessary to obtain the girl's consent, who should make the decision for her? How far should her biological parents' rights be delegated in the absence of knowledge of their fate? If those rights are delegated, should they reside with the foster family, the broader refugee community, the officials of the host country, or representatives of the agencies that funded the refugee camp?

The issue was resolved through the intervention of workers from the donor agency, who mobilized elders in the refugee community. The elders opposed the arrangement because they felt that the foster family was profiteering in regard to the bride price, and the workers and the refugee community together blocked the marriage. Such alliances are not always possible, of course. The questions that this case study raises concerning who is ultimately responsible for children whose ties with their families and communities have been disrupted remain unanswered. Furthermore, this case study, like the others, raises fundamental questions concerning the nature of childhood itself and the rights that children should be accorded—rights that are themselves defined by how childhood is conceived.

Concepts of Childhood and the Rights of the Child

Neither the nature of childhood nor its age parameters are universally agreed upon. Nevertheless, the United Nations, with the support of fifteen countries, in 1989 adopted the Convention on the Rights of the Child, which prohibits the world community from permitting people under fifteen years of age to engage in or to support armed conflict. Implicit in this convention is a notion of childhood as a developmental stage that ends at age fourteen, a notion that has both historical and cultural ties. In the Middle Ages, for example, childhood ended when one was between five and seven years of age. "Once he had passed the age of five or seven the child was immediately absorbed into the world of adults. . . . Children from the age of five could already wear a sword, which was not simply for ornament or prestige" (Aries, 1962).

Roe (1994) points out that children in nonwestern agrarian societies, in contrast with children in urban areas in the West, are assigned formal roles in the family economy when they are as young as three and that families cease to classify them as children when they are as young as five. In such developing countries as South Africa the induction of children into economic roles begins early in rural and working-class families, and in black townships the category of child is often secondary to that of youths, which includes people as young as ten (Straker, 1989).

While ideas concerning the age at which childhood ceases have varied throughout history and continue to vary across cultures, ideas concerning the precise nature of childhood have also varied. Childhood traditionally has been seen as a time of obligations and duties. Westerners, however, see childhood as a time of innocence and vulnerability and children as having certain privileges and entitlements (Straker, 1989). This construction is consistent with the broader ideology of rights in the West. This perspective holds that certain rights are based on universal moral principles that transcend immediate social contexts (Roe, 1993). It supports notions of individualism, valuing people independently of their place in society. In line with this, it sees children as holding rights independent of the family and community, including the right not to be involved in wars waged by families and communities, even if these are construed to be fought for the long-term benefit of children. Proponents of this perspective fail to acknowledge that it too is culture bound and inextricably linked to the economic and political systems that underpin Western societies.

Societies that perceive children as bound into families and communities may not accord children such rights, for the survival of children in such societies is seen as dependent on the survival of families and communities. There may, therefore, be an obligation for children to contribute to this survival.

Thus, the views that communities adopt regarding the involvement of children in war arise from their general perceptions of ethics and their attitudes toward the nature of childhood and the morality of war. I would have to put myself in the "rights" camp. I recognize that this is not a politically neutral act, however, and that I am not choosing a principle that transcends all social situations and whose goodness or rightness is self-evident. I recognize it as a value judgment, a moral choice informed by my background and worldview, as are my views concerning the morality of war.

The Morality of War

Few societies and groups do not believe that war is morally justifiable under certain circumstances (du Toit, 1990). What these circumstances may be, however, differs considerably across cultures and throughout history; war between countries has been justified almost since history began, as has the use of violence by the ruling party to maintain the status quo. Nevertheless, wars of liberation against ruling classes have only recently gained legitimacy (Bax, 1987).

An excursion into the literature on the notion of a "just war," from Constantine the Great to the present day, leads one into a morass of theories riddled with contradictions and definitional problems of concepts like "good" and "true." Indeed, under scrutiny even such seemingly straightforward notions as self-defense grow in complexity and come to defy definition and easy understanding; universal pacifism begins to emerge as the only safe foothold on a very slippery slope.

Yet universal pacifism, as a transcendental moral principle, has historically been embraced by very few. On a personal level it is extremely demanding, and on a social level there is much evidence of the strategic value of exercising violence to promote values that a society holds dear—for example, equality and social justice (du Toit, 1990). In deciding whether war ever is justifiable, and if so under what circumstances, the writings of theologians, philosophers, secular ethicists, and historians are so contradictory as to be of little value.

For those working in contexts of war or civil conflict, an interrogation of their own position in regard to this question is essential, for it has practical implications for those they work with. My own position is full of contradictions. I espouse the principle of universal pacifism as an ideal, yet I know that when physically threatened I might respond with violence. I know too that, faced with the frustrations that black South Africans suffered under apartheid, I might have engaged in revolutionary action. I recognize also that there have been times when the exercise of violence has been successful in furthering values I cherish.

I believe that I share these contradictions between my values and what my de facto reactions might be with many others, including those who face violence daily and who deal with its lived reality rather than merely contemplate it. These contradictions, uncomfortable as they may be, are in their own way helpful. They provoke a continual debate about the morality of war and violence, ensuring that questions concerning ethics remain in the forefront as one engages in clinical practice with those caught in the crossfire of war. It is important to note, however, that extreme situations bring into sharp relief certain ethical issues that are implicit in all therapeutic contexts and that need attention.

Kinzie and Boehnlein (1993), in a discussion of their work with adult survivors of massive violence, stressed the importance of six ethical principles that apply to all clinical practice: fidelity, nonmaleficence, beneficence, justice, self-interest, and autonomy. These principles have special implications for the treatment of children in war zones.

Fidelity

Fidelity implies trust, predictability, and consistency, each of which has implications for therapeutic relationships.

Trust. Therapeutic relationships are predicated on the individual's trust that the therapist has the ability and willingness to act in the patient's best interests. In most therapeutic contexts this trust develops silently as the therapist proves his professional and personal competence by creating a safe and containing emotional space. In war, however, the therapist may have to create a safe physical space as well. He may also have to prove his political commitment and involvement as well as his professional competence.

Yet the ability of therapists to provide these proofs may be compromised by war and political repression, when therapists themselves may be subject to police harassment and detention. Obviously this limits both their political involvement and their ability to ensure anyone else's physical safety. The possibility of being harassed and detained compromises therapists' ability to guarantee confidentiality, which in turn affects patients' ability to trust.

Furthermore, political repression and violence by their very nature foster suspicion and mistrust. Informers are ubiquitous in these contexts, and requests that one talk about oneself and one's activities frequently spark mistrust in those unfamiliar with the talking cure. The issue of trust in the therapeutic relationship therefore has to be dealt with overtly, and both parties have to decide how far to trust each other, not only in regard to the exposure of emotion, the usual area of risk in therapy, but in regard to the revelation of basic information. This applies as much to children as to adults.

Children in war often must keep secrets in order to protect family members, and for these children talking about their trauma may carry connotations of betrayal—and all the guilt and anxiety that this inspires—beyond what might be normal in other therapeutic contexts. The heightened need to censor information must be recognized as legitimate, given the dangerous circumstances to which these children are exposed. Indeed, if therapists are to fulfill the ethical principle of fidelity in this context they should facilitate circumspection, not push against it. This is especially true in view of the fact that their own ability to guarantee confidentiality is compromised. Therapists should focus on the fears and anxieties underlying this circumspection and help the children find ways to master them.

Predictability and consistency. Concerning the treatment of survivors of massive violence in a post-traumatic context, Kinzie and Boehnlein (1993) state that "therapists should not only be dependable and consistent but should maintain their obligation to treat these patients over time." This clearly represents an ideal that may not be attainable when traumatic stress continues. Physical safety in such situations takes priority. Treatment centers in countries under political repression are frequently raided, and receiving ongoing treatment at a predictable time and place may put individuals at risk.

Therapists are thus under pressure to modify the frame of therapy. One therapist in South Africa, for example, was contacted periodically by a messenger from another township, then blindfolded and taken to meet with a group of young activists living in a forest. Both the time and the place of therapy were determined by those seeking help rather than those giving it, a reversal of the rules that usually govern therapeutic contracts. Similarly, the initial act of trust in this encounter was made by the therapist rather than the patients.

Therapists are also under pressure to use brief-term interventions or even single sessions. Straker (1988), in collaboration with colleagues, has outlined a therapeutic model for single sessions that involves three phases: establishing trust and developing ground themes; facilitating catharsis and mastery; and planning for the future and closure.

In the first phase, once the obstacles to establishing trust have been explicitly addressed, individuals are invited to talk about their plight in general, nonpersonal terms. Through this process, ground themes, which it may be therapeutic to pursue, are identified, and an assessment is made as to how useful or damaging it will be to move into more emotive issues. This assessment includes an evaluation of the internal and external resources that individuals have available to them to assist in the containment of feelings that may emerge in the second phase. Every attempt is made to ensure that feelings that may be overwhelming are not provoked, but if such feelings do emerge, efforts are made to facilitate containment and mastery of them.

The issue of mastery is explored not only in regard to the individuals' inner world but also in regard to their external situation. This leads to the final phase of therapy: dealing with the return to unsafe situations and checking how the therapeutic process has been experienced. In dealing with the return, efforts are made to link the individuals with social-support systems sensitive to their needs and able to provide physical protection.

Requiring individuals to talk about their trauma and to reexperience the associated affect in a single therapeutic interview may have negative consequences (Kinzie and Boehnlein, 1993). Therapists in these contexts need to find ways to ensure against such outcomes, for to do nothing may have equally negative consequences. It has been shown that the sooner the effects of trauma are addressed, the better the long-term prognosis (Raphael, 1986).

Nonmaleficence

The imperative of the principle of nonmaleficence is to do no physical or emotional harm, or to expose others to the risk of harm. When treating survivors of political violence who are also activists, it is important to recognize that the very act of seeking help at a clinic may expose them to physical harm. Before 1990, South African activists wounded in battles with the state would not visit hospitals or clinics lest they be detained; instead they sought out sympathetic doctors in private practice. Even in the early 1990s, before South Africa's first democratic election, seeking help at certain clinics was risky. Different parts of townships and neighborhoods were associated with different political allegiances, and clinics that operated in these areas came to be perceived as allied with particular groupings. This pressured the clinic staff to be partisan and to withhold treatment from the "enemy."

Personnel at clinics in South Africa's war zones had to analyze the possible consequences before treating a group member who was seen as an enemy in the surrounding community. Included in this analysis was a consideration of the potentially dangerous consequences for clinic staff, who could be seen as collaborators by other patients at the clinic and by people in the surrounding community. This would be weighed against the consequences of withholding treatment from another human being. In my experience most detriment-benefit analyses in this context resulted in the withholding of treatment unless there was an urgent need for medical intervention. Even then attempts were made to offer treatment at venues other than the clinic itself.

Beneficence

This principle, closely allied with nonmaleficence, prescribes that the chosen action be the one that provides the most benefit at the lowest cost.

Psychological benefits and costs are not easy to quantify. Nevertheless, therapists in all contexts need to assess the costs and benefits of their interventions, taking into account the research literature on the efficacy of different approaches and how their personal conflicts may affect their efficiency.

Therapists working in contexts of war, however, have recourse to relatively little research on the treatment models that have evolved in such contexts. This is partly because war and violence do not lend themselves to the implementation of well-designed studies. Nevertheless, those working in contexts of continuing rather than post-traumatic stress generally agree that for treatment to be effective it must take into account the context that has created the distress and must do this overtly and explicitly. This has implications not only for how distress is treated but also for how it is conceptualized. Certainly it cannot be considered simply a symptom of individual disorder (Becker, 1993), even if the form of its manifestation is classified as such under DSM IV or ICD 10. Individual distress must instead be clearly conceptualized as a symptom of the social disorder that generated it.

The treatment that follows from this conceptualization, while not denying individual distress, focuses on its relation to social processes and attempts not only to mobilize the individual's intrapsychic resources but also to involve alternative processes within such social institutions as the family, school, and church (Becker, 1993). The language used in this process includes such terms as networking, empowerment, and activism rather than rehabilitation and cure.

There are, however, dangers inherent in this approach. A focus on empowerment in the collective, for example, might lead one to downplay the individual's vulnerabilities and woundedness. However, these dangers are perhaps less grave than those involved in labeling individuals as disordered and subjecting them to secondary victimization. There is also a hidden advantage in not focusing too sharply on individual vulnerabilities, because survival in a hostile environment often requires a certain level of defensiveness and denial. Nevertheless, pain at an individual level must still be given its full weight, never trivialized or subtly criticized.

When dealing with individual distress in contexts of continuing trauma, where the constant availability of therapists cannot be guaranteed, it is also important to mobilize interpersonal support systems and the individual's own ideological commitments; these can serve important containing functions. For this reason it is often useful to work in groups and to help individuals express their pain through collective narratives, historical documentation, and testimony rather than more conventional therapeutic techniques. This again applies to children as well as to adults. Children can be invited to develop plays and collective collages to depict their experiences. But the therapeutic purpose of these endeavors should never be subverted for political reasons, though there may be occasions when the use of such material for political purposes can have a therapeutic value. That is, the material produced in such plays and collages should never be used to advocate on behalf of the oppressed unless the individual authors express the wish that this be done. When such wishes are expressed, the use of this material for witnessing or for legal testimony may well serve a therapeutic purpose.

Justice

As has been pointed out, confrontations with dilemmas pertaining to justice frequently occur when working with survivors of war. Atrocities and inhumane behavior are almost invariably reported and may lead to conflict between the principle of justice on a social level and the principle of beneficence on the level of the individual patient. Conflict may also arise between the principles of justice and self-interest. Exposing atrocities committed by organs of the state may jeopardize not only the client's safety but also the therapist's and that of the institute in which he works. Yet to do nothing makes the therapist a bystander to atrocities and human rights violations.

Therapists themselves need to become politically involved, as the material they hear when working with survivors of war almost inevitably raises issues pertaining to justice. In my experience therapists who are themselves politically active are best able to separate therapeutic from political objectives and to work effectively with survivors of war (Straker and Moosa, 1994). It is important for therapists to be in touch with and to understand their own emotional reactions to the material they have heard lest they be tempted to act out and consequently risk compromising those they work with. Furthermore, if their feelings remain unexamined, therapists may inadvertently encourage patients to act them out, thereby endangering themselves. It is appropriate for therapists to have strong reactions when dealing with survivors of war. When they cease having such reactions, they may be showing the numbing associated with post-traumatic stress disorder (PTSD) following their own secondary traumatization; this numbing needs to be investigated.

In resolving these dilemmas I have indicated support for the views of Eth (1992), who states that therapeutic relationships cannot be exploited in the context of the treatment of traumatized refugees, even for the common good. The social obligation to campaign for justice, which may be stimulated in therapists by the material they hear from patients, must be enacted outside the therapeutic context. There must be a clear separation of the therapeutic enterprise from political activism, and therapists should not use material heard in therapy for political purposes except when patients, cognizant of all the implications, request that they do so. In these instances therapeutic material may be used in campaigns for social justice.

When, however, the material is produced by children, the rules are different. One must question whether children can ever be cognizant of the implications that may flow from publication of their material. It is obvious that younger children cannot fully comprehend these implications, and the question then follows, Should therapists accede to requests from caretakers that therapeutic material be used for political campaigns?

The answer to this question must be informed by the principle of beneficence applied in regard to the children themselves. I acknowledge, however, that my answer is influenced by my view that children have rights outside of their families and communities.

In considering whether to facilitate the publication of their material for political purposes, therapists need to explore the meaning of this decision within the therapeutic relationship itself. In addition, they should explore privately, if not explicitly, the implications of requests—for their own self-interest and that of the therapeutic institute for which they work.

Self-Interest

If therapists are to continue to function both as creative human beings and as effective therapists, they have an ethical obligation to consider their own self-interest. This is especially important in contexts of war and political repression, in which therapists are subject to vicarious as well as direct traumatization. In these contexts therapists need to be aware of the limits to their own courage and of their need for support from others.

In caring for themselves, therapists in these contexts need to recognize the social nature of their distress and not personalize it as a sign of their own disorder. They need to network, to use their values and ideological commitments to direct their work, and to document their experiences as therapists.

Autonomy

The principle of autonomy holds that individuals should be free to act as they choose provided their actions do not harm others or limit the freedom of others to do the same. This principle does not refer to the common good but to individual rights, and as such it is bound to the ideology of individualism predominant in Western cultures. So it is not surprising that it poses the most problems for those working in contexts of war. By its nature, war requires the sacrifice of individual interests and even the supreme sacrifice of human life to the common good. The state of war severely limits individual autonomy, affecting both therapists and patients. In this context therapists must confront the question of acceptable limits on their own autonomy. They must examine to what extent they should consider themselves ethically bound—not only to limit their autonomous action so as not to harm others, but to surrender their freedom and adhere to the prescriptions of the liberation movement whose goals they support.

In regard to those who seek help, the notion of informed consent, which is inextricably linked with autonomy, becomes more complex in contexts of war, particularly when children are involved. In the South African war of liberation, many individuals, including large numbers of youths younger than fifteen, chose to become activists. They often participated against the wishes of their parents but with the support of many elders in the liberation movement.

The question arose as to whether they should be regarded as children in the conventional sense or, given the "adult" decisions and activities they were involved in, whether therapists should accept their definition of themselves as freedom fighters and treat them accordingly.

If their definition was not accepted, a secondary question arose: Who should be consulted concerning them, given that they rejected parental authority by accepting the authority of older members of the liberation struggle?

Once again, there are no easy answers. The U.N. Convention and the ethical principles described above provide a framework within which these dilemmas can be considered, but they cannot provide hard and fast answers.

Conclusion

It is important to note that ethical frameworks are often applied retrospectively to decisions that have had to be made in the moment. As such, these frameworks provide a description of how therapists make decisions; the frameworks do not provide a set of prescriptions for such decisions. This lack of prescriptive directives is inevitable given that the ethical principles that these frameworks encompass often conflict and do not lend themselves to easy hierarchical ordering. In the final analysis, ethical decisions that therapists make in the moment must represent the outcome of a personal interrogation of deeply held values that dictate which ethical principle will take priority, in what circumstances, and with whom.

Furthermore, practical considerations must be brought to bear on actual decisions in real situations. Thus individuals who hold different value positions may make similar decisions in particular circumstances, as was clear in the vignette about the unaccompanied refugee girl.

In sum, good clinicians, like good philosophers, should engage in dialogue concerning crucial ethical issues and should view the process as indispensable both in coming to specific decisions regarding particular children in war and in formulating more general policies in this regard. In this process of debate, clinicians should clearly recognize that the views they themselves hold are as culturally and historically bound as the views of those with whom they may disagree. By acknowledging this fact a priori, it becomes more likely that positions which first appear to be opposites will move closer together at a higher level of deliberation. Through this process, progress will also be made toward preventing the splitting of inner cognitions and fantasies, such that the self and its allies are seen as all good and the other is seen as all bad, mirroring the categorical thinking and fantasizing that encourage and support wars in the first place.

REFERENCES

Aries, P. 1962. *Centuries of childhood*. London: Penguin Books.

Bax, D. 1987. From Constantine to Calvin: The doctrine of the just war. In C. Villa-Vicencia, ed., *Theology and violence: The South African debate,* 147–173. Johannesburg: Skotaville Publishers.

Becker, D. 1993. The deficiency of the PTSD concept when dealing with victims of human rights violations. In R. Kleber, C. Figley, and B. Gersons, eds., *Beyond trauma: Selected papers from the first world conference on traumatic stress.* New York: Plenum Press.

du Toit, A. 1990. Discourse on political violence. In C. Manganyi and A. du Toit, eds., *Political violence and the struggle in South Africa,* 87–131. Johannesburg: Southern Book Publishers.

Eth, S. 1992. Ethical challenges in the treatment of traumatized refugees. *Journal of Traumatic Stress* 5:103–111.

Gross, B. H., Southland, M. J., Lamb, H. R., and Weinberger, S. E. 1987. Assessing danger and responding appropriately: Hedbund expands the clinicians' liability established by Tarasoff. *Journal of Clinical Psychiatry* 48:9–12.

Karasu, B. 1991. Ethical aspects of psychotherapy. In S. Bloch and P. Chodoff, eds., *Psychiatric ethics,* 135–167. Oxford: Oxford University Press.

Kinzie, J., and Boehnlein, J. 1993. Psychotherapy of victims of massive violence: Countertransference and ethical issues. *American Journal of Psychotherapy* 1:90–102.

Lifton, R. 1976. Advocacy and corruption in the healing professions. *International Review of Psychoanalysis* 3:385–398.

Raphael, B. 1986. *When disaster strikes*. London: Hutchinson.

Roe, M. D. 1993. Queries about protecting children in war settings. *Peace Psychology Bulletin* 3(1):12–18.

Ross, W. 1930. *The right and the good*. Oxford: Clarendon Press.

Steere, J. 1984. *Ethics in clinical psychology.* Cape Town: Oxford University Press.

Straker, G. 1988. Child abuse, counselling, and apartheid. *Free Associations* 14:7–38.

——. 1989. From victim to villain: A "slight" of speech? Media representations of township youth. *South African Journal of Psychology* 19:20–27.

Straker, G., and Moosa, F. 1994. Interacting with trauma survivors in contexts of continuing traumatic stress. *Journal of Traumatic Stress* 7, no. 3, 457–465.

United Nations Convention on the Rights of the Child. Unofficial summary of articles, 1991. *American Psychologist* 46:50–52.

CHAPTER THREE

What Do We Need to Know to Understand Children in War and Community Violence?

JAMES GARBARINO AND KATHLEEN KOSTELNY

The previous chapters raise the questions, What is a child? and What is normal development? To address these issues more fully, it is crucial to have a framework for conceptualizing the development of the child, the expectable environment(s), and the optimal environments in which the child grows up. James Garbarino and Kathleen Kostelny draw on their extensive experience studying and working with children in several war-torn areas of the world and in areas of violence in Chicago. Their model allows for a description of the destructive effects of violence on child development and of the forces within the child and his or her surround that promote resiliency and even creative transformation. Their emphases on the child's need to make meaning of the world and on the role of spiritual and philosophical dimensions in the child's mind are not always seen in accounts of child development. But they are vital to comprehending the experiences of psychic survival and transcendence that some children have even in horrible situations, such as the Holocaust and the Cambodian genocide. Interviews with and autobiographical accounts of these now grown children point to how their quest for meaning in a seemingly arbitrary and utterly cruel world helped to sustain and nourish them at critical junctures. The view of development elaborated in this chapter allows us to comprehend the survival value of acts of altruism, both on the part of children and on the part of adults toward children, and to understand how altruism feeds sustaining ideals that in turn may nourish the ability to give to others.

The authors present, in effect, the question of which theory or theories of development one should rely on, and which is or are truly useful. Garbarino and Kostelny have constructed a framework that draws on several theoretical approaches: (1) an Eriksonian model of developmental stages over the life cycle, with its own mix of psychoanalytic and sociocultural assumptions; (2) a Piagetian model of intellectual development; (3) some modern models of intelligence (Sternberg, 1985, and Vygotsky, 1986); and (4) a human ecological model emphasizing the role of spiritual and political meaning in organizing the inner world of the child.

The choice of developmental models of those who work with children is of course influenced by their training and intellectual background (teacher, therapist, parent, researcher, policy planner) as well as by the setting in which they work. Garbarino and Kostelny have tried to develop a model that takes into account both the inner world of the child and the external nutriment of family, school, and society. They argue, in effect, that we need a model that supports the power of helpful outside interventions in correcting the skewed development that accompanies war and violence. We need a model that is realistic and optimistic in its support of the child's aspirations and that serves to empower and encourage the adults in the child's world.

Practical guides that implement the thinking expressed in this chapter include Mona Macksoud, Helping children cope with the stresses of war: A manual for parents and teachers *(New York: UNICEF, 1993), and Naomi Richman,* Helping children in difficult circumstances: A teacher's manual *(London: Save the Children, 1991).*

This chapter focuses on preadolescent children, as does chapter 6. Chapters 2 and 7 focus on adolescents and young adults.

Children are not simply short adults. There is a human kinship that unites children and adults, but there are significant cognitive, emotional, linguistic, and physical differences that separate us. Adults who seek to understand children in war must recognize these differences. Children who seek to make sense of the world must contend with the differences in their efforts to get their needs met. After recognizing this gap, however, we as adults must seek to bridge it through accessing our own childhoods and searching developmental science for knowledge, empathy, and understanding. We must listen to children and see children as they are.

What do we need to know to understand children in war? We need a developmental perspective. Our goal in this chapter is to present such a developmental perspective to build a foundation for understanding children in situations of war and communal violence. We address the meaning of child development, the roles of "social maps" and context in development, the interplay of social experience and biological forces, and the critical role of intervention in promoting resilience.

What Is Child Development?

In the broadest sense, child development is the process of becoming fully human, whatever that means in a particular child's culture. Experiences combine with a child's biological givens, and from this mixture emerges a complete person, ready for the challenges of day-to-day life. This may mean as a student, as a worker, as a friend, as a family member, and as a citizen, but also as a soldier and as a refugee. To succeed in these roles children need to be rooted in the basic skills of life in their community. War both intensifies the challenge (by increasing the difficulty of becoming competent) and alters the range of roles for the child (for example, by displacing student with soldier). Children need to become socially competent: They must know who they are. They must have a secure and positive sense of their own identity. They must become proficient in thinking and speaking clearly. They must learn to understand the many ways people communicate with one another. It is in the context of this broad conception that we must understand the impact of war on child development.

Our understanding of children in war would be incomplete if it stopped with basic social competence, however. Beyond the demands of everyday social competence, children need a sense of wonder to sustain cognitive development. They need to appreciate the magic of being alive. We want them to do more than just learn to read. We want them to experience the joy of great literature and the pleasure of reading just for fun. We want them to do more than just cope with human relationships. We want them to know love and friendship. We want them to be able to do more than just exist. We want them to know and to appreciate the miracles of existence. We are as concerned with the quality of their inner, spiritual life as we are with the mechanics of their development.

How is all this to happen? First, we must recognize that it is not going to happen automatically. It is up to the adult caregivers to approach children "developmentally." This is of special relevance to children in war, where threats to development abound, threats that include both the trauma of direct assault and of debilitating neglect.

The Developmental Approach
The Child's Changing Potentials

What does it mean to approach a child developmentally? It means that we recognize that child's changing capacity. As children develop, their intellectual, physical, and emotional potentials change. The range of what is possible increases and alters, and these changes in the child's capacity are what child development is all about. Many experts believe that these changes take place in a regular sequence in which the child faces first one issue, then another. Erik Erikson (1950) described eight stages of development, beginning with infancy and extending through old age. Table 3.1 outlines the first four stages, which apply to childhood in Erikson's approach, and the key developmental issues that the child faces in each. Facing these issues is connected to cognitive development as much as it is to emotional development, to social processes as much as to psychological ones. Underlying it all is the foundation of brain growth and development, as ever more complex experiences stimulate and sustain higher levels of brain function.

The child's capacity to experience trust depends on his or her ability to recognize continuity and regularity in care and caregivers. To *feel* that the world is a regular and safe place, the child must *know* when it is not. To become autonomous the child must *know* who she or he is. To become confident about fantasy and reality the child must *know* the difference between them. To take on the role of student the child must *know* the basic behaviors required for mastery. There is a feedback process at work here. If basic needs go unmet, they thwart higher-order development. A terrorized child exists in a state of alarm that prevents opportunities for more sophisticated reflection and learning. An unloved child does not "know" trust in the feeling part of his or her brain. In sum, the processes of knowing are inextricably bound to the processes of feeling, with the brain providing the context for all these translations of experience into knowledge.

Children living amid war and communal violence face special challenges in meeting Erikson's stages. Basic trust is particularly difficult to achieve when parents are psychologically unavailable, and parents are at increased risk of being psychologically unavailable in a war zone or among refugee and displaced populations. For example, a mental health survey in a Cambodian refugee camp reported that nearly 50 percent of the mothers were "seriously depressed" (Garbarino, Kostelny, and Dubrow, 1991b). Children of seriously depressed mothers are less likely than other children to develop secure attachments in the first year of life (Osofsky, 1995). Neglect is common, leading to the prospect of inhibited brain development.

The trauma of life in a war zone may impede resolution of the autonomy versus shame issue. Regression is a typical response among young children affected by war; toiletting and speech problems are common. Both are threats to the basic competence that underlies autonomy.

Meeting the third challenge—initiative versus guilt—depends in part on negotiating a settlement between fantasy and impulse, on the one hand, and reality and restraint, on the other. War and communal violence undermine this process by releasing the dark forces of aggression, by disrupting culturally normal relationships, and by overturning or disarming social structures, thus placing young children in jeopardy.

Finally, war and communal violence disrupt schooling and ordinary vocational development for children. During war, schools are often closed or destroyed. In Mozambique more than 2,000 schools were destroyed, robbing

Table 3.1. Stages of Child Development, Formulated by Erik Erikson

Stage I: Infancy—Basic Trust vs. Mistrust (birth to 18 months)

The infant needs to develop a sense of security, a feeling that the world is a trustworthy place. This comes from establishing a safe and nurturing relationship with primary caregivers—most notably parents (usually the mother). This period emphasizes basic sensory and intellectual growth.

Stage II: Toddler—Autonomy vs. Shame (18 to 36 months)

The toddler needs to develop a sense of being able to do things on his or her own. This includes walking well and beginning to master basic communication through words and gestures. Relationships with parents, siblings, and caregivers are important in providing opportunities for learning and demonstrating these basic skills. Learning to control bodily functions is important. Piaget observed the emergence of basic intellectual operations through the senses of touch, sight, smell, and hearing in this period.

Stage III: Preschool—Initiative vs. Guilt (3 to 5½ years)

The preschooler needs to become confident about testing the limits of individual freedom and group responsibility, of fantasy and reality, of what feels good and what is permissible. Intellectual skills become more sophisticated and language matures rapidly. There is a need to come to terms with social reality in a significant way, but in a manner that does not frighten the child from believing in his or her self-worth.

Stage IV: Elementary School—Industry vs. Inferiority (5½ to 12 years)

This is the time when children take up the important tasks of becoming active participants in the culture beyond the family. Being a student means learning basic academic and social skills and learning how to live in groups with adult guidance. Children develop their characteristic style for working on projects and for presenting themselves to the world. This is a time of consolidating the child's inner life in preparation for the special challenges that adolescence brings. Piaget identified important maturing of the child's ability to think and reason, thus laying the foundation for more fully adultlike reasoning, the task to be mastered in adolescence. Freud called this period the latency stage to indicate that the powerful urges of infancy and early childhood were under control while the sexual impulses of puberty were yet to surface.

Source: Erik Erikson, *Childhood and society* (New York: Norton, 1950).

500,000 children of the opportunity for education. In Cambodia, teachers were singled out as special targets for execution (Garbarino, Kostelny, and Dubrow, 1991b). Moreover, children who experience war and communal violence often have difficulty concentrating in school, and they evidence learning and behavior problems in the classroom (Garbarino, Kostelny, and Dubrow, 1991b; Dyson, 1989).

The Capacity for Change

Approaching a child developmentally also means that we recognize the capacity for change. A child's life is not predetermined; there is no unalterable genetic code that determines what and who a child will be. Each child contains the potential to become many different children, and caring adults can do much to shape which one of those children will come to life. Assuming that development is fixed and predetermined at birth is a recipe for developmental disability and failure.

For example, when genetically identical twins are raised together, or in very similar communities, they grow up to be very similar, even to the extent of having very similar IQ scores. When genetically identical twins grow up in very different environments, however, their IQ scores are likely to be much less similar. One study reported a correlation of 0.85 for identical twins reared separately but in similar communities but only 0.26 for identical twins reared separately in dissimilar communities (Bronfenbrenner, 1986). While genetic heritage usually makes an important contribution to cognitive development, other biological influences can be powerful as well—for example, nutrition that affects brain growth. Moreover, we must recognize that the social environment that a community provides goes a long way toward determining whether biological potential will bloom or wither, whether the biological underpinnings of cognitive development will be fulfilled or denied by experience (Bronfenbrenner, Moen, and Garbarino, 1984). The human brain develops through the use to which it is put. If experience limits the brain to self-defensive survival efforts, without opportunities for higher experiences, potential growth and development are thwarted and future opportunities are lost.

Drawing Social Maps

Most important, we must recognize that development is the process by which the child forms a picture or mentally draws a map of the world and his or her place in it. This map of the world in all its cognitive *and* affective dimensions contains the brain's working hypotheses and conclusions about reality.

A child's development ranges across many domains—linguistic, cognitive, affective, and physical. But it comes together in the child's emerging capacity to form and maintain social maps (Garbarino and associates, 1992). These representations of the world certainly reflect the cognitive competence of the child (knowing the world in the scientific sense of empirical fact). But they also indicate the child's moral and affective inclination. They indicate characteristic ways of feeling about the world.

"What happens when the soldiers come at night?" we asked one young girl.
"The little ones are frightened," she replied.
"And you?" we asked. "Are you frightened?"
"No," she responded bravely. "Only the little ones."

"And what do you do then?" we continued.

"I comfort them," she answered. She is eleven years old. (Garbarino, Kostelny, and Dubrow, 1991b)

Fear is a common theme for children living in a war zone: they wrestle with it, deny it, deal with it. It must be addressed in their social maps. "What do you want to be when you grow up?" we asked a ten-year-old boy. "I don't know. . . . It doesn't matter. . . . I'll probably be killed like my father," he replied sadly (Garbarino, Kostelny, and Dubrow, 1991b).

Future orientation is a frequent casualty among children in war zones, particularly those who have first-hand experience with severe personal loss. "Terminal thinking" results when the probability of death takes the place of an expectation of life, and a child's social map is altered profoundly. We can see evidence of this in Harris Survey results indicating that 35 percent of urban sixth- through twelfth-graders reported that they worry they will not live to old age because they fear they will be shot (compare Garbarino, 1995).

The child's social map is initially the product of experience, a working conclusion about the world born of encounters. But this social map increasingly becomes the cause of the child's experience as well. By creating expectations ("I am surrounded by enemies") it stimulates behavior ("I must trust no one"). By recognizing patterns ("My comrades will protect me") it creates motives to act ("Loyalty to the freedom fighters is most important"). In a war zone, the role of danger in the social maps of children is of course a special concern.

Young children must contend with dangers that derive from two sources not nearly so relevant to adults. First, their physical immaturity places them at risk for injury from trauma that would not be sustained by adults, who are larger and more powerful. Second, young children tend to believe in the reality of threats from what most adults would define as the fantasy world. This increases their vulnerability to perceiving themselves as being in danger. These dangers include monsters under the bed, wolves in the basement, and invisible creatures in the dark corners of bedrooms. But their belief in fantasy also gives them access to magical sources of strength and protection through highly personalized lenses.

We were visiting an orphanage in Baghdad shortly after the Persian Gulf War. "Do any of these boys have fathers?" we asked. "Of course," replied the matron. "Saddam is their father." Later, at an early childhood center we noted Iraqi leader Saddam Hussein's picture in the classroom. When we asked about it a child responded, "Uncle Saddam protects us. He protected us during the bombing." Here the child's magical thinking is augmented by the adults' magical thinking.

Trauma arises when the child cannot give meaning to dangerous experiences in the presence of overwhelming arousal. This orientation is contained in the American Psychiatric Association's definition of post-traumatic stress disorder, which refers to threatening experiences outside the realm of normal experience. Herman (1992) sees trauma this way: as coming "face to face with both human vulnerability in the natural world and with the capacity for evil in human nature."

While adults have developed mechanisms for self-regulation, children are more vulnerable to arousal (van der Kolk, 1987). Brain stem development, for example, is not complete until age eight or nine, and this creates vulnerability to overwhelming arousal. When Bruce Perry (1994) studied children removed from the intense and chronic stress of living in David Koresh's Branch Davidian complex in Waco, Texas, he found that they had seriously elevated heart rates, which indicated a chronic state of overwhelming arousal in the face of danger. How do children make sense of such threats, particularly given their immature cognitive capacities?

Normal children exposed to normal experiences often produce fascinating cognitive solutions to everyday issues. For example, children often develop concepts of divinity that reveal their cognitive immaturity (which is not to say that adults are immune from naïve theology). One boy illustrated this when he explained to his mother that God sat at a giant control board in heaven and controlled everyone and everything by turning knobs. This, he explained, was why we get more "interesting" weather at night (for example, thunderstorms), because with so many people asleep, God had more time to play around with the knobs that controlled clouds, wind, rain, and lightning.

Experiences that are cognitively overwhelming and that produce overwhelming arousal may evoke a process in which understanding these experiences has pathogenic side effects. That is, in coping with traumatic events, the child is forced into patterns of behavior, thought, and feelings that are themselves "abnormal" when contrasted with those of the untraumatized child. Children are particularly vulnerable to the trauma caused by threat and fear. For example, in a study by Davidson and Smith (1990), those children exposed to trauma before age ten were three times more likely to exhibit PTSD than were those exposed after age twelve.

Children and youth exposed to acute danger may require processing over a period of months (Pynoos and Nader, 1988). If the traumatic stress is intense enough, it may leave permanent psychic scars (Terr, 1990). This is particularly true among children made vulnerable because of disruptions in their primary relationships, most notably with parents. These effects include excessive sensitivity to stimuli associated with the trauma, and diminished expectations for the future (Terr, 1990).

But chronic danger imposes a requirement for *developmental* adjustment: accommodations. These are likely to include persistent PTSD, alterations of personality, major changes in patterns of behavior, or ideological interpretations of the world that provide a framework for making sense of ongoing danger (Garbarino et al., 1992). This is particularly true when that danger comes from the violent overthrow of day-to-day social reality, as is the case in war, communal violence, or chronic violent crime.

Beyond any individual strengths that come to a child at birth, the key to successful adaptation and "resilience" lies in the balance of social supports from and for parents and other adults. It lies in parental capacity to buffer social stress by offering children a positive path to follow in dealing with that stress. The quality of life for young children thus becomes a social indicator as well as a measure of personal worth. This hypothesis emerges from a wide range of research and clinical observation, and is manifest in Papanek's (1972) assessment of children in World War II London: "Children measure the danger that threatens them chiefly by the reactions of those around them, especially of their trusted parents and teachers."

Adults as Teachers

Adults are crucial resources for children who are attempting to cope with chronic danger and stress. Generations of studies focusing on the experience of children living in war zones testify to the importance of adult responses to danger as mediating factors in children's responses (Garbarino, Kostelny, and Dubrow, 1991b). So long as adults offer a role model exuding loving, calm, positive determination, most children can cope with a great deal of stress associated with war or community violence. Although children may be traumatized by their experiences, the adults around them will be able to serve as a resource and to support them in rehabilitative efforts.

Once adults begin to decompensate and to panic, however, children suffer. This is not surprising, given the importance of the images of adults contained in a child's social map. Traumatized children need help to recover from their experiences (Terr, 1990), and emotionally disabled or immobilized adults are unlikely to be able to give children what they need. Such adults are inclined to engage in denial, to be emotionally inaccessible, to exude powerlessness, and to misinterpret the child's signals. Messages of safety are particularly important in establishing adults as sources of protection and authority for children living in conditions of threat and violence. These observations of the role of adults in teaching children how to respond to war and community violence derive from developmental phenomena explored by Lev Vygotsky (1986).

In Vygotsky's approach, child development is fundamentally social: development proceeds most effectively through interactive teaching. He focuses on what he calls the zone of proximal development: the difference between what the child can accomplish alone and what the child can accomplish with the guidance of a competent adult. How is this relevant to the child's ability to cope with trauma?

In the case of acute trauma—a single horrible incident that violates the normal reality of the child's world—the child needs psychological first aid in the form of help in believing that "things are back to normal." This therapy of reassurance is a relatively easy teaching task, but the child who lives with chronic trauma (for example, the horror of war) needs something more. This child needs to be taught how to redefine the world in moral and structural terms.

The child needs assistance in processing the existing world if he or she is to avoid drawing social or psychologically pathogenic conclusions: "The world is a hostile and dangerous place," "Adults have lost control of the world," "Kill or be killed," "Don't trust anyone," "My enemies are subhuman." Here the role of the teacher is crucial for the well-being of the child and for the well-being of the community in which that child is a citizen. War creates a socially toxic environment for children, and children need adults to help them avoid psychic poisons (Garbarino, 1995).

In children's desire to integrate their horrible experiences with their hopes, we have noted significant sex differences. Boys often say that they wish to be soldiers to avenge their lost loved ones through violence. Girls, however, are more invested in reestablishing and maintaining community (Garbarino, Kostelny, and Dubrow, 1991b).

A New Model of Intelligence: Foundations for Caring and Resilience

In thinking about children mastering the developmental challenge of living with war or community violence, we are drawn to models of cognitive development that capture the range of human abilities involved. Robert Sternberg (1985) takes the concept of intelligence from an abstract quality to a feature of real-life situations, and in so doing he recognizes that there are several strategies for making sense of the world. He concludes that the best model contains three themes.

The first theme is raw analytical power, a theme that Sternberg calls componential because it concerns the whole set of components contained in "traditional" thinking about intelligence. It refers to what goes on inside a person's head as one solves problems, criticizes hypotheses, makes sense of sensory data, and so forth. This is information processing in the image of a computer.

The second theme is experiential and refers to the ability to combine the knowledge and ideas at hand creatively and insightfully. The emphasis here is on rearranging what one has experienced or learned as a way of mastering the world. Sternberg finds that three abilities make up the experiential: being able to see what is the relevant information about a puzzling situation (selective encoding), being able to put a set of facts together in a way that sheds light in a consistent way (selective combinations), and being able to see new analogies between objects or events previously thought unconnected or dissimilar (selective comparison).

Sternberg calls the third theme contextual because it represents the ability to understand a particular environment's expectations and to arrange to meet or change them. Here the emphasis is on mastering the social realities as a way to solve problems. Sternberg's approach to contextual intelligence is based on how well people understand possible matches between situations and self. It involves seeing how social realities are organized and how to make them work toward one's goals (which may include reshaping or redirecting those social realities).

Sternberg points out that conventional tests of intelligence play to the componential theme, but life offers an opportunity for the contextual to emerge. One of the important implications of Sternberg's approach is this principle: you know only as much about a person's intelligence as you permit yourself to know by the range of assessments you make. A narrow look at information processing may permit only expression of the componential, just as a test confined to creativity and insight will be good only for uncovering the experiential. And, assessing only situationally defined competence (on the streets or at school) will measure only the contextual. Sternberg reports that even though modern assessments of IQ are good for measuring componential intelligence, once someone is in the normal range (100 or higher) IQ differences do not account for much in life success. However, this conclusion heightens the importance of preventing IQ deficiencies of the sort associated with early deprivation, such as may occur during wartime—nutritional deficiencies and separation from parents, for example.

The real thrust of Sternberg's approach is to argue that each person needs to do as much as possible to enhance all three themes and to arrange life to play to strengths and shield weaknesses. For example, Sternberg finds that instruction can boost experiential intelligence just as it can to some degree boost componential and contextual intelligence. In a diverse environment there are many opportunities to accomplish this. The keys are to avoid a debilitating deficiency of componential intelligence, to be encouraged to develop experiential intelligence, and to have access to opportunities to learn social realities that provide important material and resources that constitute intelligence. The threats are thus early deprivations that suppress componential intelligence, repressive environments that stultify creativity and foster rigid thinking, and situations that allow one to be sidetracked or dead-ended into settings that are cut off from a society's principal resources.

Preconditions for Optimal Development

What does it take for a child to form a realistic and positive map of the world, a map that will lead the child into the world with confidence for love, trust, responsibility, and beauty? It takes a world that offers each family the means to meet a child's basic needs (Garbarino and associates, 1992). A child needs a family with access to health care so that he or she can grow strong and healthy. A child needs a family with adequate employment and income, which provides the basis for prosocial contextual intelligence. And, most of all, a child needs day-to-day love, predictability, and stability in important caregiving relationships. Such positive stability is crucial, especially in the early years, when critical brain growth and development occurs.

Whether children experience these ingredients is critical to their development. Threats to the physical health of a child can jeopardize mental and emotional development. Poverty and neglect can stunt intellectual development and impose stress that undermines social development. Instability of child-care arrangements can threaten the child's sense of security and continuity. War can do all this damage and more.

Much of our thinking about how children develop intellectually relies on the pioneering work of the Swiss psychologist Jean Piaget. Piaget's view of development is based on the idea that children form concepts that represent reality. As their brains mature and as they experience the world, they either fit these experiences into existing concepts (a process that Piaget called assimilation) or they adjust the schemes to make sense of new or incongruous ideas (a process that Piaget labeled accommodation). Thus, for example, the child develops a scheme "dog" to cover four-legged furry creatures and understands that German shepherds, collies, and dachshunds are all dogs. But the child must alter his or her concept of dog to acknowledge the fact that some four-legged furry creatures are not dogs but rather are horses, cows, cats, or llamas.

But the child cannot develop in a social vacuum. There is more to development than maturation. Development is a social process, and it is through relationships that the child learns about the world and how it works (Vygotsky, 1986). Who points out that this four-legged furry creature is not a dog but a cat? Who reassures the child when he or she is frightened? Who affirms the child's need to play and daydream? Who guides and helps the child in learning society's rules and beliefs? Who encourages the child to think creatively?

Child development (including brain development) proceeds through and because of social relationships. The earliest and most important of these are between infant and parents (and others who care for the child). These "attachment" relationships are the training ground and foundation for social relationships. Problems in early attachments tend to translate into general social problems, cognitive deficiencies, and emotional difficulties. Deprive the child of crucial social relationships and the child will not thrive and move forward developmentally but will fall back, regress, and stop developing.

To move development forward, children need responses that are emotionally validating and developmentally challenging (Garbarino, Guttmann, and Seeley, 1986). When the child rolls a toy car across the table and says, "Car go," she needs a person to respond with a smile and say, "Yes, honey. That's right, the car is going. And where do you think the car is going?" The child needs people to teach him or her how to be patient, how to follow through, how to behave responsibly, as well as how to tell dogs from cats, A's from B's, and 1's from 2's. A child needs people who care for that child, know that child, and who validate that child emotionally.

The good teacher understands the distance between what a child can accomplish alone and what that child can do when helped by an adult or a more competent peer—the zone of proximate development (Vygotsky, 1986). It is the critical territory for interventions that seek to stimulate and support a child's cognitive development. When a child's environment does not help him reach his full potential "naturally," intervention is needed to change that fact by, one hopes, altering the child's permanent environment rather than inoculating the child against that environment (a strategy of dubious validity and limited success). The key is to shift the child's environment into the zone of proximal development, where it can operate effectively. This means shaping the behavior of adults in the child's life.

Teaching as the Key to Development

It is not so much the capacity for learning that distinguishes humans from other species but rather the capacity to teach. All animals can learn, but only humans consciously set out to teach as a way of facilitating development. Human beings construct elaborate and sophisticated cultures, which they teach to children in ways that are marvelous to behold. It is because humans teach that we do not need to reinvent the wheel each generation or discover fire over and over again. This intergenerational transmission is a kind of cultural DNA. Children learn from adults in many ways, some of which are inadvertent on the adult's part, but deliberate teaching plays a special role in the learning process.

What does all this mean for understanding child development in general and cognitive development in particular? Children's development will not move forward most efficiently if we simply turn them loose to "go forth and learn!" nor if we plan every detail in their existence. Children need to be treated like honored dignitaries from a foreign land who do not yet understand the language or know the customs. They need to be loved and respected and to be taught the ropes.

The Accumulation of Risk

Of the many domains of child development research emerging in the past two decades, the studies of risk and resilience are particularly important for understanding children in war. This research teaches an important developmental lesson: risk accumulates, opportunity ameliorates (Garbarino and associates, 1992). An emergent model of risk by Sameroff and colleagues (1987) has found that most children can cope with low levels of risk, but it is the accumulation of risks that jeopardizes development, particularly when no compensatory forces are at work.

Risk accumulates, opportunity ameliorates. This is a central conclusion we draw from our observations of children coping with war and communal violence. Children can cope with one or two major risk factors in their lives, but when risk accumulates—with the addition of a third, fourth, and fifth factor—we see a precipitation of developmental damage (Garbarino and Kostelny, 1996). This model highlights the importance of context in understanding the differences observed among children living in war zones and under forms of community violence. It highlights the common observation that children who are victims of family violence are hurt most by war and community violence. For most children experiencing community violence, the experience takes place within a larger context of risk. Such children often are poor, live in disrupted families, contend with parental incapacity brought on by depression or substance abuse, are raised by parents with little education or few employment prospects, and are exposed to domestic violence (Garbarino, Kostelny, and Dubrow, 1991b; Kotlowitz, 1991).

This constellation of risk by itself creates enormous challenges for young children. For them, the trauma of community violence is often the final straw. This is a crucial issue in war zones around the world and among the approximately 20 percent of American children who live with a significant accumulation of risk.

Factors Leading to Resiliency and Coping

As opportunity factors accumulate, resilience increases (Dunst and Trivette, 1992). Convergent findings from studies of life course responses to stressful early experience suggest a series of ameliorating factors that can be applied to children growing up in war zones (Losel and Bliesener, 1990):

- active attempts to cope with stress (not just reactions to stress);
- cognitive competence (at least an average level of intelligence);
- experiences of self-efficacy and corresponding self-confidence and positive self-esteem;
- temperamental characteristics that favor active coping attempts and positive relationships with others (for example, high level of activity, goal orientation, sociability) rather than passive withdrawal;
- a stable emotional relationship with at least one parent or other reference person;
- an open, supportive educational climate and parental model of behavior that encourages constructive coping with problems; and
- social support from people outside the family.

An example of this phenomenon is Candida, a Nicaraguan who was kidnapped at age nine by the contras. Her parents were killed, and Candida was forced to live on the run with the contras. Eventually she escaped and was adopted by her father's cousin. "Sixteen when we met her, she is known as the 'solidad,' the one who is not yet married. She told us she had more important things on her agenda. Sure, she has boyfriends, but she plans to become a civil engineer. She excels in school, especially at math, and has finished six grades in less than three years. She had the opportunity to study abroad—government policy dictates that war orphans are entitled to the best education—but she preferred to study in Nicaragua and stay with her family. She is very active in politics and is very proud that she could vote in the elections. While she hopes there won't be a war, she will join the struggle if necessary" (Garbarino, Kostelny, and Dubrow, 1991b).

The task of dealing with the effects of war and community violence on children falls to the people who care for these children—their parents and other relatives, teachers, and counselors. But these adults take on this task while facing enormous challenges of their own. Whether in war zones around the world or in

American communities, we have found that human service professionals and educators working in high-violence areas are themselves often traumatized by their exposure to violence. In one study in Chicago we found that 60 percent of the Head Start staff members surveyed had experienced traumatic events connected with violence (Garbarino et al., 1992). For these individuals, efforts to create a safe zone in the school are crucial to their ability to perform their important functions in the lives of high-risk children. For this safe zone to help children focus on their schoolwork, it must exist as part of their social maps.

Our efforts to understand the impact of war and chronic community violence on children and youth around the world highlight several concerns—unmet medical needs, the corrosive effects of poverty and violence on personality and brain development, academic achievement, and so forth. But from our perspective, the most important of these is that the experience of trauma distorts the development of values—suppressing higher-order thinking about human relations and stimulating more primitive approaches.

We offer this observation based on the recognition that the dual nature of trauma (overwhelming arousal *and* overwhelming cognitions) implies a twofold model of its consequences. PTSD represents the wound that is "narrowly" psychological (and that may extend to other specifically psychological effects—compare Garbarino et al., 1992). As our discussion of social maps implies, however, there is a second wound, the philosophical hurt that may arise from the experiencing of trauma, particularly chronic trauma related to war and community violence.

Victims of trauma who are protected from the philosophical wounds can manage the psychological symptoms. They may carry permanent symptoms, but they are able to organize their behavior effectively in prosocial patterns as co-workers, citizens, and family members. In short, they function, albeit with an emotional limp (Garbarino, Guttmann, and Seeley, 1986). However, those who suffer from psychological symptoms *and* the philosophical wounds of distrust, terminal thinking, and antisocial hostility are likely to end up as "emotional cripples," unable to function (Garbarino, 1995). These are the individuals for whom trauma and neglect have undermined a sense of positive connection to higher morality and purpose, for whom sustaining spiritual resources are inaccessible.

Unless we reach children and youth with healing experiences and offer them a moral, political, and spiritual framework within which to process their experiences, traumatized children are likely to be drawn to groups and ideologies that legitimize and reward their rage, fear, and hateful cynicism. This is an environment in which violent peer groups (for example, gangs and militia) flourish and community institutions deteriorate.

At the heart of this moral deterioration is declining trust in adults on the part of children and youth in high-violence communities (Garbarino, 1995). As one youth living in a small city experiencing a proliferation of gangs put it to us recently: "If I join a gang I'll be 50 percent safe, but if I don't, I'll be 0 percent safe." He does not put his trust and faith in adults. That is what he is telling us if we are prepared to listen. There are self-serving, antisocial individuals and groups in any society prepared to mobilize and exploit the anger, fear, alienation, and hostility that many traumatized children feel. *They* are listening. Are *we*?

Implications for Intervention in Situations of War and Community Violence

Having sketched what we mean by child development, we can turn to a developmentally grounded approach to intervention in a more systematic way.

Lesson No. 1 "Those who have the most learn the most." When early childhood education programs such as Head Start were offered in a given community, not everyone participated and not everyone benefited equally. It was the more highly motivated people, those who already had their heads a bit above water, who used these opportunities and whose children gained the most. We can presume that the same is true in situations of war and community violence.

Lesson No. 2 "The greater the challenge, the greater the payoffs." There is a law of increasing returns at work in programs aimed at children in war zones and areas of community violence. Each child protected from developmental delays and educational failure means a later savings of many thousands of dollars in costs to society. These savings flow from more productive employment, better health, and less delinquency. Reaching the most affected people should be a priority. But as we move from the easiest to the hardest cases, we experience a simultaneous increase in both program costs and program benefits. Providing effective intervention for the most deprived populations will remain a challenging proposition in any society at war. At the most extreme point of the spectrum this means that controlling the most devastated individuals through *permanent* supervisory relationships, while costly, may be the only way to avoid disastrously antisocial or self-destructive behavior.

Lesson No. 3 "We can't inoculate children against future failure." Effective programs cannot prevent later failure. But they can prepare children to take advantage of later opportunities—in school and in the world of work. Without this preparation, many children are bound to fail because they lack the cognitive and affective skills needed. Investing in powerful intervention programs is, therefore, a necessary condition for programs later in life to work. The first years of life are crucial for healthy brain growth and development. No investment is more cost-effective.

Lesson No. 4 "Earlier is better." Programs that are delayed until adolescence are generally not as effective as programs that begin during childhood. The earlier intervention begins, the better are its chances of succeeding. The odds of promoting more developmentally enhancing social maps increases when intervention occurs during the early period of brain growth and development.

Lesson No. 5 "No narrowly based program can do it alone." For intervention programs to succeed, they should be part of a well-coordinated campaign to prevent developmental delays, to prevent health problems that disproportionately affect and inhibit the development of children in war zones and areas of community violence, and to upgrade the conditions of life in high-risk social environments of which violence is often just one negative feature. Research reveals that it is the accumulation of risk factors, not the presence or absence of any one factor, that tells the story about a child's development (Sameroff et al., 1987).

Lesson No. 6 "If parents are not part of the solution, they are part of the problem." We must collaborate with parents. This means that high-risk parents must be brought into the process of intervention as much as children. These parents may themselves have incorporated the damages faced by their children if war or community violence has been chronic.

Lesson No. 7 "Doing the job well requires well-trained professionals." Developing and running the necessary intervention programs require a high level of professional expertise. Managing a program for middle-class children who come from stable, highly motivated families living in peaceful environments is difficult enough, but successfully operating an intervention program for high-risk children living in a war zone or area of community violence is far more challenging for staff members. They cannot be trained or hired cheaply. What is more, they must receive intensive expert supervision to deal with the unconscious and conscious issues raised by working with traumatized populations (for example, powerlessness, rage, empathy overload).

Conclusion

War and communal violence have direct effects on child development (such as the psychological impact of trauma) as well as indirect effects (the loss of key relationships). Placing these effects within a context of normal development is useful in two ways: it opens our eyes to the many domains in which war and community violence may take its toll, and it illuminates the many necessary elements of intervention to help children cope effectively.

REFERENCES

Bronfenbrenner, U. 1986. The ecology of the family as a context for human development: Research perspectives. *Developmental Psychology* 22:723–742.

Bronfenbrenner, U., Moen, P., and Garbarino, J. 1984. Families and communities. In R. Parke, ed., *Review of child development research.* Chicago: University of Chicago Press.

Davidson, J., and Smith, R. 1990. Traumatic experiences in psychiatric outpatients. *Journal of Traumatic Stress Studies* 3 (July):459–475.

Dunst, C. J., and Trivette, C. M. 1992. Risk and opportunity factors influencing parent and child functioning. Paper based on presentations at the Ninth Annual Smoky Mountain Winter Institute, Asheville, N.C.

Dyson, J. 1989. Family violence and its effect on children's academic underachievement and behavior problems in school. *Journal of the National Medical Association* 82: 17–22.

Erikson, E. 1950. *Childhood and society.* New York: Norton.

——. 1992. *Towards a sustainable society: An economic, social and environmental agenda for our children's future.* Chicago: Noble Press.

——. 1995. *Raising children in a socially toxic environment.* San Francisco: Jossey-Bass.

Garbarino, J., Dubrow, N., Kostelny, K., and Pardo, C. 1992. *Children in danger: Coping with the consequences of community violence.* San Francisco: Jossey-Bass.

Garbarino, J., Guttmann, E., and Seeley, J. 1986. *The psychologically battered child.* San Francisco: Jossey-Bass.

Garbarino, J., and Kostelny, K. 1993. Children's response to war: What do we know? In L. Leavitt and N. Fox, eds., *The psychological effects of war and violence on children.* Hillsdale, N.J.: Lawrence Erlbaum, 23–40.

——. 1994. Developmental consequences of living in dangerous and unstable environments: The situation of refugee children. In *The psychological well-being of refugee children,* 2nd ed. Geneva: International Catholic Child Bureau.

——. 1996. The effects of political violence on Palestinian children's behavior problems: A risk accumulation model. *Child Development* 67:33–45.

Garbarino, J., Kostelny, K., and Dubrow, N. 1991a. What children can tell us about living in danger. *American Psychologist* 46:376–383.

——. 1991b. *No place to be a child: Growing up in a war zone.* Lexington, Mass.: Lexington Books.

Garbarino, J., and Manly, J. In press. Free and captured play. *International Play Journal.*

Garbarino, J., and associates. 1992. *Children and families in the social environment.* 2nd ed. New York: Aldine, 1982.

Herman, J. L. 1992. *Trauma and recovery.* New York: Basic Books.

Kostelny, K., and Garbarino, J. 1994. Coping with the consequences of living in danger: The case of Palestinian children and youth. *International Journal of Behavioral Development* 17(4):595–611.

Kotlowitz, A. 1991. *There are no children here.* New York: Doubleday.

Losel, F., and Bliesener, T. 1990. Resilience in adolescence: A study on the generalizability of protective factors. In K. Hurrelmann and F. Losel, eds., *Health hazards in adolescence.* New York: Walter de Gruyter.

McClane, J., and McNamee, G. 1987. *Early literacy.* Cambridge, Mass.: Harvard University Press.

Olds, D., Henderson, C., Chamberlain, R., and Tatelbaum, R. 1986. Preventing child abuse and neglect: A randomized trial of nurse home visitation. *Pediatrics* 78:65–78.

Osofsky, J. 1995. The effects of violence exposure on young children. *American Psychologist* 50:782–788.

Paley, V. 1987. *Boys and girls: Superheroes in the doll corner.* Chicago: University of Chicago Press.

Papanek, V. 1972. *Design for the real world: Human ecology and social change.* New York: Pantheon.

Parents as Teachers. 1989. The National Center. Missouri Department of Elementary and Secondary Education. Jefferson City, Mo., 1988.

Perry, B. 1994. Evolution of emotional, behavioral, and physiological responses in children acutely exposed to violence. Presentation at 41st Annual Academy of Child and Adolescent Psychiatry, New York.

Pynoos, R., and Nader, K. 1988. Psychological first aid and treatment approach to children exposed to community violence: Research implications. *Journal of Traumatic Stress Studies* 1(4):445–473.

Sameroff, A., Seifer, R., Barocas, R., Zax, M., and Greenspan, S. 1987. Intelligence quotient scores of 4-year-old children: Social-environmental risk factors. *Pediatrics* 79:343–350.

Sternberg, R. J. 1985. *Beyond IQ*. New York: Cambridge University.

Terr, L. 1990. *Too scared to cry*. New York: HarperCollins.

Van der Kolk, B. A. 1987. *Psychological trauma*. Washington, D.C.: American Psychiatric Press.

Vygotsky, L. 1986. *Thought and language*. London: MIT Press.

Weikart, D. 1983. Prevention strategies for healthy babies and healthy children. Testimony before the Select Committee on Children, Youth, and Families. U.S. House of Representatives. June 30.

CHAPTER FOUR

Post-Traumatic Stress Disorder and Other Stress Reactions

WILLIAM ARROYO AND SPENCER ETH

William Arroyo and Spencer Eth provide a specifically clinical psychiatric focus to the question of how children respond to and deal with trauma. In their work they discuss the discourse of the book diagnostic categories and epidemiological terms such as prevalence, risk factors, psychopathology, and treatment. They offer an eminently practical set of recommendations for diagnostic criteria, and they indicate what is known about effective and relevant forms of treatment, whether dialogical or pharmacological. They also begin a more refined discussion of the concept of trauma and a more detailed examination of the pathways by which trauma can produce psychopathological conditions.

Their discussion of trauma draws heavily on a developmental model, similar in many respects to that presented in the previous chapter. At the same time, they take up a number of problems attendant on using a model that is based primarily on psychopathology. They speak of adverse effects on growth and development, not only traumatic stress syndromes, and they consider the issue of the boundaries between normal stress reactions and psychopathological reactions. They also consider the complex interplay between physiology and psychology, raising the issue that disorders induced by psychological distress can leave a physiological mark and may need treatment that addresses both domains.

They are also aware of the limitations of current diagnostic schemas, such as those laid out in the Diagnostic and Statistical Manual (DSM-IV) of the American Psychiatric Association, especially in regard to children. In general, these schemas do not reflect the intensity, severity, and chronicity of the devastation wrought by war and persecution on children of different ages, and they are in need of both empirical and philosophical refinement. This issue and the impact of the political climate and political motivations for violence are reflected in chapter 2 and have been elaborated by David Becker, who works primarily in

Chile with victims of persecution under the Pinochet dictatorship (see, for example, E. Lira, D. Becker, and M. I. Castillo, Psicoterapia de víctimas de represión política bajo dictadura; Un desafío terapeútico, teórico y político *[San Francisco: American Association of Science, 1989]).*

Arroyo and Eth skillfully summarize the state of the art of medicine, drawing on their extensive experience in the United States and elsewhere. At the same time, they remind us of how much more solid knowledge is needed.

Major stress reactions in children, especially traumatic stress syndromes, are a focus of concern throughout the world. The cause of the concern from a clinical perspective is related to the associated risks of psychopathology and of adverse impact on the growth and development of children. Life-threatening incidents, both natural and man-made disasters, are unfortunately not uncommon worldwide. Some of these events are associated with chronically stressful situations that may also affect growth and development.

Research on psychological trauma in children lags behind that on adults, and many studies have been elaborations of investigations conducted with adult populations. Although the research on adults has provided a good framework from which to launch research on children, there are problems in attempting to apply the same paradigms to children. Major differences between the two populations exist in the area of development, the range of reactions and their phenomenology, and the mediators of stress reactions.

In this chapter we address common stress responses in children, the various stress-related disorders in children, prevalence information on these disorders, their developmental implications, and various treatment methods.

Review of Literature on Post-Traumatic Stress

Garmezy and Rutter (1985) classify stress studies into five major categories: (1) loss; (2) chronically disturbed relationships; (3) events that change the family status quo; (4) events that require social adaptation; and (5) acute traumatic events. Hill (1994) suggests that a more clinically relevant approach to assessing the effects of stress might be to narrow the study variables to the amount of threatened or actual loss, the amount of anxiety caused, and the amount of adaptation required by the child—all considered in a developmental context.

Both warfare and communal violence provide contexts in which a child is potentially exposed to acute and severe stressors, with possible subsequent periods of chronic adversities. Several factors will determine the success of the child's attempt to adapt to these situations, including the child's perception and vulnerabilities, and the availability of protective factors.

The child's cognitive appraisal of the situation or stressor is crucial because it determines in large part how effective he or she will be in mobilizing internal defensive mechanisms or external resources, and whether a post-traumatic syndrome will develop. For example, it is rare for all individuals who are exposed to the same life-threatening stressor to experience the same psychic trauma. Each person has a subjective way of perceiving, making it impossible to predict exactly who will develop psychic trauma; one can only conclude with certainty that all are at higher risk than are those who have not been exposed.

Psychic trauma refers to a sense of profound helplessness in the face of overwhelming danger, anxiety, and arousal when confronted with an external situation in which there is a high risk of death or injury to oneself or to another. The constellation of post-traumatic symptoms includes behavioral, cognitive, and physiological clusters. The course of the symptomatic picture is also variable and may be mediated by many factors. Some of the features of psychic trauma may last from a few days to many years; also, they do not necessarily correlate with the psychiatric diagnosis a child may receive.

Terr (1991) characterizes childhood trauma as involving four primary characteristics: "strongly visualized" or "repeatedly perceived" memories; "repetitive behaviors"; "trauma-specific fears"; and "changed attitudes about people, aspects of life, and the future." She adds that childhood trauma may be Type I, or the "single-blow" type, referring to the reactions that can follow a single event that has not been preceded by other traumatic events. This type is characterized by detailed memories, "omens," and misperceptions. Long-standing or repeated exposure to extreme events induces Type II trauma. Along with repeated child abuse, life in a war zone or violent urban area may provide the context in which children develop this type of syndrome. Type II reactions can be characterized by massive denial, psychic numbing, self-hypnosis, dissociation, aggression toward self, identification with the aggressor, and personality changes. Children with Type I trauma who experience major secondary adversities as a consequence of the original event may develop a Type II profile. In some instances acute stressors have minor complications, but in others the complications may assume a chronic adverse course in which there is an accumulation of the effects of many stressors. This may characterize children living in a war zone and being exposed to a myriad of stressors, and children living in a neighborhood where violence is rampant. In these instances either there may be no stress-free time in which to recover, or the first major stressor may predispose the child to more severe reactions with subsequent stressors.

Response patterns among children exposed to stress are variable. However, the disaster literature reports patterns in children exposed both to acute stressors and to high and chronic levels of stress—common in both communal and war-related violence. Vogel and Vernberg (1993) conclude that group scores on general behavior checklists are seldom significantly elevated after disasters. However, there is an increase in the prevalence of fears, often specific to the event. For example, a child who lived in a war zone may become fearful when exposed to people in military uniforms, which the child associates with violence (Arroyo, 1988); a child who survived a destructive hurricane may become anxious when near bodies of water (Yule, Udwin, and Murdoch, 1990). A fear of the recurrence of, for example, a sniper incident (Pynoos et al., 1987) or civil unrest (Eth, Arroyo, and Silverstein, 1993) may arise. Fear may become debilitating, as is commonly seen in PTSD.

We noted separation difficulties, clinging, and other dependent behaviors in clinical work with Los Angeles earthquake survivors (Arroyo and Eth, 1994), and others have made similar observations in different disasters (Sullivan, Saylor, and Foster, 1991). Separation difficulties are more evident in younger children but may also be present in subtler forms in older children (Vogel and Vernberg, 1993). Vogel and Vernberg have observed that parents who become anxious as a result of trauma may encourage clinging types of behavior and proximity to their children, ostensibly to protect them; this protective stance may also serve to diminish the parent's anxiety. Reenactments of certain elements of the critical incident in play or "post-traumatic play" (Terr, 1981) are commonly seen in preschoolers and school-aged children as a form of repetition compulsion that does not relieve the trauma-related anxiety. At other times the play may be part of reconstructive fantasies of the victims or survivors, such as reported in reroofing of buildings after a hurricane (Saylor, Powell, and Swenson, 1992), which may be an important element in the recovery phase.

Disturbances of sleep patterns are frequently encountered, along with reluctance to sleep alone, night terrors, nightmares, and repeated dreams about the disaster or event; these can be correlated to the severity of other symptoms (Pynoos et al., 1987). Increased irritability and tantrums are also common (Ollendick and Hoffman, 1982). Enuresis and other signs of regression may be prevalent in preschool and elementary school children (Gleser, Green, and Winget, 1981). Vague and multiple somatic complaints are often found; in more severe cases these symptoms may last for several months (Nader et al., 1990) and may affect school attendance. Feelings of responsibility and guilt may be expressed by those who witnessed violent deaths (Pynoos et al., 1987). Anxiety and depression are noted in children who have been exposed to disasters (Yule, Udwin, and Murdoch, 1990). In most instances, symptoms developed in response to a disaster begin to diminish after the event (Vogel and Vernberg, 1993), and recovery may be complete within eighteen to thirty-six months. Risk factors for symptom chronicity include the dose of exposure and psychological connection to the victims (Nader et al., 1990). Recent data suggest that dissociation symptoms experienced in the immediate aftermath of the traumatic event and subsequent life stress predict a severe course (Koopman, Classen, and Spiegel, 1994).

The initial attempts to study the effects of war on children, based on the reactions of children during World War II, concluded that separation from parents may have contributed more to the temporary psychological distress than the war itself (Freud and Burlingham, 1943). This finding may be confounded by recently disclosed information that many of these evacuated children were apparently abused (Wicks, 1988); this was not known previously, probably because of minimal child-protection statutes in Great Britain in the 1940s. The quality of the caretaking was likely to have been poor, and this factor should always be scrutinized in evaluating the evacuation of a population of children from proximal battlefields. Ayalon (1983) found a high level of anxiety among children in areas where the Arab-Israeli conflict is endemic. Others have found high rates of PTSD among children exposed to war (Saigh, 1991). Chronic symptoms were found in some Southeast Asian youngsters exposed to extreme war-related violence several years after the exposure (Kinzie et al., 1986).

The preponderance of the literature on the reactions by children to urban violence has focused on discrete episodes of violence. Though many youngsters from urban areas are exposed to a series of violence, children's reactions to such violence had not been studied until recently (Richters and Martinez, 1993; Martinez and Richters, 1993). These new investigations found that exposure to violence both in the community and at home was correlated with distress symptoms primarily in younger children (first- and second-graders) and older children (fifth- and sixth-graders), that the older children's distress and depression were associated with exposure to violence affecting known victims, and that younger children who had higher levels of distress also had more guns and drugs in the home. They also concluded that parents generally tended to underestimate their children's level of distress; this, of course, would have clinical implications in the area of emotional support provided to the children by their parents. In addition, it was found that exposure to violence was more common in households in which the parents were less educated. Martinez and Richters (1993) warn, however, that they did not determine whether the symptoms preceded or followed their subjects' exposure to violence; also, it is conceivable that the children's symptoms may have made them more vulnerable to further exposure to violence.

The literature on chronic adverse environments also has implications for children and families exposed to repeated stressors. Some of these stressors are closely related to the attributes of the child, others may be related to parents, and still others to economic conditions. As in the case of single severe stressors, the stress of chronically adverse environments tends to undermine the coping skills, adaptation, and possibly growth and development of children. Rutter (1978, 1985, 1987) found several variables that cumulatively proved to be significantly associated with psychiatric disorder in children. These included severe marital discord, low socioeconomic status, large family size or overcrowding, paternal criminality, maternal psychiatric disorder, and the placement of a child under the care of social services. Twenty-one percent of the children with four or more of these factors manifested a psychiatric disorder. Kolvin and his colleagues (1988) found that poor mothering, overcrowding, and marital disruption were powerful indicators of adversity and psychiatric morbidity. Some of these factors may be evident in children from war zones and violence-ridden neighborhoods.

Prevalence of Stress Reactions

The studies regarding the prevalence of stress reactions among children exposed to acute, potentially traumatic events are variable, and a comparison of these studies is problematic. The rates for PTSD, the most frequently studied stress-related syndrome, for example, seem to vary greatly, and widely differing methodologies have been employed to measure them. The sample (and control sample, if any), criteria, rating instruments, type of stressor, time lapse between the occurrence of stress and actual data collection, and the population's proximity to the event are rarely comparable. Another difficulty is that many of these studies propose hypotheses based on a linear causal model, which tends to underestimate the influence of other factors or contexts that are considered in a transactional model.

The prevalence of stress-related disorders in children exposed to warfare is considerable, according to most recent studies. A recent estimate by UNICEF suggests that 80 percent of the primary victims of war are women and children (Lee, 1991). Ayalon (1983) found high rates of anxiety among Israeli children, and Saigh (1989) found that nearly a third of his subjects aged nine to thirteen years developed PTSD. The levels of PTSD did not vary much, regardless of whether the subjects were direct or indirect victims. In a study of Cambodian children (Kinzie et al., 1986), 50 percent of adolescent refugees met the criteria for PTSD six years after leaving their homeland, though a five-year follow-up showed that the symptoms appeared to be diminishing.

Children who survive disasters also have variable rates of prevalence as a function of methodologies and other factors described above. In the Buffalo Creek, West Virginia, disaster of 1972, 37 percent of the children aged two to fifteen probably met criteria for the diagnosis of PTSD in a study made two years after the event (Green et al., 1991). In that disaster, the collapse of a slag mining dam caused flooding that killed one hundred twenty-five people. Thousands were left homeless. A suit filed against the mining company on behalf of six hundred residents (including two hundred children) for "psychological impairment" was settled out of court. Bloch, Silber, and Perry (1956) demonstrated that about 30 percent of children showed mild to severe reactions as a result of a tornado in Vicksburg, Mississippi. In a study on the effects of an airplane disaster in Lockerbie, Scotland (Parry Jones, 1991), 66 percent of fifty-four children from the area of the crash were found to have PTSD; 88 percent had sleep disturbance; and more than 50 percent had disturbances in concentration, mood, and anxiety regulation.

The context of the events may be another important variable in understanding reactions to stress. If these events occurred in an impoverished area where, for example, the infrastructure of a community is destroyed, the degree and duration of suffering and impairment could be quite different from those found in the industrialized countries, where most of these studies have been conducted.

The issue of the cultural relevance of PTSD and other anxiety-related disorders has been raised by several authors (Marsella, Friedman, and Spain, 1993; Guarnaccia and Kirmayer, 1993; Rogler, 1992). Although it is clear from the fundamental theory on which PTSD is based that a life-threatening event may precipitate a cluster of symptoms of severe stress, there is a great deal of variation in the symptoms of stress among cultural groups. Much more research is needed to elucidate these variations.

Diagnostic Categories of Stress-Related Mental Disorders

Intense debate has raged for many years on whether PTSD and other stress-related reactions are normal or psychopathological responses. O'Donohue and Elliot (1992) question whether PTSD is a mental disorder. The same inquiry can be made for the less severe category of adjustment disorder. Current thinking appears to support the belief that even though these syndromes may be expectable reactions to catastrophic stressors, it is prudent to classify them as mental disorders (American Psychiatric Association, 1994) because of their associated emotional distress and psychosocial disability.

A question regarding stress reactions in children that has not been answered fully is to what extent there is a developmental progression of reactions to stress (Yule, 1994). Although the literature in general suggests that the extent is considerable, there are no normative data to support this notion. The lack of data makes it particularly challenging for clinicians and investigators to provide an accurate diagnosis. The fact remains, however, that youngsters with these stress-related diagnoses do indeed suffer along with their families.

Children may develop one or more of a variety of DSM-IV psychiatric disorders associated with exposure to psychosocial stressors. Some authors (Davidson, 1993; Terr, 1991) believe that several diagnostic categories are potentially trauma related. Most of the following categories have been studied primarily in adults and have few, if any, criteria specifically applicable to children, though children can also receive these diagnoses.

The diagnostic criteria of PTSD reflected in the DSM-IV (American Psychiatric Association, 1994) have been modified for applicability to children. The stressor criteria require that, in addition to having experienced or witnessed a life-threatening event, a person must respond with intense fear, helplessness, or horror. In children the response may be disorganized or agitated behavior. In the reexperiencing cluster of symptoms, the phenomenon of repetitive play, in which themes or aspects of the trauma are expressed, may be substituted for recurrent distressing recollections. Children may have frightening dreams without recognizable content, and they may also exhibit diagnostically significant traumatic reenactments. A new general criterion is that the symptoms of PTSD cause clinically significant distress or impairment in social, occupational, or other important areas of functioning. The disorder may be further classified into subtypes: acute (duration of less than three months), chronic (duration of three months or more), and delayed (onset at least six months after the stressor).

A new category, acute stress disorder, is included in DSM-IV (American Psychiatric Association, 1994). The criteria are similar to those for PTSD except that the dissociative symptoms of derealization and depersonalization are included; the symptoms must last for at least two days but not more than four weeks, and they must begin within four weeks of the traumatic event. This condition cannot be merely an exacerbation of a preexisting Axis I disorder. There are no specific diagnostic modifications for children who exhibit this disorder.

In *brief psychotic disorder* (brief reactive) a person's response to a major stressor involves psychotic symptoms of sudden onset of less than one month's duration. The disorder ends with a return to the premorbid state. The identical criteria apply to all age groups.

Nightmare disorder is characterized by frequent awakenings from sleep because of recurring frightening dreams. These REM-sleep dreams cause significant distress or result in social or occupational dysfunction.

Sleep terror disorder is characterized by recurrence of sleep terror, awakenings from sleep usually beginning with a panicky scream or cry, autonomic arousal, and intense fear. The individual is difficult to awaken during these non–REM sleep episodes.

Separation anxiety disorder is characterized by excessive anxiety regarding separation or anticipated separation from the child's primary caretaker. This disorder usually has its onset during the preschool years.

Reactive attachment disorder is characterized by markedly disturbed and developmentally inappropriate social relatedness before age five.

Dissociative amnesia is characterized by an inability to recall important personal information, usually of a traumatic or stressful nature. It is more likely to occur among older teenagers than among young children who have experienced a single traumatic event. It may be difficult to diagnose in very young children because it may be confused with developmentally appropriate childhood amnesia.

Dissociative fugue is characterized by an inability to recall one's past and by confusion about one's identity associated with sudden unexpected travel away from home. This rare disorder is more common in adolescence than in preadolescence.

Conversion disorder is a condition in which one's physical or sensory function suggests a medical illness, for which there is a lack of corroborative medical evidence. It is apparently an expression of an unconscious psychological conflict, and the symptoms are not intentionally produced. The usual onset is in adolescence. The same criteria apply to all age groups.

Depersonalization disorder is a state in which one experiences an altered sense of self through a feeling of detachment from, and of being an observer of, one's own mental processes or body. The onset is usually in adolescence, and the same criteria apply to all age groups.

Adjustment disorders are emotional or behavioral symptoms developed in response to identifiable stressor(s) that may be single, multiple, recurrent, or continuous, and may accompany specific developmental events. The symptoms have an onset within three months of the stressor. The disorder is further classified according to the predominant symptom—that is, anxiety, depressed mood, disturbance of conduct, mixed disturbance of emotions and conduct, mixed anxiety and depressed mood, and unspecified.

Specific phobia is a specific fear. Trauma-specific fears are common in traumatized children and adolescents (Terr, 1991). In children the anxiety may be expressed by crying, freezing, tantrums, or clinging. Children may not recognize that the fear is excessive or unreasonable.

Panic disorder consists of discrete episodes of intense anxiety or discomfort, with or without agoraphobia. The disorder is more common in adolescence than in childhood; the criteria are the same for all age groups.

Major depressive episodes may follow the violent death of a loved one. The criteria for children include irritable mood and failure to gain weight as expected (American Psychiatric Association, 1994). Other diagnostic criteria that apply to all age groups include depressed mood, diminished interest or pleasure in most daytime activities, insomnia or hypersomnia, fatigue, diminished concentration, and recurrent thoughts of death.

Somatization disorder consists of clinically significant, recurrent, and multiple somatic complaints of several years' duration. This is more commonly seen in adolescence than in childhood. The criteria are the same for all age groups.

Substance abuse disorders are more common among older adolescents. The same criteria apply to all age groups.

Borderline personality disorder is characterized by instability of self-image, interpersonal relationships, and mood, and marked impulsivity. This is more commonly seen in late adolescence and adulthood than in childhood. Personality disorders are rarely diagnosed in the prepubertal child.

Dissociative identity disorder is one in which more than one distinct identity or personality takes control of the person's behavior. In children the symptoms are not attributable to imaginary play.

Other diagnostic considerations, especially when working with culturally diverse populations and immigrant populations, are the so-called culture-bound syndromes (American Psychiatric Association, 1994), which may be confused with those listed above. These include *ataque de nervios, bilis* or *colera, boufee delirante, ghost sickness, latah, locura, nervios,* and *susto.*

Developmental Considerations of Trauma

Psychic trauma has various implications for a child's level of functioning and the strategies of intervention used. For space reasons we limit our discussion to the effects of psychic trauma on development rather than other types of stress. There is a dearth of empirical research on the effects of psychic trauma on development; the extant work is primarily of a clinical nature and suggests that there are differential developmental effects (Eth and Pynoos, 1985; Pynoos, 1993; Arroyo and Eth, 1994).

The cognitive immaturity of infants, coupled with their limited communicative ability, presents nearly insurmountable obstacles to the evaluation of trauma during infancy with the available techniques, which are dependent on verbal expression in clinical settings. However, Drell, Siegel, and Gaensbauer (1993) strongly suggest that there is a recognizable constellation of symptoms found in traumatized infants—including hypervigilance, exaggerated startle, developmental regression, clinging behavior, body dysregulation, and nightmares. They suggest that growth and developmental progress may be compromised by the duration and severity of these symptoms. This presentation can be further modified by the response of the child's mother, for example, who may have been traumatized simultaneously by the same event. For example, a mother whose husband has been killed by an intruder may become too impaired to meet the needs of her infant; a prolonged and severe reaction in mother could seriously jeopardize the growth and development of her infant.

Traumatized preschool children (ages three to five) exhibit such avoidance behavior as social withdrawal, which could disrupt their progress toward independence from their primary caretaker and jeopardize the acquisition of social skills necessary to negotiate this particular developmental period. The type of traumatic attachment largely manifested by pervasive anxiety in the toddler approximates the inhibited attachment disorder described by Zeanah, Mammen, and Lieberman (1993).

Young primary-school-age children may regress to skills more consistent with the preschool-age group and may thereby become targets of ridicule by their peers. For example, a boy who has acquired developmentally appropriate language skills and elimination habits begins to engage in baby talk and soils himself after being exposed to a major stressor. He will soon elicit disparaging remarks from his peers, become socially ostracized, and lose opportunities for further prosocial development.

Repetitive play that is assaultive in nature may be a manifestation of the reexperiencing phenomenon in traumatized children. For example, a girl who lives in a war zone and witnesses the violent interrogation of a family member by a military officer may later engage in similar behavior with her peers. Such behavior would likely invite disciplinary action by her teacher and social ostracism by her peers, which could hurt her social development.

The academic performance of a traumatized child from a war zone may deteriorate as a result of psychological trauma, as has been demonstrated in some disasters (Tsui, 1990). Learning could become seriously compromised in the traumatized student who manifests hypervigilance, impaired concentration, and exaggerated startle to loud noises. Marginal students may become school failures or dropouts.

The traumatized older adolescent usually manifests the symptoms and behaviors found in traumatized adults (Eth, 1989). In addition, a traumatized adolescent may exhibit such antisocial behaviors as truancy, sexual promiscuity, and substance abuse. Life-endangering acts involving the use of firearms, automobiles, and illicit substances could constitute reenactment behavior. The consequences will be aversive in the areas of his social life, education, and family.

Children exposed to discrete traumatic events and those raised in environments of chronic danger and stress—crime-ridden urban areas and areas of endemic political violence, for example—may be at risk of having their moral development disrupted (Garbarino, Kostelny, and Dubrow, 1991). Each child or youth who is exposed to trauma, be it acute or repetitive, is compelled to search for an explanation of the event in order to more effectively cope with the related stress. The child who becomes injured or whose family member sustains an injury must attempt to make sense of the assault. Adults and peers may offer their perspective to the child. Such perspectives, however, may or may not be comprehended by the youngster or may be misconstrued, depending on the child's cognitive developmental level, prior life experiences, political ideology, religious and possibly cultural influences. Some of these factors are known to be operative in adults (Pines, 1989; Punamaki, 1987). Although interpersonal violence is universally discouraged in modern societies, there are exceptions. The commonest example is violence used in self-defense, and this rationale is frequently invoked by proponents of warfare.

Coles (1987) believes that children who live in politically unstable environments do not routinely become amoral; in fact, some children develop a precocious and strong moral sensibility. Fields' research (1987) indicates that the moral development of most children in Northern Ireland and the Middle East is stunted compared with that of children of the same age from more peaceful communities. In many instances a vendetta mentality became the operative community norm. Similar views predominate in urban areas where hate crimes are common. Such mental frameworks may be consistent with a particular ethnic, racial, religious, or political group, and relevant social contingencies may operate to reinforce such moral beliefs. At times, a complication or a symptom found in PTSD—such as irritability, hypervigilance, or reenactment of the trauma—can prompt retaliation or vigilante justice mentality.

Garbarino, Kostelny, and Dubrow (1991) suggest that appropriate moral development requires a social environment that stimulates moral issue–focused discussions, relevant social interactions, and discussion of moral positions corresponding to a stage of moral development beyond that of the particular child. Gilligan (1982) adds that when this process occurs in a nurturant context, progress in moral development will occur. In other instances the child's community, such as school, may provide the essential ingredient for progress in moral development. Moral development and principles may in some instances be buttressed by or be in conflict with one's political ideology. Fanatically embraced ideology may alter or undermine one's moral principles (Bettelheim, 1943).

Mediators of Stress Reactions

Symptoms of psychological trauma and related stress rarely have their onset in a vacuum. Each youngster has a unique context of biological, developmental, psychological, and social factors that, in combination with the potential effects of the offending stressor, will determine the phenomenology of the child's reaction. These determinants are often classified as risk and protective factors (Sameroff, Seifer, and Zax, 1982; Rolf et al., 1990; Garmezy, 1993). Risk factors generally refer to factors associated more often than by chance with a disease process or disorder—for example, PTSD or major depressive disorder. A more recent field of study (Garmezy, 1993) concerns protective factors that tend to support the development of adaptive behaviors. Risk and protective factors may vary with developmental phase. The risk and protective factors discussed in this section focus on post-traumatic stress disorder.

In a study of the Buffalo Creek disaster, Green et al. (1991) concluded that after seventeen years the factors that appeared to be related to PTSD symptoms were the appraisal of the "life element" (those who remained alive), which was evident in the older children's reactions; the level of functioning of the parents, which correlated more with the reactions of the older children's group (aged eight to seventeen) than with those of the youngest group (aged two to seven); and the level of irritability in the home across all age groups.

Research on protective factors or resilience is relatively less developed than that on risk factors. Children who rebound from the initial psychological impact to resume patterns of adaptation and competence are sometimes called resilient. Apart from the research on child abuse, there is limited study in this area as it relates to psychological trauma in children. The work of Farber and Egeland (1987) with abused and neglected infants has implications for infants and toddlers repeatedly exposed to other types of potentially traumatic events. Farber and Egeland found that a subset of children exhibited levels of competent functioning when tested between the ages of twelve months and forty-two months. The size of the subset declined, however, implying that the continuation of abuse over time may have been responsible for deterioration in functioning. This study may apply to children exposed to recurrent violence in war zones and in certain communities. Garmezy (1993) suggests that prolonged and cumulative stress may be a prime factor in the loss of resilience over time. Luthar and Zigler (1991) suggest that behavioral competence does not necessarily imply emotional adjustment, because youngsters in emotional distress may exhibit appropriate behavior. Garmezy (1993) warns that emotional distress per se in a child does not equate with the absence of developmentally appropriate adaptive or competent behaviors.

In a literature review, Garmezy (1985) suggests that three salient classes of factors facilitate effective adaptation and coping by children who are exposed to stressful life situations. These are temperament factors, which include activity level, reflectiveness, cognitive skills, and a positive responsiveness to others; factors related to families, including warmth, cohesion, and the presence of a caring and responsible adult; and external support, which for children may be a teacher, a neighbor, a peer's parent, or a member of a church or children's service agency.

Under wartime conditions in a very impoverished country, the integrity of the family, the quality of its caregiving, and community resources are compromised to such an extreme degree that children are predisposed to the development of severe stress reactions.

The traumatic loss by death of a loved one places a youngster at high risk for a morbid grief reaction, which is generally a more complex and prolonged process than is an episode of uncomplicated bereavement (Eth and Pynoos, 1985).

Infants and toddlers may display strong separation anxiety and other symptoms of distress if they are removed from their parents' care, especially as a consequence of an emergency, such as evacuation during wartime. The risk for trauma may be increased in these situations. Evacuation in some disasters has been associated with higher psychological distress in children (Milne, 1977; Dohrenwend et al., 1981). If relocation occurs without sufficient support, it too may increase the risk for psychopathology. Injury to a child or to a close family member also places the youngster at risk for a more severe psychological disturbance (Gillis, 1991). Lingering signs of injury serve as a painful reminder of the original event.

Extensive property damage during a disaster correlates with short-term reactions (Finch and Belter, 1991) but less so with long-term effects (McFarlane, 1987; Gleser, Green, and Winget, 1981). But during wartime symptoms may well endure.

Sex differences among disaster victims tend to be minimal before late elementary school age, when girls tend to report more anxiety, depression (Gleser, Green, and Winget, 1981; Yule, 1992b), PTSD symptoms (Green et al., 1991; Yule, 1992a), and overall symptoms (Gleser, Green, and Winget, 1981). Girls also tend to exhibit a higher frequency of internalizing symptoms than do boys (Gleser, Green, and Winget, 1981; Steinglass and Gerrity, 1990), although boys are more likely to exhibit externalizing symptoms (Gleser, Green, and Winget, 1981).

Prior traumatic symptoms are not consistently shown to influence the risk for future psychopathology. In at least one study there appears to be a direct relationship (Earls et al., 1988), but it is not clearly shown in another (Hanford et al., 1986). Pynoos et al. (1987) report that the overall severity of reactions is not directly related to prior trauma, but there is a suggestion that specific symptoms may be related to prior traumas.

Community support is also likely to affect the response of children to disasters (Galante and Foa, 1986). The less helpful the community, the higher the risk for the development of psychological distress.

Clinical Interventions

The approaches and techniques used to treat stress-related disorders in children include crisis intervention, critical-incident stress debriefing, individual treatment, group intervention, family intervention, medication, and combinations of these. Each approach may have its own theoretical base. Systematic evaluations of treatment effectiveness or outcome in comparison with other interventions are virtually absent in the literature. In this section we limit our discussion to two major types of intervention: group intervention strategy and pharmacotherapy. We discuss other treatment approaches elsewhere in this chapter.

Group Treatment

There are various group techniques that can be used in responding to a disaster, principally critical incident debriefing (Yule and Udwin, 1991) alone or debriefing followed by psychological first aid. We describe the latter in some detail.

Psychological first aid for children can originate from different locales. School-based intervention is preferable for several reasons, and it can be modified for the needs of a particular classroom. School is a familiar, comfortable, and natural venue for many children. School personnel often welcome the assistance of mental health specialists, especially following a catastrophic event, and parents generally appreciate the education provided regarding children's reactions to stress. Mental health consultants can use the natural networks of support consisting of other students, teachers, and school personnel, and they can help the school personnel to minimize the effects of the particular stressors (Yule and Gold, 1993).

Prior to the delivery of such service, a liaison must be established with the community entity—the school, religious organization, or recreation center, for example. This initial contact should be followed by a gathering of information regarding the event, such as number and age of the people affected, degree of exposure, and extent of injuries and damage. This data must be collected and assessed before the school or other agency can be entered.

Various group treatment techniques have been described and recommended for use during the acute phase or early aftermath of traumatic events, such as earthquakes (Galante and Foa, 1986) and community violence (Eth, Arroyo, and Silverstein, 1993). The goals of the intervention (Arroyo and Eth, 1991) are: (1) the resumption of the normal routine—for example, school activities—at the particular site; (2) critical incident debriefing of the children and caretakers; (3) education of children and responsible adults regarding stress reactions; and (4) identification of those individuals who may require close monitoring and professional mental health referral.

Information should be provided to the responsible adults about the range of normal stress reactions and the course of the emotional recovery. Strategies to help the children cope more effectively in school and at home should also be discussed. It's equally important to discuss the expectable stress reactions of adults, because their ability to cope with the event will undoubtedly influence the recovery of the children, school, and larger community. The responsible adults should struggle to convey a sense of security and mastery in order to modulate children's anxiety and to assure them of the physical and emotional safety of their environment.

Adults should openly discuss with children and adolescents information regarding the event, the spectrum of reactions, efforts to ensure their safety, methods to cope more effectively with the stress, strategies to prevent a recurrence or to diminish the impact, and methods to help promote recovery in the larger community. The expression of feelings and fears should be encouraged, and resources for support should be presented. Activities such as drawing (Arroyo and Eth, 1991), storytelling, or play (Galante and Foa, 1986) can be used with preschool or elementary school youngsters to accomplish these goals. We have had mixed success in using these methods with secondary school students.

These classroom interventions can serve as models of open discussion for responsible adults to facilitate effective communication with children. A discussion of death may be indicated if community members died as a result of the event. Adults commonly feel unprepared to speak with children about the death of a loved one or about the violent death of community members as a result of politically related violence.

Medication

Pharmacotherapy is rarely the treatment of choice during an acute phase of trauma. More often it is recommended as an adjunctive form of symptom relief, primarily to help the child become more receptive to and more capable of participating in other forms of therapy.

Several authors (Kolb, 1987; Krystal et al., 1989; Ver Ellen and van Kammen, 1990) have elucidated our preliminary understanding of the psychobiological basis of PTSD. It appears that at the least noradrergic, serotonergic, endogenous opioid, hypothalamic-pituitary-adrenocortical, and diurnal sleep cycle are involved. The acoustic startle response reflex is disrupted in PTSD, suggesting dysregulation of brain stem pathways to the thalamus and amygdala (Krystal et al., 1989). The syndrome of learned helplessness found in animals exposed to inescapable shock is analogous to the constellation of symptoms of depression often associated with PTSD (van der Kolk, 1987).

The use of pharmacotherapy in the treatment of PTSD has been controversial. Some authors discourage pharmacotherapy because it may interfere with the psychological processes and resolution of the psychological conflicts thought to be inherent in psychic trauma. Others (Marmar et al., 1993) believe its role should be adjunctive to psychotherapy, and that by reducing the intensity of symptoms it could effect a state of receptivity to psychotherapeutic techniques. However, only a few psychotherapeutic techniques have been the subject of systematic investigation (Allodi, 1991; Foa, Olasov Rothbaum, and Steketee, 1987), and these studies have involved adult subjects exclusively.

Although many different medications have been used in the treatment of PTSD, placebo-controlled studies in adults are limited to a handful (Solomon, Gerrity, and Muff, 1992). Even fewer such studies have been completed with children and adolescents.

In the case of a child or adolescent who develops a normal stress response, medication is seldom indicated. The exception might be that of a youngster who has a co-morbid psychiatric illness.

Benzodiazepines have been recommended in adults for the symptomatic treatment of acute catastrophic stress reactions (Forster and Marmar, 1991). Their primary effect is to promote sleep and diminish anxiety, while other core symptoms of PTSD may be unaffected. Research has not established the superiority of any particular benzodiazepine (Dubovsky, 1990), and short-term use is advised in order to avoid dependence on this class of drugs. Research involving benzodiazepines for the treatment of anxiety disorders in children and adolescents has been limited to anxiety disorders other than PTSD (D'Amato, 1962; Krakowski, 1963; Lucas and Pasley, 1969). A small number of these investigations have been double blind (Lucas and Pasley, 1969). The literature suggests that benzodiazepines may help relieve symptoms of anxiety in children and adolescents.

Caution is advised in the use of benzodiazepines with children and adolescents because of the potential for abuse by older children, siblings, and caretakers (Allen, Rapoport, and Swedo, 1993). Benzodiazepines are metabolized faster in children than in adults (Coffey, Shader, and Greenblatt, 1983). Long half-life benzodiazepines may be preferable to short half-life ones because of decreased dosing frequency and milder withdrawal reactions. Recommended dosages (Allen, Rapoport, and Swedo, 1993) are: diazepam (or Valium) (half-life 30 to 60 hours), 0.12–0.80 mg/kg body weight qhs (or divided as bid or tid); lorazepam (or Ativan) (half-life 12 to 18 hours) 0.02–0.10 mg/kg body weight per day (or divided as bid or tid); and alprazolam (or Xanax) (half-life 12 to 15 hours) 0.005–0.050 mg/kg body weight per day (or divided as tid or qid).

Antidepressants, including tricyclics and monoamine oxidase inhibitors (MAOIs), and serotonin specific reuptake inhibitors (or SSRIs) may also be useful in the treatment of adults with PTSD. In placebo-controlled studies of adults, these agents were found to be effective in treatment of the positive symptoms (reexperiencing and arousal symptoms) (Frank et al., 1988; Davidson et al., 1990). Another study (Shestatsky et al., 1988) found no difference between phenelzine and placebo. An open trial (Marmar et al., 1993) with fluoxetine was found to be efficacious. There are no placebo-controlled studies on the use of antidepressants for the treatment of PTSD in children and adolescents. However, there are earlier

studies (Gittelman-Klein and Klein, 1971) suggesting that tricyclics may be helpful in the treatment of school phobia and separation anxiety disorder, while later
investigators (Bernstein, Garfinkel, and Borchardt, 1990) are less encouraging.
Again, these medications should be used cautiously with children who have PTSD.
The decision to prescribe these medications should be based on the child's diagnosis, individual medical history, and family medical history. If a patient has a
cardiac conduction defect and a tricyclic is under consideration, then a pediatric
consultation should be entertained. The usual dietary restrictions must be followed for MAOIs.

Recommended dosages (Allen, Rapoport, and Swedo, 1993) are: imipramine (or Tofranil) 1–3 mg/kg in divided doses; if above 3 mg/kg blood levels
then EKGs should be monitored, 5 mg/kg usually not exceeded; desipramine or
(Norpramin), same as imipramine; nortriptyline (or Pamelor) 0.5–1.5 mg/kg in
divided doses, blood levels and EKGs should be monitored, should not exceed 2.5
mg/kg. Recommended dosage (McCracken and Cantwell, 1992) for MAOIs are:
phenelzine (or Parnate) 30–90 mg per day in divided doses and tranylcypromine
10–40 mg per day in divided doses. The most widely used SSRI in adults is
fluoxetine (or Prozac) at a dose of 10 or 20 mg per day.

According to several reports (Kinzie and Leung, 1989; Kolb et al., 1984),
adrenergic blockers (such as propranolol) and adrenergic agonists (such as clonidine) have been effective in relieving the reexperiencing and arousal symptoms of
fear-enhanced startle in adults. There are no controlled studies on the use of these
two agents in children and adolescents. Propranolol has been successfully used in
the treatment of PTSD in some cases of sexual and physical abuse (Famularo,
Kinscherff, and Fenton, 1988). Both propranolol and clonidine should therefore
be considered components of a comprehensive treatment plan of the acute catastrophic and uncomplicated PTSD reactions. Propranolol should be used cautiously
for children with diabetes mellitus, because of possible induction of hypoglyce-
mia, and in children with asthma, because of possible induction of bronchospasm.

Recommended dosages (Allen, Rapoport, and Swedo, 1993) are: propranolol (Inderal) initial dose of 0.8 mg/kg per day in two or three divided doses
gradually increased to the maximum dose tolerated or 2.5 mg/kg per day, which-
ever comes first. Monitoring of the pulse and blood pressure can help to establish
the minimum effective dosage. An adequate trial consists of at least two weeks at
the maximum dose. Propranolol should be tapered over two to three weeks when
discontinued. Clonidine (or Catapres) (Hunt, Capper, and O'Connell, 1990)
should be increased gradually, beginning with an initial dose of 0.05 mg per day
and increased every third day until a daily total dosage range between 3 and 5
microgram/kg is achieved. It should be administered in three or four divided
doses daily.

According to case reports (Kutcher and Mackenzie, 1988; Biederman, 1987)
clonazepam (or Klonopin) has been successfully used in the treatment of children
with panic disorder. Recommended dosages are 0.02–0.01 mg/kg qhs or divided into two or three doses daily.

Although there are no systematic studies done with respect to co-morbid states, anecdotal reports suggest that standard pharmacological treatments should be used when PTSD complicates another psychiatric condition.

Conclusion

It should be apparent that children can develop a broad spectrum of symptoms related to stress that represent a variety of discrete syndromes. The sources of stress can be a single terrifying life-threatening event or a series of repetitive major stressors, as is common in war zones and in some major urban areas of the world. At times, these single events or series of events precipitate sources of stress or secondary adversities, which in turn may progress into a chronically stressful environment that contributes to the development of a diagnosable psychiatric disorder. Fortunately, in most instances, the constellation of symptoms is brief in duration.

At times it is tempting to consider these clinical phenomena exclusively in a paradigm of linear causality. However, it appears that a transactional model, in which many factors are influential, is more applicable; more studies of risk factors, coping behaviors, protective processes or resilience, and perpetuating mechanisms should enhance our understanding in the years ahead. These stressful circumstances and psychiatric disorders can undermine the growth and development of children. They can affect a youngster's socialization, mastery of cognitive tasks, and moral maturation. Precise delineation of their impact on the various developmental lines warrants further investigation, and longitudinal studies would be especially helpful.

The therapeutic intervention strategies described in the literature are based more on anecdotal reports and theoretical frameworks than on empirical research. Treatment outcome and evaluation studies are generally lacking in the these areas. However, given the disheartening incidence of severe stressors, there will undoubtedly be many more opportunities to study these clinical phenomena and improve our ability to help affected children.

REFERENCES

Allen, J. A., Rapoport, J. L., and Swedo, S. E. 1993. Psychopharmacologic treatment of childhood anxiety disorders. In H. L. Leonard, ed., *Child and adolescent psychiatric clinics of North America: Anxiety disorders,* 795–818. Philadelphia: W. B. Saunders.

Allodi, F. A. 1991. Assessment and treatment of torture victims: A critical review. *Journal of Nervous Mental Disorder* 79:4–11.

American Psychiatric Association. 1994. Anxiety disorders. In *Diagnostic Statistical Manual of Mental Disorders,* 4th ed., 393–444. Washington, D.C.: American Psychiatric Press.

Arroyo, W. 1988. War traumatized Central American children. Paper presented at meeting at Catholic University of America, Washington, D.C.

Arroyo, W., and Eth, S. 1991. Group treatment model of post-traumatic stress disorder. Paper presented at American Psychological Association Conference, San Francisco, August. 19.

———. 1994. Assessment following violence-witnessing trauma. In E. Peled, P. G. Jaffe, and J. L. Edleson, eds., *Ending the cycle of violence: Community response to children of battered women*. Newbury Park, Calif.: Sage.

Ayalon, O. 1983. Coping with terrorism: The Israeli case. In D. Meichenbaum and M. E. Jaremko, eds., *Stress reduction and prevention*, 293–339. New York: Plenum.

Bernstein, G., Garfinkel, B., and Borchardt, C. 1990. Comparative studies of pharmaco-therapy for school refusal. *Journal of the American Academy of Child and Adolescent Psychiatry* 29:773–781.

Bettelheim, B. 1943. Individual and mass behavior in extreme situations. *Journal of Abnormal Social Psychology* 38:17–452.

Biederman, J. 1987. Clonazepam in the treatment of prepubertal children with panic-like symptoms. *Journal of Clinical Psychiatry* 48(supp.):38–42.

Bloch, D. A., Silber, E., and Perry, S. E. 1956. Some factors in the emotional reactions of children to disaster. *American Journal of Psychiatry* 133:416–422.

Coffey, B., Shader, R. I., and Greenblatt, D. J. 1983. Pharmacokinetics of benzodiazepines and psychostimulants in children. *Journal of Clinical Psychopharmacology* 3:217–225.

Coles, R. 1987. *The political life of children*. Boston: Houghton Mifflin.

D'Amato, G. 1962. Chlordiazepoxide in management of school phobia. *Diseases of the Nervous System* 23:292–295.

Davidson, J. 1993. Issues in the diagnosis of post-traumatic stress disorder. In J. M. Oldham, M. B. Riba, and A. Tasman, eds., *Review of Psychiatry*, vol. 12, 141–156. Washington, D.C.: American Psychiatric Press.

Davidson, J., Kudler, H., Smith, R., et al. 1990. Treatment of post-traumatic stress disorder with amitryptyline and placebo. *Archives of General Psychiatry* 47: 259–266.

Dohrenwend, B. P., Dohrenwend, B. S., Warheit, G., Barlett, G. S., Goldsteen, K., and Martin, J. L. 1981. Stress in the community: A report to the President's Commission on the accident at Three Mile Island. *Annual New York Academy of Science* 365:159–174.

Drell, M. J., Siegel, C. H., and Gaensbauer, T. J. 1993. Post-traumatic stress disorder. In C. H. Zeanah, ed., *Handbook of Infant Mental Health*, 291–304. New York: Guilford Press.

Dubovsky, S. L. 1990. Generalized anxiety disorder: New concepts and psychophar-macologic therapies. *Journal of Clinical Psychiatry* 51(supp.):3–10.

Earls, F., Smith, E., Reich, W., and Jung, K. G. 1988. Investigating psychopathological consequences of a disaster in children: A pilot study incorporating a structured diagnostic interview. *Journal of the American Academy of Child and Adolescent Psychiatry* 27:90–95.

Eth, S. 1989. The adolescent witness to homicide. In E. P. Benedek and D. G. Cornell, eds., *Juvenile homicide*, 87–113. Washington, D.C.: American Psychiatric Press.

Eth, S., Arroyo, W., and Silverstein, S. 1993. School consultation following the Los Angeles riots. Presented at American Psychiatric Association conference, San Francisco, May 23.

Eth, S., and Pynoos, R. S. 1985. Developmental perspective on psychic trauma in childhood. In C. R. Figley, ed., *Trauma and its wake*, 36–52. New York: Brunner/Mazel.

Famularo, R., Kinscherff, R., and Fenton, T. 1988. Propranolol treatment for childhood post-traumatic stress disorder, acute type. *American Journal of Disorders in Children* 142:1244–1247.

Farber, A. E., and Egeland, B. 1987. Invulnerability among abused and neglected children. In E. J. Anthony and B. J. Cohler, eds., *The invulnerable child,* 253–288. New York: Guilford Press.

Fields, R. 1987. Terrorized into terrorist: Sequelae of PTSD in young victims. Paper presented at the meeting of the Society for Traumatic Stress Studies, New York, October 25.

Finch, A. J., Jr., and Belter, R. W. 1991. Impact of a natural disaster on children and their families. Paper presented at American Psychological Association conference, San Francisco, August 10.

Foa, E. B., Olasov Rothbaum, B., and Steketee, G. S. 1987. Treatment of rape victims. Paper presented at the National Institute of Mental Health State of the Art in Sexual Assault Research, Charleston, S.C., September 18.

Forster, P., and Marmar, C. R. 1991. Benzodiazepines in acute stress reactions: Benefits, risks, and controversies. In P. P. Byrne and D. S. Cowley, eds., *Benzodiazepines in clinical practice: Risks and benefits,* 73–88. Washington, D.C.: American Psychiatric Press.

Frank, J. B., Giller, E. L., Kosten, T. R., et al. 1988. A randomized clinical trial of phenelzine and imipramine for post-traumatic stress disorder. *American Journal of Psychiatry* 145:1289–1291.

Freud, A., and Burlingham, D. T. 1943. *Children and war.* London: Medical War Books.

Galante, R., and Foa, D. 1986. An epidemiological study of psychic trauma and treatment effectiveness for children after a natural disaster. *Journal of the American Academy of Child Psychiatry* 25:357–363.

Garbarino, J., Kostelny, K., and Dubrow, N. 1991. What children can tell us about living in danger. *American Psychology* 46:376–383.

Garmezy, N. 1985. Stress-resistant children: The search for protective factors. *Journal of Child Psychology Psychiatry* 4(supp.):213–233.

——. 1993. Children in poverty: Resilience despite risk. *Psychiatry* 56 (February): 127–136.

Garmezy, N., and Rutter, M. 1985. Acute reactions to stress. In M. Rutter and L. Hersov, eds., *Child and adolescent psychiatry: Modern approaches,* 2nd ed., 152–176. Oxford: Blackwell.

Gilligan, C. 1982. *In a different voice.* Cambridge, Mass.: Harvard University Press.

Gillis, H. M. 1991. Children's responses and symptomatology following the Stockton, California, schoolyard shooting. Paper presented at American Psychological Association conference, San Francisco, August 12.

Gittelman-Klein, R., and Klein, D. 1971. Controlled imipramine treatment of school phobia. *Archives of General Psychiatry* 25:204–207.

Gleser, G., Green, B. L., and Winget, C. 1981. *Prolonged psychological effects of disaster: A study of Buffalo Creek.* New York: Academic Press.

Green, B. L., Korol, M., Grace, M. C., Vary, M. G., Leonard, A. C., Gleser, G. C., and Smitson-Cohen, S. 1991. Children and disaster: Age, gender, and parental effects on PTSD symptoms. *Journal of the American Academy of Child and Adolescent Psychiatry* 30:945–951.

Guarnaccia, P. J., and Kirmayer, L. J. 1993. Literature review on culture and the anxiety disorders. In J. E. Mezzich, A. Kleinman, H. Fabrega, Jr., B. Good, G. Johnson-

Powell, K.-M. Lin, S. Manson, and D. Parron, eds., *Cultural proposals for DSM-IV: Submitted to the DSM-IV task force by the steering committee, NIMH-sponsored group on culture and diagnosis,* 135–149. Published by the editors.

Hanford, H. A., Mayes, S. D., Mattison, R. E., Humphrey, F. J., Bagnato, S., Bixler, E. O., and Kales, J. D. 1986. Child and parent reaction to the Three Mile Island nuclear disaster. *Journal of the American Academy of Child Psychiatry* 26:346–356.

Hill, P. 1994. Adjustment disorders. In M. Rutter, E. Taylor, and L. Hersov, eds., *Child and adolescent psychiatry: Modern approaches,* 3rd ed., 375–391. Oxford: Blackwell.

Hunt, R. D., Capper, L., and O'Connell, P. 1990. Clonidine in child and adolescent mood disorders. *Journal of Child and Adolescent Psychopharmacy* 1:87–102.

Kinzie, J. D., and Leung, P. 1989. Clonidine in Cambodian patients with post-traumatic stress disorder. *Journal of Nervous and Mental Disorders* 177:546–550.

Kinzie, J. D., Sack, W. H., Angell, R. H., Manson, S., and Rath, B. 1986. The psychiatric effects of massive trauma on Cambodian children. *Journal of the American Academy of Child and Adolescent Psychiatry* 25:370–376.

Kolb, L. C. 1987. A neuropsychological hypothesis explaining post-traumatic stress disorders. *American Journal of Psychiatry* 144:989–995.

Kolb, L. C., Burris, B. C., and Griffiths, S. 1984. Propranolol and clonidine in the treatment of post-traumatic stress disorders of war. In B. A. van der Kolk, ed., *Post traumatic stress disorder, psychological and biological sequelae.* Washington, D.C.: American Psychiatric Press, 1984.

Kolvin, I., Miller, F. J. W., Fleeting, M., and Kolvin, P. A. 1988. Risk/protective factors for offending with particular reference to deprivation. In M. Rutter, ed., *Studies of psychosocial risk: The power of longitudinal data,* 77–95. Cambridge: Cambridge University Press.

Koopman, C., Classen, C., and Spiegel, D. 1994. Predictors of post-traumatic stress symptoms among survivors of the Oakland/Berkeley, California, firestorm. *American Journal of Psychiatry* 151:888–894.

Krakowski, A. J. 1963. Chlordiazepoxide in treatment of children with emotional disturbances. *New York State Journal of Medicine* 63:3388–3392.

Krystal, J. H., Kosten, T. R., Southwick, S., et al. 1989. Neurobiological aspects of PTSD: Review of clinical and preclinical studies. *Behavioral Theory* 20:177–198.

Kutcher, S. P., and Mackenzie, S. 1988. Successful clonazepam treatment of adolescents with panic disorder. *Journal of Clinical Psychopharmacy* 8:299–301.

Lee, I. 1991. Second international conference on wartime medical services. *Medicine and War* 7:120–128.

Lucas, A. R., and Pasley, F. C. 1969. Psychoactive drugs in the treatment of emotionally disturbed children: Haloperidol and diazepam. *Comprehensive Psychiatry* 10:376–386.

Luthar, S. S., and Zigler, E. 1991. Vulnerability and competence: A review of research on resilience in childhood. *American Journal of Orthopsychiatry* 61:6–22.

McCracken, J. T., and Cantwell, D. P. 1992. Management of child and adolescent mood disorders. In D. P. Cantwell, ed., *Child and adolescent psychiatric clinics of North America: Mood disorders,* 229–256. Philadelphia: W. B. Saunders.

McFarlane, A. C. 1987. Post-traumatic phenomena in a longitudinal study of children following a natural disaster. *Journal of the American Academy of Child and Adolescent Psychiatry* 26:764–769.

Marmar, C. R., Foy, D., Kagan, B., and Pynoos, R. S. 1993. An integrated approach for treating posttraumatic stress. In J. M. Oldham, M. B. Riba, and A. Tasman, *Review of psychiatry,* vol. 12, 239–272. Washington, D.C.: American Psychiatric Press.

Marsella, A. J., Friedman, M. J., and Spain, E. H., 1993. Ethnocultural aspects of post-traumatic stress disorder. In J. M. Oldham, M. B. Riba, and A. Tasman, eds., *Review of psychiatry,* vol. 12, 157–181. Washington, D.C.: American Psychiatric Press.

Martinez, P., and Richters, J. E. 1993. The NIMH community violence project: II. Children's distress symptoms associated with violence exposure. *Psychiatry* 56:22–35.

Milne, G. 1977. Cyclone Tracy: II. The effects on Darwin children. *Australian Psychology* 12:55–62.

Nader, K., Pynoos, R., Fairbanks, L., and Frederick, C. 1990. Children's PTSD reactions one year after a sniper attack at their school. *American Journal of Psychiatry* 147:1526–1528.

O'Donohue, W., and Elliot, A. 1992. The current status of post-traumatic stress disorder as a diagnostic category: Problems and proposals. *Journal of Traumatic Stress* 5:421–439.

Ollendick, S. G., and Hoffman, M. 1982. Assessment of psychological reactions in disaster victims. *Journal of Community Psychology* 10:157–167.

Parry Jones, W. 1991. Children of Lockerbie. Paper presented at Guys Hospital meeting, London.

Pines, R. 1989. Why do Israelis burn out: The role of the intifada. Paper presented at the International Conference on Psychological Stress and Adjustment, Tel Aviv, January.

Punamaki, R. 1987. Psychological stress responses of Palestinian mothers and their children in conditions of military occupation and political violence. *Quarterly Newsletter of Comparative Human Cognition* 9:76–84.

Pynoos, R. S. 1993. Traumatic stress and developmental psychopathology in children and adolescents. In J. M. Oldham, M. B. Riba, and A. Tasman, *Review of psychiatry,* vol. 12, 239–272. Washington, D.C.: American Psychiatric Press.

Pynoos, R. S., and Eth, S. 1986. Witness to violence. *Journal of American Child Psychiatry* 25:306–319.

Pynoos, R., Frederick C., Nader, K., Arroyo, W., Steinberg, A., Spencer, E., Nuñez, F., and Fairbanks, L. 1987. Life threat and post-traumatic stress in school age children. *Archives of General Psychiatry* 44:1057–1063.

Richters, J. E., and Martinez, P. 1993. The NIMH community violence project: I. Children as victims of and witness to violence. *Psychiatry* 56:7–21.

Rogler, L. H., 1992. The role of culture in mental health diagnosis: The need for programmatic research. *Journal of Nervous Stress Disorder* 180:745–747.

Rolf, J., Masten, A. S., Cicchetti, D., Nuechterlein, K. H., and Weintraub, S. 1990. *Risk and protective factors in the development of psychopathology.* Cambridge, Eng.: Cambridge University Press.

Rutter, M. 1978. Family, area, and school influences in the genesis of conduct disorders. In L. A. Hersov, M. Berger, and D. Schaffer, eds., *Aggression and anti-social behavior in childhood and adolescence,* 95–113. Oxford: Pergamon.

———. 1985. Resilience in the face of adversity: Protective factors and resistance to psychiatric disorder. *British Journal of Psychiatry* 147:598–611.

———. 1987. Psychosocial resilience and protective mechanisms. *American Journal of Orthopsychiatry* 57:316–331.

Saigh, P. A. 1989. The development and validation of the children's post-traumatic stress disorder inventory. *International Journal Special Edition* 4:75–84.

——. 1991. The development of post-traumatic stress disorder. *Behavioral Research and Therapy* 29:213–216.

Sameroff, A, J., Seifer, R., and Zax, M. 1982. Early development of children at risk for emotional disorder. *Monographs of the Society for Research in Child Development* 47(7).

Saylor, C. F., Powell, P., and Swenson, C. 1992. Hurricane Hugo blows down the broccoli: Preschoolers' post-disaster play and adjustment. *Child Psychology and Human Development* 22:139–149.

Shestatsky, M., Greenberg, D., and Lerer, B. 1988. A controlled trial of phenelzine in post-traumatic stress disorder. *Psychiatry Research* 24:149–155.

Solomon, S. D., Gerrity, E. T., and Muff, A. M. 1992. Efficacy of treatments for post-traumatic stress disorders. *Journal of the American Medical Association* 268:633–638.

Steinglass, P., and Gerrity, E. 1990. Natural disasters and post-traumatic stress disorder: Short-term versus long-term recovery in two disaster-affected communities. *Journal of Applied Social Psychology* 20:1746–1765.

Sullivan, M. A., Saylor, C., and Foster, S. C. 1991. Post-hurricane adjustment of pre-schoolers and their families. *Advances in Behavioral Research and Therapy* 13:163–172.

Terr, L. 1981. Forbidden games: Post-traumatic child's play. *Journal of the Academy of Child Psychiatry* 20:741–759.

——. 1991. Childhood traumas: An outline and overview. *American Journal of Psychiatry* 148:10–20.

Tsui, E. P. 1990. The Jupiter sinking disaster: Effects on teenagers' school performance. Master's diss., University of London, Institute of Psychiatry.

van der Kolk, B. 1987. Drug treatment of post-traumatic stress disorder. *Journal of Nervous Mental Disorder* 13:203–213.

Ver Ellen, P., and van Kammen, D. P. 1990. The biological findings in post-traumatic stress disorder: A review. *Journal of Social Psychology* 20:1789–1821.

Vogel, J. M., Vernberg, E. M. 1993. Task force report—Part 1: Children's psychological responses to disasters. *Journal of Clinical Child Psychiatry* 22:464–484.

Wicks, B. 1988. *No time to wave good-bye.* London: Bloomsbury.

Yule, W. 1992a. Post-traumatic stress disorder in child survivors of shipping disasters: The sinking of the "Jupiter." *Psychotherapy and Psychosomatics* 57:200–205.

——. 1992b. Resilience and vulnerability in child survivors of disasters. In *Vulnerability and resilience: A festschrift for Ann and Alan Clarke,* 182–198. London: Jessica Kingsley.

——. 1994. Post-traumatic stress disorder, in M. Rutter, E. Taylor, and L. Hersov, eds., *Child and adolescent psychiatry: Modern approaches.* 3rd ed., 392–406. London: Black-well.

Yule, W., and Gold, A. 1993. *Wise before the event: Coping with crises in schools.* London: Calouste Gulbenkian Foundation.

Yule, W., and Udwin, O. 1991. Screening child survivors for posttraumatic stress disorders: Experiences from the "Jupiter" sinking. *British Journal of Clinical Psychiatry* 30:131–138.

Yule, W., Udwin, O., and Murdoch, K. 1990. The "Jupiter" sinking: Effects on children's fears, depression, and anxiety. *Journal of Child Psychology Psychiatry* 31:1051–1061.

Zeanah, C. H., Mammen, O. K., and Lieberman, A. F. 1993. Disorders of attachment. In C. H. Zeanah, ed., *Handbook of infant mental health,* 332–349. New York: Guilford Press.

CHAPTER FIVE

Refugee Children

JOSEPH WESTERMEYER AND KAREN WAHMANHOLM

In this chapter Joseph Westermeyer and Karen Wahmanholm continue the clinical emphasis on PTSD *and other stress reactions. They base the chapter primarily on their experience with groups of refugee children resettled in the United States. They provide detailed and practical guidelines and clinical examples of both assessment and treatment for a variety of conditions. The authors repeatedly call attention to the neurological and other physical damage caused by deprivation, exposure to disease, and injury from bullets, shells, and land mines. These forms of damage are an integral part of violent dislocation, persecution, and flight, but they may not appear until years later. The authors make dramatically clear how careful, timely assessment and treatment of problems can limit the amount of disruption in a child's development while enormously enhancing the functioning and adaptation of the family.*

The authors describe the treatments and support services that are needed, including educational and psychotherapeutic interventions, family meetings, and psychopharmacological modalities. At the same time, their brief clinical vignettes highlight the poignancy of the struggles of the children and their families, their determination, and their resourcefulness. (We recommend as supplementary reading the narrative accounts of Southeast Asian refugees encountering mental health and medical personnel in the United States that are found in Le Ly Hayslip's When Heaven and Earth Changed Place *[1989] and her* Child of War, Woman of Peace *[1993], and Gail Sheehy's* Spirit of Survival *[1986], an account of her adoption of a Cambodian girl.) Both the clinical vignettes and the systematic discussion of assessment and treatment emphasize the need to pay close attention to cross-cultural differences and barriers and at the same time provide practical suggestions for dealing with these problems.*

The authors show how political forces not only precipitate the refugee situation but also af-fect how a nation deals with new arrivals. They pose a major ethical and policy dilemma: Should the United States continue to take in almost all the refugees who arrive but short-change many of them on services they may desperately need, or should America take in a smaller number and aim at improving the quality of the services offered? This problem, knotty enough in its most narrowly construed form, grows even more complex when one realizes to what degree U.S. military, economic, and diplomatic policies are involved in the creation or exclusion of large refugee populations.

Our purpose in this chapter is to alert the reader to the special mental health problems experienced by refugee children. In times of peace and social stability it is difficult to imagine that children can become not only the inadvertent but also even the *intended* victims of political and military struggle (Goudvis, 1993). Unfortunately, today we see the imprisonment and torture of children; the forced conscription of children into military units as combatants, laborers, and sexual victims; the abuse of children as a way to punish or torture their parents and other family members; the targeting of child victims on the basis of their parents' ethnicity, religion, education, or occupation; the focusing on children as bearers of political ideologies that are invidious to their elders; the raising of children in refugee camps, with insecurity, poor adult role models, inadequate education, and lack of job opportunities.

As parents become aware of such victimization of children for political and military purposes, they may choose to flee their homeland for the sake of the children. Sometimes parents send their children out of the country while they remain behind, as occurred during the 1980s in Indochina, when poverty-stricken families sent out their older children and adolescents in the hope that they would eventually be able to provide financial support for the family left behind.

Before, during, and after refugee flight children undergo many of the same depredations and challenges as their elders. The perceptions and effects of these events can be markedly different for children and adults, however. For example, a few weeks of poor nutrition can have minimal effect on adults but lifelong or even fatal effects on children. Conversely, flight from home, occupation, and social network can be devastating for adults, whereas the children (if well cared for and kept safe) may view it as an exciting adventure marked by family coopera-tion and mutual support.

Refugee children are not merely smaller or younger versions of their elders. Child and adolescent developmental concepts and hallmarks—biological, psy-chological, social, and cultural—are keys to understanding the effects of flight and relocation. Refugee experiences occur at a time when children are especially vulnerable in certain ways but flexible in others. Refugee children have advantages over their elders in their ability to acculturate to a new society. They have disadvantages in that they are prone to such problems as loss or impairment of their parents at a time when they are dependent on them (Krogh and Montgomery, 1993). Since progress from childhood to adulthood is gradual, refugee-related events during adolescence or young adulthood can have effects that resemble effects more typical of younger children or older adults (Carlin, 1979). For example, in a culture fostering prolonged dependence on parents or extended family, loss or separation from family even late in adolescence can precipitate conditions that one would expect to occur earlier in cultures fostering early individuation. Conversely, even preteen or early-teen refugees can become involved with drug abuse, prostitution, or crime as venues for survival if they lose the protection, guidance, and material support of their families.

Special definitions and terms apply to refugee children. "Children" includes newborns through people aged twenty-one. There are many categories or types of "refugee children." Some were refugees as children but are now adults. Others were refugees as children and are still minors. Children born to refugee parents share many of the characteristics of refugee children even though they are not refugees themselves; that is, they live in two cultures (the culture of their parents, and the culture of the society in which they live), they are exposed to the same potential family problems (for example, alexithymia and depression), and family bereavement over numerous losses is typically present. One subgroup of refugee children is "unaccompanied minors," whose parents are not present because the children left (or were forced to leave) without their parents or because the parents died or were killed during flight. All large refugee flights have produced hundreds and even thousands of unaccompanied children (Ahearn and Athey, 1991). Depending on one's definitions, the number of "refugee children" in the United States may range from a few hundred thousand to perhaps a few million.

The U.N. definition of refugees includes people who have fled their homeland because of persecution based on their race, religious belief, political persuasion, culture-ethnicity, education, or socioeconomic status. Refugees who flee from one part of their own country to another part are referred to as internal or in-country refugees. Some refugees flee outside their country, often to a nearby "country of first refuge," perhaps with the intention of returning to their homeland or moving to a third "country of resettlement," which is usually some distance from the country of origin.

Demography

Each cohort of refugees or "refugee wave" tends to have its own demographic characteristics. In general, most refugee groups include more women and children than men, often because the male members of the group have been conscripted into the military, imprisoned or detained, or killed. At any given point in time, about half the refugees in the world are children and adolescents under age eighteen (Williamson, 1988). Among a group of 67,499 Vietnamese refugees in the United States in 1976, 46 percent were aged seventeen or younger (Kelly, 1977).

This demographic distribution among refugees calls for special methods of assistance, such as meeting the nutritional needs of children and women (with vitamins and minerals, for example), taking special health measures (such as immunization and prevention or care of infectious disease), establishing security measures to protect them, and providing socialization, education, and eventual occupational training so that the refugees will be able to support themselves. Unless refugee aid takes these special needs into account, malnutrition, infectious disease, cultural anomie, illiteracy, ignorance, absence of occupational training, inactivity, and social alienation may result; in fact, these social problems have become the hallmarks of refugee camps around the world.

Some refugee flights have consisted largely of older adolescents and young single adults. The Hungarian and Czechoslovakian flights of the 1950s are examples. Following the defeat of the centrist-rightist governments in Vietnam and Laos in 1975, the first wave of refugees included many young soldiers who fled without family support or other occupational skills. These groups present special needs for education, job training, acculturation to the new country, and socialization into adult roles and responsibilities.

In many refugee-producing countries, the refugees flee to adjacent nations, where the food, climate, culture, and perhaps the language are familiar to them. However, children in such settings are generally restricted to guarded refugee camps, highly artificial environments. Children in other resettlement countries are able to attend school and range freely through the society but are subject to other problems (discussed below). As a result of their political and historical ties to the countries involved, resettlement countries tend to "specialize" in certain cultural groups. Examples follow:

England: Anglophone Africans, South Asians
France: Algerians, Francophone Southeast Asians
Germany: Afghanistanis, Kurdistanis, Eastern Europeans of German ancestry, West Africans
Holland: Indonesians
India: Tibetans, Hindus from Pakistan
Italy: West Africans
Scandinavia: Southeast Asians, South Asians, Middle Easterners, Africans, Latin Americans
Spain: Latin Americans, North Africans
Switzerland: Tibetans, South Asians, Eastern Europeans
United States: Southeast Asians, Middle Easterners, Latin Americans, Africans, Eastern Europeans

Refugee cohorts, even those from the same country, can differ greatly in socioeconomic status. For example, three major waves of Vietnamese refugees relocated to the United States between 1975 and 1990. The first wave was the most highly educated, with many government leaders, professionals, business-people, and military officers. The third wave was the least educated, with many illiterate farmers and fishermen who fled to escape grinding poverty.

Etiology
Trauma

Children are not immune to the violence and trauma of war and political persecution. However, the horror that many of us feel toward such harm to children can interfere with providing adequate care for them. Clinicians who treat children should consider the possibility that they have witnessed or experienced violent acts and inquire specifically about it. In the following case, pediatricians had evaluated the children, given them a "clean bill of health," and referred them for psychiatric care because of presumed nonorganic psychiatric conditions.

An eleven-year-old Vietnamese boy was referred to the University of Minnesota department of psychiatry because of his inability to learn English and to progress in school, despite having spent three years in the United States. Psychological testing at school and a physical exam by a pediatrician had failed to uncover any problems. The pediatrician noted a small scar on the child's forehead, however, and the parents stated that the child had been wounded in the head during a North Vietnamese assault on their town. The child had been evacuated, given hospital care, and had recovered. The parents did not know the nature of their son's injury, although they observed that he did less well in school after the injury and seemed to "forget things." An X-ray of the skull revealed a 1.5-centimeter piece of jagged shrapnel in the boy's brain, on the side opposite the scar on his forehead. Brain imaging revealed ablation of much of both frontal lobes.

Working with the school, we developed an educational program taking the child's brain damage into account. This included putting him into an elementary English as a second language class in which he received considerable individual tutoring, including work with pictures and hand signs that would encourage use of other parts of his brain to build a link between concepts and would utilize diverse forms of developing symbols representative of concepts (for example, visual-image, visual-written, auditory-verbal, tactile, kinesthetic). The school was urged to permit him to develop at his own pace and to provide abundant opportunities for success and positive feedback.

The family knew that the child was different from their other children and readily accepted his organic deficit, which they had suspected in any event. Moreover, they were heartened that such a child could receive special education and that his maximum potential would be the goal. Within several weeks both the school and the family reported progress in the child, citing improved academic performance, more age-appropriate behavior at home and at school, and improvement in his peers' and siblings' view of him (that is, as less disabled, more "normal").

Infectious Disease

Unless they have been immunized, children are more likely than adults to acquire an infectious disease under flight conditions, since they have not yet developed as many antibodies as adults have. Exposed to crowded refugee conditions, poor sanitation, and exhaustion, they run a high risk of infection (Hodson and Springthorpe, 1976). Infections also contribute to malnutrition, because body and protein stores used to fight the infection may not be replaced (Olness, 1977).

Some of these infections, such as measles or meningococcus, can cause direct brain impairment through meningitis or encephalitis. Other infections can produce brain damage through prolonged high fever, febrile seizures, dehydration, and malnutrition. Absence of medical facilities can have disastrous effects even in conditions that would probably have been resolved readily had timely and adequate medical care been available. The following are case examples from our clinical experience.

A one-month-old Hmong child accompanied his parents (both health care workers) on their flight through the jungle out of Laos. During the trek the child became febrile over a several-day period, with temperatures that the mother estimated to be 103 to 104 degrees Fahrenheit. On two occasions the child had prolonged seizures. Later in childhood he manifested hyperactivity, poor concentration, low grades in school, a preference for playing with younger children, temper tantrums well into his school years, and behavioral problems at home and school. Intelligence testing in the United States revealed an IQ of 119. He did well on a regimen of methylphenidate, a special school program, and family counseling with an emphasis on behavioral modification.

Over the long term, the above patient did well; he completed high school, married, and became employed. The following case exemplifies the type of individual who will require lifelong social, financial, and psychiatric services.

At the age of six a Cambodian girl underwent a prolonged period of severe malnutrition, malaria, and recurrent high fevers. She came to the United States at age nine and was referred for evaluation two years later, when she had failed to learn English or acquire other academic skills (for example, mathematics and writing). On evaluation, she demonstrated good social skills and a fairly good vocabulary in Cambodian. However, numerous neurological soft signs (for example, frontal lobe signs and dysdiadochokinesia)

and hard signs (unequal deep-tendon reflexes) were present, she had difficulty adapting to novel tasks, and an assessment of her social and academic
function suggested an intellectual age of about five years. Brain imaging
revealed that much of one cerebral hemisphere was atrophied, with scattered
areas of atrophy in the other hemisphere. Placement in a program for mild to
moderately retarded children of her own age resulted in progress consistent
with her remaining abilities.

Refugee children may be at risk for such epidemic diseases as hepatitis-A,
hepatitis-B, tuberculosis, and various gastrointestinal parasites and bacteria carried by their elders and newly arriving relatives. But refugee parents may avoid
immunization for their children even after they relocate to the United States.
They may view as "normal" such pediatric conditions as chronically draining ear
infections, which can lead to lifelong hearing impairment. If refugee parents are
suspicious or fearful of medical interventions, they may not obtain medical attention for their children in a timely fashion.

Malnutrition

Children are more likely than adults to suffer permanent problems as a result
of malnutrition during preflight adversity, flight, or refugee camp experiences. In
the chaos of refugee flight a balanced, nutritious diet may not be available for
days, weeks, or months.

Poor nutrition affects children more rapidly and more seriously than adults,
for three reasons. First, children and adolescents have a higher metabolic rate than
do adults, meaning that they require more calories relative to body weight simply
to remain alive. Second, food above and beyond basic metabolic needs is necessary for normal growth and development in children and adolescents. And third,
children are more apt than adults to suffer permanent biodevelopmental damage
(for example, brain damage and small stature) as a result of malnutrition.

Pellagra and beriberi, both "wet" (edematous) and "dry," are most likely to
occur in older children and young adolescents, perhaps because of their high
nutritional needs during this period. Those who survive these malnutritions are
apt to have concentration and memory problems, at least for a time following
their recovery. Younger children have small nutritional needs, and neonates and
infants may still be breast-feeding—a nutritional risk for the mother, but an
advantage for the infant whose mother remains reasonably well nourished.

Malnutrition may remain a threat for some refugee children even after their
resettlement in the United States. Many refugee families do not provide adequate
fruits and vegetables, food items that are considerably more expensive in the
United States than in refugee-producing countries. In many refugee families in
the United States, children eat excessive amounts of salt and meat and too few
fruits and vegetables. Carotene blood levels are apt to be low. Development of
diet-induced cardiovascular disease, as has occurred among Japanese-Americans
(Marmot and Syme, 1976), poses a risk for later life.

Age and the Effect of Pathogenic Factors

These factors can have devastating physical or psychological consequences, depending on the age and developmental stage of the child when the circumstances occur and how long the conditions persist. At the same time, refugee children may have some advantages over their elders because their developmental stage may make them more adaptable and flexible. Their acculturation may be in some ways easier.

Child and adolescent refugees differ from their adult peers in that they must simultaneously acculturate to the new society while being socialized within the family. For infants, the process may involve a bicultural socializing—to the culture at home and to the prevailing society. For the newly arrived older adolescent, the process mainly involves acculturation, with perhaps some socialization in high school, college, the Job Corps, or the military.

The age at which the child encounters trauma, infectious disease, or malnutrition may influence the pathological picture. Younger children have the advantage of more "plastic" brains than older people, so that remaining brain tissue may take over certain brain functions after a brain injury. Older children may have acquired more knowledge or skill prior to the injury, and some of this "archaic" knowledge or skill may persist even after brain injury.

Family Factors in Pathogenesis

Trauma to or loss of parents. Injury to or the death of a child's parent or parents can have lasting consequences, especially if the child's security is threatened or if he or she does not have the opportunity to grieve the losses, as in the following case.

A fifteen-year-old Laotian boy presented with a several-week history of anxiety, depression, and thoughts of suicide. He had been in the United States for four years and had made a highly successful adjustment in his family, among peers, and in school. His crisis was precipitated by the belated report of his father's death in a concentration camp for former military officers. No funeral ceremonies had been held, and the boy—as the eldest son—felt responsible now for taking his father's patriarchal role in the family. Immediate intervention consisted of guiding him in grieving for his father in the absence of a corpse and funeral ceremonies. Next, we met with his mother to discuss her expectations of her son. Although she agreed that in Laos he would assume family leadership and responsibilities, she did not believe that was either feasible or appropriate in the United States. She wanted him to remain in school, and she expected that he would attend college. Moreover, she did not believe that he had the maturity to lead a family in so complex a society as America's. Elder male members of the extended family concurred. In a family session, the mother and extended family elders clarified what they expected of him in his present and future role in the family. Assured that the family wanted him to remain in school and to continue his academic and personal development for the next several years, he returned to his former high level of coping.

Conversely, a child can remain relatively secure and emotionally undisturbed in the midst of tumult if the family remains intact and the parents are able to discharge their parental responsibilities toward the child. The child might even perceive the events as exciting and experience them as a time of increased family closeness. The following case exemplifies this viewpoint.

An Afghan couple, both physicians, were escaping overland to Pakistan with their two preschool-age children. The trek was difficult: there were attacks by Soviet helicopters, the family had to sleep out in the cold most nights, and food was limited. The children took the flight in good spirits, despite their parents' extreme anxiety over the situation. At the end of several days of walking the four-year-old asked, "When are we getting to the hotel? We are all dirty, and we need a bath."

Child neglect and abuse. Child neglect and abuse are rare among people whose cultures value the parental role and child-raising skills and who may have fled to assure their children a viable future. However, such problems do occur in the context of migration, resettlement, adjustment problems, and associated mental disorders. Some unaccompanied minors have been subject to physical or sexual abuse or have survived prostitution. As substance abuse appeared and spread (such as opium addiction among Hmong refugees), refugee child abuse and neglect increased appreciably.

A fearful and maladaptive six-year-old Vietnamese boy was referred to our clinic by the school. He described anal intercourse and other sexual activities with his "uncle" for "as long as I can remember." The "uncle" had obtained the boy two years earlier from his sister, who had in turn obtained the boy from an orphanage.

Pseudo child abuse may present to medical and psychiatric facilities. These involve the use of various folk treatments, such as moxybustion, "coining" (rubbing the skin briskly with a coin so that an abrasion results), acupuncture, and deep kneading or pounding. Instances of lead and arsenic poisoning from administration of folk medications have also occurred.

Intergenerational conflict. Refugee children acculturate more rapidly than their parents and grandparents, and intergenerational strife may result. This varies in duration and intensity and in its effects on parents and children. From a clinical perspective, its untoward results mount during adolescence as refugee minors are trying to establish their own identities and to enter mainstream social, recreational, and work roles. Tragedies may result. For example, a Hmong father hanged himself when his son bought a new car without the father's permission but with money that the son himself had earned. Dating and marriage are often focal issues, as in the following case.

A Hmong family was referred when their fifteen-year-old daughter announced a suicide plan to her teacher. The girls' father, observing her interest in boys and dating, believed that the time had come for her to marry. He had arranged a marriage with a young Hmong man, accepted the bride price, and then proudly announced his accomplishment to the family. The girl wanted to be an airline stewardess or a nurse and did not plan to marry until her twenties. In subsequent family sessions, the mother (whose family had similarly betrothed her without her approval) revealed her support of the daughter in these matters. This left the father isolated from family support and increasingly depressed. During his treatment for depression (requiring medication and psychotherapy) and regular family sessions, the father agreed to negotiate a face-saving withdrawal from the betrothal. Moreover, both parents agreed to support their daughter in choosing her own career and marriage partner. The daughter agreed to negotiate her social activities with her parents so they could be comfortable with her decisions and behavior.

As this case demonstrates, intergenerational conflict can give rise to disciplinary methods that are generally considered excessive or inappropriate in American society. Although these cultural differences present challenges to the clinician, they also present an opportunity for negotiation, education, and clarification. Refugee parents need to know what disciplines will be supported by U.S. society, and refugee children need to know that their parents have the right and obligation to guide them in socially responsible, age-appropriate ways.

Parental acculturation failure. Parents who fail to learn English, to understand American social institutions, or to enter the workplace are at risk for mental disorder (Westermeyer, 1988a). They also cannot effectively prepare their children for life in the United States. This disability arises from their inability as parents to cooperate with the school system in the education of their children, to act as role models, and to teach relevant social survival skills to their children. Such parents put themselves at risk for crises precipitated by their acculturating children, as in the following case.

A Hmong family was referred from the emergency room after the mother had attempted suicide by swallowing pills. Although the family had lived in the United States for several years, both parents remained isolated from the majority of society and from the expatriate Hmong community by virtue of being deaf. The family crisis was precipitated unknowingly by their fourteen-year-old daughter, who had allowed a Hmong boy of the same age to carry her books home from school, as she had observed others do. When she introduced the boy to her mother at the door, the mother began weeping and tearing her clothes; she later ingested the pills. The mother had assumed that the girl had become sexually active and was trying to force a marriage on her parents. Following resolution of the family crisis (and during treatment for associated psychiatric and medical problems in the parents), the parents enrolled in a local sign-language class. They learned rapidly and were soon on their way to a more stable family life.

Parental psychiatric disorder. Adults suffering prolonged major psychiatric disorders are unable to discharge their parental responsibilities effectively, putting their children at risk for personality, interpersonal, and mental-emotional problems. This has been well documented for children of parents with schizophrenia, chronic depression, and substance abuse. Studies of parents and families who became refugees during World War II have identified tendencies in refugee parents that may adversely affect children; such parents may harbor lingering distrust of the outside world (Freyberg, 1980), may expect their children to compensate them for their own earlier losses (Trossman, 1968), and may assign names and roles of lost relatives to children, who are then expected to replace those losses (Rakoff, 1964).

Even so-called invulnerable children, who evolve out of this process with intact coping skills and high achievement, can have impaired intimate relationships and problems in caring for themselves emotionally (Anthony and Cohler, 1987).

Family Structure and Adaptive Style

Like individuals, refugee families have their own structures, functions, and histories (Dunnigan, 1982), which may foster or impede individual and family adaptation in the host country. Structures and styles that were successful in the former culture may be problem-producing in the new one if they are continued without regard for changed circumstances. Economic pursuits, sex roles, courting and marriage, child bearing, and child rearing occur within the context of the family. The family aids acculturation to the extent that it can support its members as they undergo changes in these areas. But to the extent that the family opposes such changes, it can add to the children's burdens.

Political Factors in Pathogenesis

Resettlement countries or countries of first refuge can mitigate mental health sequelae by providing a supportive, secure environment—or they can cause additional hardship through racism and harassment. Governments with limited resources may be ambivalent toward refugees, and this ambivalence may increase the insecurity of refugee families and their children. Segregation or demeaning treatment of refugees may increase children's identity confusion and contribute to difficulty in internalizing a positive ethnic identity.

Many refugees come from communities in which they were members of the dominant race or culture. And even in refugee camps, groups tend to be placed with others of the same culture. With resettlement, the reality of minority status takes hold. Indigenous neighbors may resent refugees' competition for jobs, housing, and finite health and social services, especially in lower-class neighbor-hoods. Hostility may spill over into vandalism, harassment, assault, and other manifestations of insecurity. Hostility may occur among refugee groups them-selves. The following case reveals one kind of problem that may result from interethnic tensions and carryover of refugee camp behaviors.

> An eighteen-year-old Vietnamese male student was referred by the court for evaluation after stabbing another student, a Laotian refugee. The patient's parents had reported his age as fifteen so that he might continue school to make up for the years of education that he lost while in the refugee camp. He arrived at school in the United States with a refugee camp attitude, believing that each group had to provide for its own security rather than rely on administrators to resolve disputes. He assaulted the fellow student after re-portedly being harassed for being Vietnamese.

Psychopathology
Organic Mental Disorders

Refugee children are at risk for brain injury from numerous sources. Most of these injuries occur after birth; among American children, such damage usually occurs perinatally. The later onset can influence personality and social develop-ment, leaving children at risk for maladjustment and psychiatric disorder.

> A fifteen-year-old male Laotian high school student presented with an acute psychosis. At age ten, while living in a refugee camp, he had a high sustained fever with convulsions and two days of coma. Subsequently he showed a personality change: greater impulsiveness, irritability, and self-centeredness, and problems with authority. During his preteen and early adolescent years he experienced mounting problems in peer relationships, in dealing with authority figures, and with sexuality, although he continued to achieve top grades in school until shortly before his mental illness.

These acquired disorders can begin in the United States. Refugee children may be at greater risk of being injured in car accidents (because their parents are unfamiliar with American traffic), being hurt while riding their bicycles and motorcycles (also because of unfamiliarity), and suffering neglected infections (because of parents' lack of knowledge about the medical system).

> A four-year-old Tai-Phouan boy from Laos was seen because of behavioral changes resulting from a car accident six months earlier. He had sustained a linear skull fracture and was unconscious for several hours, but he recovered without evident neurological damage. His mother and aunt died in the accident; only he and his father (the driver) survived. Family assessment revealed that the father had a major depression. The father received treat-ment for depression and counseling in child rearing, and the boy improved. However, abnormal EEG findings and psychometric abnormalities persisted

in association with hyperactivity. Two years later, on reevaluation following treatment, the father was remarried and not depressed. The son was in school, not hyperactive, and performing well.

Mood Disorders

Depression. In both epidemiological and clinical studies of adult refugees, major depression is the psychiatric disorder with the highest incidence and prevalence (Westermeyer, 1988a, 1988b). This may not be the case among refugee children—although the data are sparse (Kim and Chun, 1993)—perhaps because of the low prevalence of major depression among children generally. It may also be due to the difficulty of recognizing depression in children, with its often different manifestations (for example, hypersomnia rather than insomnia, social conflict rather than withdrawal, aggressiveness rather than self-punitiveness) and its variable presentation with the child's age (Ionescu-Tongyonk, 1977; Philips, 1979; Welner, 1978). Depression in refugee children and adolescents often accompanies other problems, such as learning, conduct, or substance-use disorders; this can make it difficult to recognize the existence of depression.

A ten-year-old Hmong girl born in the United States to refugee parents was placed in a foster home following the death of her mother from meningitis (her father had died of a cancer several years earlier). She manifested numerous symptoms after her mother's death: nightmares; night terrors; fear of being alone; fear of flushing toilets; aversion to bathing; a need to please adults; inability to reveal anger to adults, with episodic rages against her siblings; stealing from mother surrogates and envied peers who still had both parents; and lying to cover her stealing and to avoid displeasing adults. After a year in a stable family setting, the first five symptoms disappeared, whereas the others persisted (albeit at a lower rate). On psychiatric evaluation she immediately revealed the idea that her misbehavior had caused her mother to die and that she feared that other adults would abandon her if she expressed anger. She manifested a profound depressed mood with prolonged weeping—something she had hidden from adults and peers for fear that it would alienate them. When several psychotherapy sessions failed to alleviate her depression, imipramine was begun and increased to therapeutic blood levels (150 mg). She improved considerably during nine months of weekly psychotherapy (talking rather than play therapy), permitting gradual discontinuation of medication. Among her issues were rage at her parents for dying and leaving her, as well as at the relatives who failed to meet her needs after her mother died.

Mania. Like depression, mania can be difficult to recognize in adolescents, even within American society (Ballenger, Reus, and Post, 1982). Across cultural and language boundaries the classical adult picture can be even more difficult to appreciate. Alienation, failure to acculturate, antiauthority stances, inappropriate sexuality, and similar attitudinal-behavior problems may predominate. Psychological symptoms are present (for example, racing thoughts, grandiosity, and simple hallucinations) but must be inquired after since they are rarely volunteered. Vegetative symptoms (for example, hyposomnia and weight loss) may be absent. Cognitive symptoms, such as lapses in judgment or fluctuations in attention, may be hard to identify because normal adolescents may episodically manifest similar lapses and fluctuations. To a large extent the key to this diagnosis lies in considering it.

> A seventeen-year-old Vietnamese boy was referred because of irascibility, frequent arguing with peers, failure to respond to limit setting, and academic failure. Over the previous year his behavior had led to expulsion from three schools and from four foster families. Over several months he had been seen in psychotherapy three times a week by a psychoanalyst who employed intensive psychoanalytic psychotherapy. At the time of our assessment the patient had been suspended from school, and his foster parents were threatening to separate because of family conflicts introduced by the patient. Lithium reduced most of the patient's severely disruptive behavior within a few days, so that he was able to return to school. Further history revealed that the patient's family had forced him to leave Vietnam because his public harangues against the new Communist regime (and other manifestations of mania) endangered the family's status with local officials. Following his stabilization on lithium, psychotherapy was directed at his grief and rage over being sent from his homeland, rationales and methods for adjusting to his situation, and short-term goals to facilitate his long-term goals (for example, graduation from high school, accommodation to his foster family, cooperation with teachers, and making friends). He has since established communication with his family in Vietnam and is now midway through college. During a brief "lithium vacation" his symptoms reappeared within a few weeks, so he continues on lithium with infrequent supportive sessions.

Substance-related disorders. Initially after resettlement the prevalence of substance abuse among refugee youths tends to be low to nil. As time goes on many refugee youths acquire patterns of substance abuse from local American youths or from adults within their own expatriate group.

Learning Disabilities and Attention Deficit Disorder

These disorders can be difficult to assess in recently arrived refugee children or in those whose English-language abilities remain poor. They should be considered in refugee children who do poor academic work or fail over time to learn English on a level with peers. Medical, neurological, and psychiatric evaluation should be considered in such cases, since the standard psychometric measures have dubious validity, and organic mental disorder may be present. Neurological signs, a history of central nervous system damage, and psychiatric evaluation can lead to remedial recommendations to family, school, or other resources. The case vignettes in this chapter exemplify this process.

Mental retardation. Retarded refugee children often have achieved social and behavioral stability in their country of origin. Their flight to or resettlement in another country can disrupt this stability, with behavioral, emotional, or mental consequences. Factors such as family stability and continuity of role appear to be important in weighing for or against morbidity in this group. The following case typifies the kind of problem that can result, as well as means for rehabilitation.

> A fourteen-year-old Hmong boy with moderate mental retardation presented in the emergency department after assaulting family members. Examination revealed paranoid hallucinations and delusions. Previously he had gotten along well in the family. During the family's recent flight from Laos, the father died when he stepped on a land mine. Since arrival in the United States, the patient's mother and three older siblings had been out of the home regularly, attending school and English-language courses. After having been arrested for meandering through traffic, the patient had been locked up alone in the home (he previously had been with relatives twenty-four hours a day). Next he left water running and burned himself on the gas stove, resulting in his being locked alone in his room when family members were not present. Following a period of hospitalization and neuroleptic medication, he did well in a day program for moderately retarded adolescents.

> A mildly retarded sixteen-year-old Hmong girl was referred from the emergency department, where she had been by the police. She had been found wandering the streets at night in the middle of a Minnesota winter, lightly clothed in tropical clothes. Her family reported that she had left home after earlier threatening suicide. She had arrived in the United States only recently, and her widowed father had remarried in the previous month. The patient (the eldest daughter) and her new stepmother had not been congenial with each other. History revealed a closed head injury in childhood. Observation and history suggested a petit mal seizure pattern that had begun during the flight from Laos; eeg affirmed this diagnosis. The patient responded to individual and family therapy, along with treatment for her seizure disorder. She was able to reenter her home, begin English classes, and enter special education classes. She married at age nineteen and now has two children.

Pediatricians and school psychologists in the United States encounter many cases of congenital mental retardation, which is present from birth. But they see relatively few cases of acquired mental retardation, which begins during infancy, childhood, or adolescence. Although children with congenital MR show across-the-board deficits that are mutually consistent, children with acquired MR may demonstrate marked inconsistencies resulting from the surviving skills and knowledge present at the time of the brain insult, together with the loss of capacity from the brain insult. Children with acquired MR may possess vocabulary or stereotypic social skills that make them appear more capable than they actually are. For example, an ethnic Chinese girl from Laos had an episode of encephalitis at age fifteen, at a time when she was obtaining the highest grades in her class. Years later she could read in French, Chinese, and Laotian, as well as give the meanings of individual words. However, she could not retain what she had read for more than a few minutes, was unable to acquire new knowledge, and could not perform tasks at which she had previously shown skill (for example, cooking dinner and shopping for the family groceries).

Psychoses

The incidence of acute psychoses among refugee adolescents and children appears to be low, perhaps because psychosis in the midst of war, civil conflict, and refugee flight is so often lethal. Psychosis can occur in young refugees who are vulnerable as a result of such preexisting conditions as mental retardation or other brain insult. Treatment across cultures and languages can be difficult, but we have seen many patients return to their prepsychosis level of function, perhaps because of the role of overwhelming stress in precipitating these cases.

Schizophrenia likewise is not a common adolescent problem, but its low incidence is countered by a growing prevalence over time, as recurrently or chronically schizophrenic adolescent and young adult refugees surface for care. Refugee families typically have difficulty accepting the gravity and chronicity of the problem. This lack of acceptance can have untoward consequences for the patient, other family members, and the family finances. Refugee families may repeatedly seek help at diverse medical, social, and psychiatric facilities, thereby undermining long-term rehabilitative efforts. Families also may expend large sums on folk healing modalities, which can offer temporary hope but rarely affect the long-term course, as in the following case.

> A fifteen-year-old Lao-Hmong boy developed paranoid auditory hallucinations along with grandiose delusions. He assaulted family members, refused to attend school, destroyed the family's expensive computer, and demanded that the family purchase a wife for him. The family sought treatment at several psychiatric facilities in three different states over a two-year period. Eventually the family permitted him to remain in one treatment program, where his condition improved to the point that he could reenter high school.

Paranoid, affective, and somatic symptoms are perhaps more common in psychotic refugee patients than among indigenous psychotic patients (Westermeyer, 1989; Westermeyer, Bouafuely, and Neider, 1989; Westermeyer et al., 1989). Some families resist seeking outside help, especially if the affected adolescent is docile or withdrawn, as demonstrated by this case:

> A sixteen-year-old Vietnamese refugee came to official attention when resettlement workers found that the child was not in high school. A home visit

revealed a bizarre-acting, mute, unkempt teenager who was living in a large packing carton in a back room. Psychiatric assessment established the presence of hallucinations and delusions, and hospitalization was arranged to further assess his condition. Prior to his admission the entire family suddenly fled the state.

Eating Disorders

Anorexia and bulimia are not yet common among refugee adolescents. Overeating and obesity are more frequent in resettlement countries than in rural Third World countries. Nonetheless, eating disorders do appear among refugee adolescents in resettlement countries, usually in association with acculturation to the majority society, as observed in the patient discussed below:

> A seventeen-year-old Lao girl was evaluated for overeating, weight loss, and amenorrhea. She admitted to practicing bulimia, a behavior that she had learned from her American peers. Treatment with this well-acculturated, intelligent patient included individual psychotherapy, a day program for eating disorder, and culturally sensitive family therapy.

Conduct Disorder

Some clinical data suggest that conduct disorder may be more common among refugee adolescents than among indigenous adolescents (Kim and Chun, 1993). Previous case vignettes show examples of behavioral problems associated with various psychiatric conditions. Environmental stresses or personal catastrophes may predate these problems, as in the following case.

> A twelve-year-old Lao boy was evaluated for touching girls' genitalia in class, assaulting other children, and failing to respond to teachers' attempts to impose limitations. His history revealed that the boy's father, a former policeman, had become mentally ill and gone to live in a Buddhist temple after the Communist regime was established. The boy's mother then began a liaison with a Vietnamese soldier who eventually moved in and forced the patient and his teenage brothers out of the home. The brothers brought the boy to a refugee camp in Thailand and then returned to fight with the resistance in Laos. Soon afterward the boy was placed with an American woman who had a long history of recurrent mental illness. One of the woman's teenage sons alerted authorities that the mother was deteriorating again—appearing partially clothed in the home, leaving the bathroom door open while she bathed, and fondling the children in a seductive fashion. The boy responded to placement with a Lao family and weekly psychotherapy over a one-year period.

During psychotherapy, accomplishments included the following:

- expressing his rage at the Vietnamese stepfather for forcing him and his brothers out of the home;
- coming to accept his mother's liaison as a means of survival for her and several younger siblings;
- grieving the loss of his father and his brothers;
- giving up acting as a "pseudomature" adult and accepting the role of child, which involved learning to trust and depend on adults again;
- discussing his loss of innocence about the potential for evil and destruction in the world;
- finding reasons for him to go on and reach his best potential despite the obstacles (for example, honoring his father, making his brothers' sacrifices live on, possibly "rescuing" his mother at some time when he was an adult and able to help her).

Clinical Assessment
Culturally Sensitive Psychiatric Evaluation

Psychiatric assessment of children, adolescents, and their families should proceed in a culturally sensitive way (Lee, 1988; Szapocznik, Kurtines, and Fernandez, 1980). Culturally sensitive evaluation includes the following characteristics.

- The clinician should have general awareness of the patient's cultural values, attitudes, ideal versus behavioral norms (behaviors that a culture prescribes versus those actually practiced), and worldview.
- More specific cultural knowledge must be obtained relative to the particular symptoms, conflicts, problems, or context presented by the patient (for example, age at initiating courting and relative value accorded to independence from family versus family interdependence for older adolescents).
- The clinician should appreciate the major psycho-socio-cultural stressors and be able to recognize the strengths and resources available to the young refugee patient in his or her sociocultural situation.
- The patient's concepts of health, illness, well-being, and disease should be known to the therapist. It is often useful to ask refugee youth about their ideas regarding the cause of the problem, its probable course, and possible outcomes.

Working with a Translator

Recently arrived refugees or those who have not learned adequate English must be assessed with the aid of a translator if the clinician does not speak the child's language. In the clinical context, translators are often referred to as interpreters (because they are expected to convey connotative as well as denotative meaning) or bilingual workers (because their responsibilities generally involve much more than translation or interpretation).

The patient-interpreter relationship can be different when the patient is a child rather than an adult. From the child's perspective, transference may involve distrust, fear of being judged, or loss of confidentiality through the interpreter to the parents. Or the child may be motivated to trust the "foreign" clinician who is teamed up with someone of the child's own ethnic group (that is, the interpreter), since the child may feel caught between the clinician's culture and the interpreter's culture.

Similarly, the interpreter's countertransference can affect assessment and therapy. Interpreters may react negatively to the child's acculturation or Americanization. An interpreter may preach to or shame a refugee minor just when understanding and support are needed. Or the interpreter may discern in the child his or her own earlier struggles and seek to establish a therapeutic alliance. The clinician-interpreter relationship also can be crucial in this process, since the clinician often acts as a mentor or role model for the interpreter. The following situation provides an example of a problem related to an interpreter naïve to the psychiatric setting.

> A ten-year-old unaccompanied Vietnamese boy—recently arrived—was referred because of school refusal, apathy, and general disinterest. His Vietnamese foster family had not seen him show any emotion. In the first session, as the boy related the deaths of his parents at sea, he began weeping uncontrollably. The translator, a former teacher, became visibly upset and insisted that "we Vietnamese do not discuss such things," although the boy indicated his desire to discuss the matter further. The translator, sent by a local social agency, had not been prepared for this work and had never done psychiatric translation.

Refugee-Related Information

It is important to inquire specifically about the refugee flight. This includes asking about preflight stressors, rationales for flight, dangers and losses along the way, conditions in the refugee camp (nutrition, security, education, recreation, employment opportunities), length of time spent in the camp, and conditions of the early resettlement in the United States. Family details before, during, and after the flight should be ascertained (whether there was death, separation, divorce, nuclear or extended family, polygamy). Age at leaving the culture of origin and at arriving in the resettlement country should be determined.

Children may be beaten, tortured, wounded, or murdered in the midst of hostilities. Routine inquiry must be made regarding this possibility. In the following case, a refugee had been raped twice in the United States and had received crisis counseling, but her victimization in Asia had not been discussed.

> A seventeen-year-old Cambodian girl was sentenced to be executed by virtue of having been a student in Phnom Phen. She was struck on the head by younger adolescents, under the direction of armed guards, and left for dead. Several hours later she regained consciousness, disentangled herself

from the pile of bodies, and managed to escape. Eventually she resettled in the United States, where she repeatedly exposed herself to obviously dangerous situations, such as walking alone in dangerous neighborhoods and allowing social situations to develop in which she was alone with men she did not know well. When she came through these dangerous experiences unscathed, her chronic depression was temporarily alleviated. However, she was at times victimized during these risk-taking behaviors, leading to several beatings, two rapes, and an illegitimate child.

Premigration psychosocial adjustment must be assessed. Culture has limited influence on early and psychosocial development. In cultures where adults constantly carry, hold, or attend to the child, unusually early toilet training may be reported—although it is probably the parents who are "trained" to anticipate the child's signals of impending defecation. Later in childhood and in adolescence numerous indices of development can be heavily influenced by culture. These include courting, assuming adult responsibilities, and achieving independent decision making. In some societies one does not become a truly mature, independent adult until one's grandchildren are born. Predictably, the age at flight and relocation greatly influence these developmental hallmarks. The case in which a Hmong father committed suicide when his son decided on his own to buy a car exemplifies the son's lack of appreciation of his father's culture and the father's lack of understanding regarding his son's new values. Kremer and Sabin (1985) have come to similar conclusions based on their work with twenty-one Indochinese refugee children and adolescents.

Family Assessment

For the therapist working with refugee children, it is as important to meet, interview, and assess the family as it is when working with other children. However, it often requires longer sessions and more visits to establish rapport and mutual trust and to clear up misunderstandings, which almost always occur on both sides. Use of a translator can also retard the process, adding to the cost of and time needed for therapy. Experienced bilingual workers can often facilitate the process by interviewing the family first without the clinician, and then later with the clinician. Especially if a rigid matriarch or patriarch is dominating or obstructing the interviews, meetings with individual family members may also be fruitful. Conversely, an interview with a large extended family (which usually requires two or three hours) can aid in clarifying extended family dynamics.

We have made more home visits in the assessment of refugee families than to a similar number of native-born patients for the following reasons: unwillingness of the family to bring a disturbed family member into a public place; our wish to reduce environmental distractions in the process of conducting an assessment of certain children (for example, the mentally retarded or organically impaired); a desire to conduct an extended family session when clinic space was limited;

having been invited by the family to conduct a session at home; our wish to assess the patient's function at home when clinical resources did not facilitate that objective. In many cases, two people made these visits, most often a clinician and a bilingual worker. Solo home visitors were usually bilingual workers who visited the family in order to orient them to the assessment process, to interview them, or to negotiate some clinical matter between the family and the clinician.

In assessing refugee families, questions that the clinician will want to consider routinely are as follows:

- How stressed is the family by sources other than the patient (for example, poverty, neighborhood insecurity, intergenerational conflict, loyalties to warring groups)?
- What are their resources (for example, emotional stability, time to aid their distressed or distressing child, education, transportation)?
- How disabled are the parents (for example, are they still grieving their losses; are they angry or demoralized by their failures; are they depressed, alexithymic, substance abusing)?
- Is the family a buffer or a further traumatization to the child's health and development (for example, is this family committed to supporting and understanding the child's development or do they see the child as a means of reversing their disappointments and failures or of resurrecting dead friends and family)?

Treatment
Compliance

Compliance problems are common among refugee patients. Such problems can be reduced by appreciating the refugee's point of view, supplemented by careful education and reeducation of the parents and the child (Hoang and Erickson, 1985). If medications are prescribed, routine instructions should include the following:

- The medication must not be given to siblings, relatives, or friends. (Refugee patients may sell prescription drugs or "prescribe" them for others with like symptoms.)
- Higher doses must not be taken without physician approval. (Some people believe that if a little is good then more must be better.)
- Most psychotropic medication requires weeks to show the first effects and may need to be taken for months or even years. (Many refugees have a model of pharmacotherapy derived from aspirin or penicillin and so expect relief in hours or a few days, with cessation of the need for medication in several hours or days.) The prescribing physician must know all other medications the patient is taking, including other prescribed drugs, over-the-counter drugs, folk remedies, and illicit drugs, such as opium. Not to do so can undermine the efficacy of psychotropic medication, perhaps

make matters worse, or possibly prove fatal. (Faced with severe or disabling illness, many refugees "doctor shop" without informing the respective physicians.) Over-the-counter and herbal drugs often have antihistaminic, anticholinergic, sedative, or sympathomimetic effects. Abuse of opium, alcohol, cannabis, and other drugs retards recovery. Any of these substances may counteract or potentiate side effects or complications of psychotropic medications.

Medications alone rarely solve psychiatric problems among refugee patients. The physician should consider the use of counsel, direction, suggestion, education, and psychotherapy. The patient may need redirection, change, effort, exercise, and forbearance. Refugees and their families may expect that a pill will magically change psychopathology without any other efforts being expended. Involvement of ethnic peers in the treatment team can be critical to eliciting the compliance needed for effective treatment.

Ethnopharmacology

Pharmacodynamic and pharmacokinetic data for adults from various racial and ethnic groups (Lin, Poland, and Nakasaki, 1993) indicate that, at a fixed dose of tricyclic, Caucasians have lower tricyclic blood levels than Asians, Asian Americans, and African Americans. Caucasians also maintain lower blood levels of neuroleptics at a fixed dose. Pharmacokinetics of lithium do not appear to vary across races, although psychiatrists in Asia achieve clinical response at blood levels below those employed in the United States. Unfortunately, such studies across cultures and races do not yet exist for children. If these data extrapolate to children, lower doses of tricyclics, neuroleptics, and even possibly lithium may be effective for refugee children who are not Caucasians. However, the interpatient differences greatly exceed the interracial or interethnic differences, so the psychiatrist must not shy away from employing adequate doses.

We have adopted the following procedure for achieving therapeutic levels of medication in refugees:

- Begin at lower than usual doses.
- Increase the dose in small increments every day or two until side effects are reached.
- Monitor the patient closely (for example, symptoms checklists, blood pressure, pulse, weight, blood levels of medication—as appropriate to the diagnosis and the treatment) and then modify the dose.

Family Education and Family Therapy

One hears the opinion that Third World people cannot be treated in family or group settings. It can of course be done, but this prevalent misconception does reflect the special problems that multiperson therapy can present. Among these are the following:

- The flow, pace, and participation of so many people make the use of a translator problematic. The group leader should speak the participants' language if possible.
- The leader whose ethnicity differs from that of the group may feel overwhelmed or outnumbered, especially if he or she is inexperienced or insecure about such an effort.
- Family structure in the particular culture must be understood in order to develop rapport with the family and to avoid "cultural resistances" (Kim, 1985).
- The therapist must demonstrate respect for the family's or group's culture and avoid stereotyping (Lappin and Scott, 1982).

Unaccompanied Minors

Following placement in a foster family, refugee children from World War II entered a period during which the child and family could not communicate, followed by a period of adjustment for both the children and their families. The most common early symptoms were overeating, fear of going to sleep alone, nightmares, phobias (for example, fear of people), excessive demands, clinging to parents, resentment of the attention paid to siblings, repression of anger or aggression, exaggerated desire to please in younger children and overt rebellion in older children, and apparent sadness (Rathbun, DiVirgilio, and Waldfogel, 1958). Several social policy and legal factors have worked against placing refugee children with members of their own cultural groups, a practice that could reduce miscommunication and misunderstanding (Harding and Looney, 1977). Many foster and adoptive parents reported that the child's physical and emotional needs in the first year after placement "drained them emotionally" (Sokoloff, Carlin, and Pham, 1984). Family problems have often resulted when the unaccompanied child requires psychiatric care (Williams and Westermeyer, 1984). Common themes in psychotherapy with these children include rage at their parents, homeland, culture, and race for having "abandoned" or otherwise rejected them and grief at the loss of family, relatives, friends, home, community, language, culture, and nation (Carlin, 1979). Later, during adolescence and young adulthood, they are at risk for identity problems involving the discrepancy between racial and ethnic identity (Westermeyer, 1979).

Many of these children respond to security, concern, a stable family environment, and firm application of clearly stated limits (writing them down may help). Foster or adoptive families should be of the same race and culture as these children whenever possible. Children who are maladaptive in an American family may become adaptive in a more culturally and racially appropriate family. All these children should be thoroughly evaluated biomedically and psychosocially prior to family placement. Their adjustment should be monitored at regular intervals throughout adolescence by a mental health professional (that is, a psychiatric nurse at master's level, a psychiatric social worker at master's level, a clinical psychologist, a psychiatrist). For those placed in American families, weekend ethnic programs and ethnic summer camps are desirable.

Interracial Children

A news article on Amerasian children from Vietnam depicted the children as successful and adjusting well to the United States (Lawlor, 1988). Anecdotal information from several relocation agencies is at odds with this glowing report, however. In one relocation agency, twenty-one of twenty-three children required social or psychiatric services because of disturbed or disturbing conditions in the first year of resettlement. Family and personal problems in this group included illiteracy (some had not been permitted to attend school); dropping out of school, running away, family violence, attempts at suicide, pregnancy, substance abuse, delinquency; and psychiatric and personality disorders in mothers (for example, sociopathy, mental retardation, and affective disorders). Sometimes the purported family is not related to the child and wants to get rid of him or her. (We have encountered such cases in which adults in Vietnam purchased "rights" to an unwanted child, solely for the purpose of acting as a "ticket to the United States.")

Occasionally an interracial refugee child still belongs to an intact family. Work with the families of these children requires what might be termed bicultural family therapy. Jalali and Boyce (1980) have described some common features of this. The family's unresolved and divergent racial and ethnic identities remain for the child to resolve in working through to a personal and often unique identity (Faulkner and Kich, 1983).

Alienated Refugee Adolescents

Alienation has been described as one type of coping mechanism available to migratory, minority, poor, or disenfranchised youth (Lampkin, 1971). A study of Cuban refugee adolescents in Miami suggests that discontent may be in part a function of identity formation problems and role stress during acculturation (Naditch and Morrissey, 1976). Early in resettlement some unaccompanied adolescents were observed rejecting both their culture of origin and the skill learning needed in their new society (Harding and Looney, 1977)

Failure to Acculturate

Refugee children and adolescents may manifest failure to acculturate in diverse ways (Krupinski and Burrows, 1986)—failing to become fluent in English, despite opportunities to do so; failing academically or dropping out of school; and entering the chronic welfare system via unemployment or pregnancy.

The causes of acculturation failure vary widely from child to child. Assessment should include biomedical, neuropsychological, and psycho-socio-cultural evaluations.

The Married Minor

In some cultures it is common for young people to marry before the age of eighteen. Refugee dislocations may force earlier marriages than might otherwise be the case. For example, a fifteen-year-old Hmong girl lost both parents in a refugee camp (her father died of natural causes, and her mother committed suicide). With no one to care for her, she became a junior wife in a polygynous household. Clinical problems encountered among married refugees under the age of eighteen follow:

- A sixteen-year-old Hmong wife suffered major depression in association with polygynous family problems.
- A seventeen-year-old Hmong wife suffered irritable bowel syndrome with symptoms of anxiety and depression in association with homemaking and child care while attempting to realize her goals for an education.
- A seventeen-year-old Hmong wife suffered migraine headaches with minor depression in association with pressure from husband and relatives to conceive a child even though she wanted to complete school.

Prevention
Maintaining a Positive Identity

Refugee children and adolescents can develop negative individual, family, and ethnic identities in association with rejection by their own homeland; downward social mobility or acculturation failure in parents; minority status in the resettlement country; harassment or rejection by the majority society; difficulty learning English and other survival skills; absence of language training and literacy in their parents' language, in the history of the homeland, and in cultural skills (cooking, sports, art, dance, music); and placement in an American foster or adoptive home whose racial and ethnic identity differs from their own.

One of the several programmatic methods that can be used to maintain a positive identity among preschool and elementary school children is a Saturday school or Sunday school to teach language, the arts, history, and ethnic skills. For older children, preteens, and early teens an ethnic summer camp with both American and expatriate staff can promulgate both identities (or the "hyphenated-American" identity). Various teams, troupes, and special associations can form around common interests and pastimes. Return visits to the country of origin may assist with identity formation in some respects, but these are often stressful as well. A return visit can stir up unhappy memories, precipitate further identity crises, and undermine idyllic notions of the home country.

Early Identification of Maladaptive Youth

Early remediation of maladjustment shortens the morbid period, often costs less than delayed remediation, and can lead to better outcomes. This is especially true among children and adolescents, in whom delay can mean missing the optimal age for specific developmental tasks. To facilitate early recognition and referral, teachers, parents, refugee relocation workers, and primary health care staff must know the signs or symptoms of acculturation failure. This is not easy. Teachers, social workers, and primary health care workers are familiar with the various disabilities of indigenous children but usually are less experienced with refugees. They may have difficulty in distinguishing between the adjusting child and the failing child. Similarly, parents may have been familiar with what to expect in the home country, but they can be overwhelmed and uncertain about what to expect in the country of resettlement.

Peer discussions can facilitate peer support, ensure mutual peer learning, and spread the hard-won lessons of family acculturation. Thus alerted to the new norms associated with acculturation, refugee families are better prepared to recognize acculturation failure. Refugee adolescents, parents, leaders, and "gatekeepers" should also be aware of the signs that can herald psychiatric disorder—social withdrawal, failure to acquire English, academic failure, change in sleep or eating patterns, personality or behavioral changes, fights, and mounting disobedience or disrespect at home or school.

Developing Services for Refugee Youth

Diagnosis is often not well related to the presenting problem among youth. For example, a child's conduct problem in the classroom could be caused by brain damage, learning disorder, mental retardation, major depression, maternal PTSD, or paternal delusional disorder. Conversely, adolescent major depression can present as academic failure, fighting, social withdrawal, suicide attempt, family disruption, and so forth. Clinical assessment must include data on the cultural, social, psychological, and biomedical levels. Family assessment and school data are additional key elements in evaluation.

An adequate array of treatment and rehabilitative services must be available. Highest priority should perhaps be outpatient consultation, with links to schools, clinics, and social agencies. Next, outpatient treatment should be available, with an array of somatotherapies, psychotherapies, and sociotherapies. An inpatient facility with staff skilled in working with refugee youths is necessary for more intensive evaluation, acute life-threatening and potentially disabling crises (for example, suicide risk, assaultiveness, and delirium), psychosis, failure of outpatient treatment, and initiation or adjustment of somatotherapies. Day program care can be useful for cases in which the youth can function at home but not at school. Long-term residential care may be necessary for a small percentage of cases refractory to less intensive and extensive approaches; these latter cases often involve multiple problems, including combinations of brain syndromes, schizophrenia, affective disorder, substance abuse, family problems, and risks to society or to the patient.

Screening for problems of mental health and social adjustment among refugee youth should occur in several contexts. Foremost is the school, where a variety of academic, behavioral, and social problems are apt to be manifest. Relocation and other social agencies encounter youth-related family and social problems, as do the clergy. Courts and detention centers request consultation related to violence, theft, drug dealing, and substance abuse. Primary care clinicians and hospitals do refer cases of psychosis and self-mutilation, child abuse, incest, and persistent somatization. Staff members in all these institutions should be sensitized to the needs and problems of refugee youths, as well as informed about the availability of local resources and expertise.

Funding for mental health services to refugee youths is a major problem. School systems may not refer cases known to warrant consultation because of their possible financial responsibility for costs incurred. They may have to urge consultation through the parents, who are often not as concerned about the problem and are reluctant to spend the money needed for a psychiatric assessment. Community mental health clinics in many areas lack staff skilled in cross-cultural assessment and care and, because of inadequate funding, may be reluctant to hire such staff. Private insurers, HMOs, and PPOs (health maintenance organizations and preferred provider organizations) in many areas are cutting back mental health benefits. Perhaps even more than the mental health system itself, the funding system obstructs and delays adequate, timely services to refugee youths.

A major problem is the absence of a national policy for refugee resettlement in general and for the mental health and social adjustment of youth in particular. Refugee youths are essentially abandoned by the federal government within months of arrival and thrown on the not-so-tender mercies of state, county, and city government. As nonvoters with special and more expensive needs, refugees do not receive services on an equity basis. In view of their special needs, the extra time and effort required in assessment and care, and the greater level of skill required, *equal* means *more* rather than simply *the same*. The lack of a national policy points up a serious deficit in the American system of government in which the federal government may choose to pass along its responsibility to the states but the states may choose not to pick up this responsibility. Consequently, an inhumane gap in services exists. Ultimately our country pays for this through refugee criminality, court costs, incarceration costs, high social welfare costs, adolescent pregnancy, unemployment, and family breakdown in refugee communities. Currently, the United States accepts more refugees for resettlement than the rest of the world combined. Americans must begin to ask, as a policy issue, whether quantity is more important than quality in making our commitment to refugees. Resources would then follow or not follow, depending on the policy. The rest of the world is watching our policies and programs. We have a responsibility to set a reasonable, ethically defensible standard.

REFERENCES

Ahearn, F. L., and Athey, J. L., eds. 1991. *Refugee children: Theory, research, and services.* Baltimore: Johns Hopkins University Press.

Anthony, E. J., and Cohler, B. J. 1987. *The invulnerable child.* New York: Guilford.

Ballenger, J. C., Reus, V. I., and Post, R. M. 1982. The "atypical" clinical picture of adolescent mania. *American Journal of Psychiatry* 139:602–606.

Carlin, J. E. 1979. Southeast Asian refugee children. In J. D. Call, J. D. Noshpitz, R. L. Cohen, and I. N. Berlin, eds., *Basic handbook of child psychiatry,* 290–300. New York: Basic Books.

Dunnigan, T. 1982. Segmentary kinship in an urban society: The Hmong of St. Paul–Minneapolis. *Anthropological Quarterly* 55:126–134.

Faulkner, J., and Kich, G. K. 1983. Assessment and engagement stages in therapy with the interracial family. In J. C. Hansen and C. J. Falicov, eds., *Cultural perspectives in family therapy,* 78–90. Rockville, Md.: Aspen Press.

Freyberg, J. 1980. Difficulties in separation-individuation as experienced by offspring of Nazi Holocaust survivors. *American Journal of Orthopsychiatry* 50:87–95.

Goudvis, P. 1993. If the mango tree could speak. Film. New Day Film Library, 22D Hollywood Ave., Hohokus, N.J. 07423.

Harding, R. K., and Looney, J. G. 1977. Problems of Southeast Asian children in a refugee camp. *American Journal of Psychiatry* 134:407–411.

Hoang, G. N., and Erickson, R. V. 1985. Cultural barriers to effective medical care among Indochinese patients. *Annual Review of Medicine* 36: 229–239.

Hodson, E. M., and Springthorpe, B. J. 1976. Medical problems in refugee children evacuated from South Vietnam. *Medical Journal of Australia* 2:747–749.

Ionescu-Tongyonk, J. 1977. Depressions and general medicine: The depressions of childhood and adolescence. *Thai Medical Journal* 1:268–277.

Jalali, B., and Boyce, E. 1980. Multicultural families in treatment. *International Journal of Family Psychiatry* 1:475–484.

Kelly, G. P. 1977. *From Vietnam to America.* Boulder, Colo.: Westview.

Kim, L. S., and Chun, C. A. 1993. Ethnic differences in psychiatric diagnosis among Asian American adolescents. *Journal of Nervous Mental Disease* 181:612–617.

Kim, S. C. 1985. Family therapy for Asia Americans: A strategic-structural framework. *Psychotherapy* 22:342–348.

Kremer, P. G., and Sabin, C. 1985. Indochinese refugee children: Problems in psychiatric diagnosis. *Journal of the American Academy of Child Psychiatry* 24:453–458.

Krogh, Y., and Montgomery, E. 1993. Conceptualizing anxiety in torture survivors: An investigation of children of torture survivors. *Torture* (supp. 1):22–24.

Krupinski, J., and Burrows, G., eds. 1986. *The price of freedom: Young Indochinese refugees in Australia.* Sydney: Pergamon.

Lampkin, L. C. 1971. Alienation as a coping mechanism. In E. Parrenstedt and W. Bernard, eds., *Crisis of family disorganization.* New York: Behavioral Publications.

Lappin, J., and Scott, S. 1982. Intervention in a Vietnamese refugee family. In J. McGoldrick, K. Pearce, and J. Giordano, eds., *Ethnicity and family therapy,* 483–490. New York: Guilford.

Lawlor, J. 1988. Amerasians start a new life in USA. *USA Today,* January 30, p. 1.

Lee, E. 1988. Cultural factors in working with Southeast Asian refugee adolescents. *Journal of Adolescence* 11:167–179.

Lin, K. M., Poland, R. E., and Nakasaki, G., eds. 1993. *Psychopharmacology and psychobiology of ethnicity.* Washington, D.C.: American Psychiatric Press.

Marmot, M. G., and Syme, S. L. 1976. Acculturation and coronary heart disease in Japanese-Americans. *American Journal of Epidemiology* 104:225–247.

Naditch, M. P., and Morrissey, R. F. 1976. Role stress, personality, and psychopathology in a group of immigrant adolescents. *Journal of Abnormal Psychology* 85:113–118.

Olness, K. 1977. The ecology of malnutrition in children. *Journal of the American Medical Women's Association* 32:79–81.

Philips, I. 1979. Childhood depression: Interpersonal interactions and depressive phenomena. *American Journal of Psychiatry* 136:511–513.

Rakoff, V. 1964. Children and families of concentration camp survivors. *Canada's Mental Health* 14:14–16.

Rathbun, C., DiVirgilio, L., and Waldfogel, S. 1958. The restitutive process in children following radical separation from family and culture. *American Journal of Orthopsychiatry* 28:408–415.

Sokoloff, B., Carlin, J., and Pham, H. 1984. Five-year follow-up of Vietnamese refugee children in the United States. *Clinical Pediatrics* 23:565–570.

Szapocznik, J., Kurtines, W. M., and Fernandez, T. 1980. Bicultural involvement and adjustment in Hispanic-American youths. *International J. Intercultural Relations* 4:355–365.

Trossman, B. 1968. Adolescent children of concentration camp survivors. *Canadian Psychiatric Association Journal* 13:121–123.

Welner, Z. 1978. Childhood depression: An overview. *Journal of Nervous Mental Disease* 166:588–593.

Westermeyer, J. 1979. The "apple" syndrome: The effects of racial-ethnic discontinuity. *Journal of Operational Psychiatry* 10:134–140.

——. 1988a. DSM III psychiatric disorders among Hmong refugees in the United States: A point prevalence study. *American Journal of Psychiatry* 145:197–202.

——. 1988b. A matched pairs study of depression among Hmong refugees with particular reference to predisposing factors and treatment outcome. *Social Psychiatry Psychiatric Epidemiology* 23:64–71.

——. 1989. Paranoid symptoms and disorders among 100 Hmong refugees: A longitudinal study. *Acta Psychiatrica Scandinavica* 80(1):47–49.

Westermeyer, J., Bouafuely, M., and Neider, J. 1989. Somatization among refugees: An epidemiological study. *Psychosomatics* 30:34–43.

Westermeyer, J., Lyfoung, T., Wahmanholm, K., and Westermeyer, M. 1989. Delusions of fatal contagion among refugee patients: Some usual and unusual aspects. *Psychosomatics* 30:374–381.

Williams, C., and Westermeyer, J. 1984. Psychiatric problems among adolescent Southeast Asian refugees: A descriptive study. *Journal of Nervous and Mental Disorders* 171:79–85.

Williamson, J. 1988. Half the world's refugees. *Refugees* 54:16–18.

CHAPTER SIX

Child Development and Adaptation to Catastrophic Circumstances

STEVEN MARANS, MIRIAM BERKMAN,
AND DONALD COHEN

In this chapter the authors focus on the effect of communal violence in the United States on the development of children. The authors, all of whom are associated with the Yale Child Study Center, approach the milieu of violence as an increasingly severe public health problem, but they also show how the individual child is affected by it.

Steven Marans, Miriam Berkman, and Donald Cohen and his colleagues have gathered statistics that document the scope of the problems faced by so many of the children growing up in urban North America today. These appalling statistics represent a perverse competition: the United States is far "ahead" of other countries in the prevalence of crime and violence and in the number of homicides and premature deaths among young people. Some of these data and others are also reviewed in chapter 7, in which Michael Greene emphasizes their impact on young adults and adolescents. Younger children who live among violence know too soon and too well that they are at risk. They know it from the fear and protectiveness their parents display; they know it from incidents that mar their daily lives.

In this chapter the authors view external violence from the perspective of the child, who under normal circumstances struggles with his own aggressive impulses and their expression or repression. They show how the worker's attunement to the child at a time of external crisis can allow the child to learn, to feel better and more secure, and to advance developmentally—not to crystallize fear, hate, and revenge fantasies that would inevitably lead to the repetition of the destructive cycle.

Furthermore, they show how such psychoanalytic work with individual children can be done in the context of an ongoing community program. This chapter builds on chapter 3 by showing examples of individual therapy with children.

The Child Development–Community Policing Program in New Haven, Connecticut, is an outstanding project that other communities, especially those with an existing infrastructure (that is, a police department and child development experts), would do well to emulate. The program spreads knowledge about and responsibility for children among more adults, providing a larger safety net and more possibilities for primary as well as secondary prevention of trauma. For the police, the cooperative program offers greater humanization of their job, more regard from the public at large, and greater personal dignity and self-respect. For mental health professionals, the program is an opportunity to apply skills beyond the consulting room, to have a wider and deeper impact on children—and the future.

Children who live in nations torn by war for many years feel that their neighborhoods are dangerous and their world unsafe. They cannot walk the streets with a sense of mastery, ownership, and security. Instead, the sight of wounded and dead bodies on the sidewalk and the sounds of nightly gunfire are daily reminders of the hazards they must negotiate; friends in caskets are evidence of what could happen to them. These children also sense that their communities are surrounded by a safe, prosperous society from which they are excluded. They often lack the supports of family or of the community and its institutions to help them deal with their anxiety and despair. It is a horrifying fact that much the same can be said of children in the American inner city.

The statistics regarding the incidence of assaultive violence are disturbing testaments to the scope of the danger confronting so many American children today.

- From 1984 to 1993 there was a 51 percent increase in violent crimes (murder, forcible rape, robbery, and aggravated assault) in the United States (U.S. Department of Justice, 1994).
- In 1993 there were 24,526 murders, 104,806 rapes, 659,757 robberies, and 1,135,009 aggravated assaults nationwide.
- Between 1983 and 1992 there was a 46.1 percent increase in arrests for possession of weapons.
- In 1991, 2.2 million people suffered nonfatal injuries from assaultive violence.
- Homicide is the second leading cause of death among fifteen- to twenty-four-year-olds.
- African American male teens are eleven times more likely to be killed by guns than are their white counterparts.

- From 1989 to 1990 Boston had a 45 percent increase in urban violence; Denver had a 29 percent increase; Chicago, New Orleans, and Dallas had increases of 20 percent (Surgeon General's Workshop on Violence and Public Health, 1991).

Studies of rates of children's exposure to scenes of violence produce equally alarming statistics.

- At Boston City Hospital it was reported that one out of every ten children seen in the primary care clinic had witnessed a shooting or stabbing before the age of six—half in the home, half on the streets. The average age of these children was 2.7 years (Taylor et al., 1992).
- In New Haven, 41 percent of a sample of sixth-, eighth-, and tenth-grade students reported having seen someone shot or stabbed in the preceding year (New Haven Public Schools, 1992).

Such exposure to violence was associated with feelings of depression and anxiety, higher levels of antisocial and aggressive activities, greater alcohol use, lower school attainment, and increased risk taking.

Violence in America is only one of the many significant environmental factors that affect the lives of many American children. For example, each year more than 1 million children feel the effects of divorce and separation (U.S. Congress, 1989); over 1 million babies are born to unwed mothers (National Center for Health Statistics, 1988); and more than 13 million children live in poverty—over 2 million more than a decade ago. While most poor children are white, minority children are much more likely to live in a poor family: 44 percent of African American and 36 percent of Hispanic children are poor, compared with fewer than 15 percent of the white children (U.S. Department of Commerce, 1990). One indicator of the outcome of so many stressors is the fact that one in five American children between the ages of three and seventeen are reported by parents to have had a developmental delay, learning disability, or behavioral problems (Zill and Schoenborn, 1988). About 30 percent of ninth-graders do not graduate from high school, and about 500,000 youngsters drop out each year (Kaufman and Frase, 1990). In the nation's urban centers as many as half of all students drop out. Dropouts are 3.5 times as likely as high school graduates to be arrested and 6 times as likely to become unmarried parents (Schorr, 1988).

In addition, children and adolescents increasingly are becoming active participants in the violence that has contributed to the climate of social adversity and despair in which they have been raised. Nationwide juvenile arrests in 1992 included:

- 3,092 children and adolescents arrested for criminal homicide;
- 4,750 arrested for rape;
- 40,499 arrested for robbery;

- 62,039 arrested for aggravated assault;
- 138,713 arrested for simple assault; and
- 47,369 arrested for weapons offenses.

Overall, between 1989 and 1993 juvenile arrests for violent crime rose about 36 percent and juvenile arrests for weapons offenses rose 66.6 percent. The vast majority of the children and adolescents accused of violent crimes are male, and a disproportionate percentage come from minority groups and poor families (U.S. Department of Justice, 1994). Though these numbers are disturbing in themselves, statistics alone do not describe the nature of the disruptions that occur in the inner lives of children who are repetitively exposed to violence in their homes and communities.

Children's Exposure to Violence in a Developmental Context

Children's exposure to interpersonal violence disrupts basic preconditions for their optimal development. Children who witness violence do so in the context of developmentally shifting modes of expressing their own aggressive impulses and feelings. Aggressivity plays a central role in development as a means of achieving a sense of power and competence; it is also a source of conflict between love and hate. Over the course of development, the more direct enactments of the toddler's hitting, biting, and kicking shift to the preschooler's fantasies and play of destructive power, to the competition on the school-age child's sports field, to the vicissitudes of affection and anger that are a part of adolescent and adult relationships (Marans and Cohen, 1993; A. Freud, 1972). However, this capacity to move from enactment to more sublimated expressions of aggressivity is undermined when the basic preconditions for feeling competent—including physical safety, stable relationships, and success in achieving desired goals—are overwhelmed by poverty, family dysfunction, overstimulation, and threatened or actual physical danger.

In the lives of all children there are expectable experiences of aggression, violence, and bodily harm at the hands of parents, siblings, and peers, or in the context of accidental injuries. With optimal development, the child is able to distinguish between fantasy and reality, between wishes and enactment, and between projections and real dangers. Again, optimally, parents and other significant adults support children in their attempts to establish these boundaries. They help children feel that the world is basically secure and safe, that there are no demons in the shadows, that their wounds will heal, that there are limits to the expression of aggressive urges, that their *wishes* to harm others cannot cause accidents that may occur, and that they can express their scary thoughts without worrying that they will be hurt in retaliation.

The potential trauma that follows the child's direct exposure to violence does not simply represent a shock that happens from outside; its impact depends on the diverse personal meanings that a given external event may carry for children in terms of their own internal concerns, past experiences, and phase-specific development.

Acute and Long-Term Effects

When children witness or directly experience real communal violence, the line between fantasy and reality is blurred: their most powerful and potentially frightening fantasies about bodily injury, loss of relationships, and loss of impulse control are enacted before their eyes. In the face of stabbings, beatings, and shootings, children may be traumatized because they cannot contain the stimulation within existing mental structures that allow for accommodation and assimilation. When the capacity to anticipate and contain exceptional events of danger is lost, the child feels that dreaded aspects of internal fantasies are vivified and are overwhelmingly real. These traumatizing experiences cannot be adequately dealt with immediately by the usual behavioral responses (fight or flight), and at the same time, the mind is unable to prepare and to rely on familiar defenses (denial, repression, avoidance, intellectualization, and so on).

When these behavioral and mental systems are immobilized—when the child is rendered passive in the face of events that are threatening to his body and mind—a cascade of psychological and physiological processes ensue. The violent events are remembered differently from other events, and the experience is handled in a special fashion. In response to the potentially traumatic circumstances of exposure to violence, children may develop specific, circumscribed symptoms involving disruptions in patterns of sleeping, eating, toileting, attention, and relating, and may also experience generalized fearfulness, disregulation of the startle reflex, and flashbacks of aspects of the violent event (American Psychiatric Association, 1994). The child's avoidant behaviors and general hypervigilance may reflect attempts to guard against the anxiety aroused by persistent, preoccupying memories of various features of the violent event, or they may appear more episodically in response to specific traumatic reminders that derive from a range of circumstances and subjective phenomena associated with the original trauma (Pynoos, 1993). In addition, a child may resort to turning a passive experience into an active response in an attempt to regain a sense of power and control when the dangers of real violence provoke feelings of helplessness and fear. That is, rather than feeling the anxiety and humiliation of being the victim or feeling vulnerable to the aggression of others, the child may become the perpetrator. Like the other post-traumatic stress–related symptoms, oppositional behavior at home and at school may be a transient means for the child to reassert his power precisely when he is feeling most vulnerable. However, when the child is regularly exposed to the dangers of violence, symptoms may no longer serve the function of restitution and recovery but may reflect a chronic adaptation in which vegetative, cognitive, and affective capacities and optimal regulation of functions are severely compromised. In a similar way, the perpetration of violence may represent another long-term adaptation to the experience of being the passive, frightened victim and to chronic exposure to violence. Alterations in character development deriving in part from identification with the exciting and powerful role of perpetrator may become a reliable hedge against the feelings of fear and helplessness that were aroused by the actual experiences of overwhelming danger. When the most powerful models in the home and neighborhood exercise *their* potency at the end of a fist or gun, aggressive enactments rather than sublimations may be an adaptive response to both internal and external sources of danger (Marans, 1994).

Impact on Families and Communities

Adults are not immune to a range of similar responses when they are confronted by communal violence. Their inability to listen and attend to children's needs in the aftermath of traumatic events may be a natural consequence of their own attempts at restitution and self-protection from feelings of vulnerability and traumatic disorganization. The potentially detrimental effects on individual and family functioning may also be mirrored in the larger community. Extended family, friends, and neighbors may be inhibited from listening to traumatic narratives and providing distressed individuals with appropriate support for reasons similar to those that inhibit parents from listening to children. In urban neighborhoods, where drug- or gang-related violence is particularly prevalent, many residents may have such a strong psychological investment in avoiding open discussion of their chronic fear and helplessness that there are few people in the community who are emotionally available to share the burdens of other community members at times of acute exposure to new episodes of violence.

Freud described the traumatic situation as one in which the individual has experienced helplessness in the face of a danger whose magnitude outweighs the "subject's estimation of his own strength" (1926, 166). In many poor urban and rural settings, the instability of families and the extended community places a special burden on existing social institutions that are called on to respond to both victims and perpetrators of violence. However, when service providers—mental health professionals, medical providers, school personnel, protective service workers, and law enforcement officers—operate in isolation in their attempts to address the multiple needs of children and families caught in the cycle of violence, they too may find themselves overwhelmed and immobilized. Alternatively, these seemingly disparate professional groups may attempt to regroup, capitalizing on knowledge gained independently, and consolidate their efforts in developing new strategies for intervening in the cycle of interpersonal violence. If mental health professionals are to play a broader role in these efforts, then clinical expertise and research must be increasingly applied to a range of services that extend beyond the consulting room. While a violent event may precipitate a host of responses that compromise children's developmental potential, it may also provide a window of opportunity for introducing psychotherapeutic interventions and the application of what we have learned in the consulting room to the coordination of diverse services that have an impact on the daily lives of children and their families. New Haven's Child Development–Community Policing Program represents one such model of interdisciplinary collaboration (Marans et al., 1995).

From the Consulting Room to the Streets: A Collaborative Response

The Child Development–Community Policing (CD–CP) Program was formed out of the joint recognition of leaders within the Yale Child Study Center and the New Haven Department of Police Service that police officers and mental health clinicians share serious concerns about the fate of children and families exposed to chronic urban violence, but that, for different reasons, neither group is able to intervene effectively. Though police officers are in daily contact with children who are victims, witnesses, and perpetrators of violence, they do not have the professional expertise, the time, or the other resources necessary to meet these children's psychological needs. Conversely, clinic-based mental health professionals may be professionally equipped to respond to children's psychological distress following episodes of violence, but the acutely traumatized children who are most in need of clinical service rarely are seen in existing outpatient clinics until months or years later, when chronic symptoms or maladaptive behavior bring them to the attention of parents, teachers, or the juvenile courts. Valuable opportunities to intervene therefore are lost at the moment when professional contact could provide both immediate stabilization and bridges to a variety of services.

The collaboration between mental health and police professionals was born out of a common-sense recognition that police officers—who not only make house-calls twenty-four hours a day but are also first on the scene of violent events—are in a unique position to help children and families who are at greatest risk of becoming the psychological casualties of violence. Similarly, when mental health professionals venture beyond the consulting room they are much better able to learn more about the impact of violence on the lives of those who are most directly involved: children, families, and the professionals themselves. Working together, police and mental health professionals have combined their observations and knowledge from the consulting room and the streets in an effort to coordinate an array of responses for children and families whose exposure to violence threatens to compromise their development and functioning.

In beginning discussions between officers and clinicians, the issue of volume and the limitations of our isolated attempts to intervene on behalf of children exposed to violence became a jumping-off point for consideration of ways that they might work together. It became clear that each group felt defeated in their individual efforts to take charge and to intervene in ways that lead to an increased mastery for themselves and for those they hope to serve. Police officers, who are regularly exposed to disturbing scenes of violence, are especially susceptible to feelings of despair in identification with the children they encounter, or to fear about the dangers that may await *them* at the next call. In this context, it is understandable that officers defend themselves against such feelings by remaining anonymous, distant, and perfunctory, turning a blind eye to the suffering of children or feeling enraged and disdainful toward the adults who have exposed them to terror. Similarly, the clinicians described cases in which children's symptomatic difficulties at school, at home, and with peers brought them to the outpatient clinic at a point when psychotherapeutic intervention alone was no match for the long history of multiple traumatic experiences that had contributed to their compromised functioning. Clinicians were also confronted by the discrepancy between their recognition of the risk factors associated with children's exposure to violence and the numbers of children who would ever actually reach the consulting rooms. It was thought that a shared frame of reference developed out of existing knowledge from the streets and the consulting room could lead to increased understanding of the needs of children traumatized by their exposure to communal violence and the possibility that collaborative action might replace professional immobilization.

To consider their potential roles in responding to the needs of children exposed to violence, police officers would need to learn more about basic principles of development and concepts of human functioning. Similarly, clinicians would need to learn more about phenomena associated with acute incidents of violence and police practices. Both groups would need to learn about the range and limitations of the other's responsibilities.

Thus, a small group of supervisory officers was exposed to a variety of clinical services and liaison activities with social services. Clinicians spent time in "ride-along" tutorials in squad cars with the supervisory officers. Both groups participated in weekly discussions about principles of development and their application to clinical and policing practices. The practical issue of increasing collaborative responses to violence was addressed through the development of a twenty-four-hour on-call service that would allow officers to receive consultation and would provide immediate clinical response to violent crime scenes in which children were involved. In addition, the fellowships for clinicians and supervisory officers were formalized and a weekly meeting was begun to discuss cases referred through the consultation service. However, it was clear that if rank-and-file officers were to participate in this new endeavor, they too would need to establish a conceptual rationale for their collaborative work with mental health professionals, not simply follow orders from supervisors about making appropriate referrals.

Developing a Common Language

In our efforts to increase the attention paid to the children exposed to communal violence it has been essential to establish a regular forum in which officers and clinicians can work out a common ground of concerns and a conceptual rationale for their collaborative work. In weekly seminars, officers and clinicians examine concepts regarding basic human needs; development of capacities for self-regulation and mastery; phase-specific sources of danger/anxiety; the link between behavior and underlying psychic processes (that is, the relation between anxiety and defenses); and individual variation with regard to potential life adaptations. It is crucial that the goal of these seminars is to demonstrate how officers' consideration of principles of development and human functioning can enhance the range of strategies in dealing with various situations and can help establish a more realistic appreciation for the impact they can have on the lives of children and families with whom they interact.

A series of ten seminars, co-led by clinicians and supervisory officers who have completed the fellowship, uses scenarios from the streets—ranging from experiences with parents and infants to involvement with adolescent gangs—to illustrate basic developmental concepts. While the discussions proceed according to a developmental sequence, they attempt to link the inner life of the child with manifest behaviors seen at the original phase of development and the ways that these phenomena may be observed throughout the life cycle. In turn, the seminars allow officers and clinicians to think about the meaning of behavior as an effective tool for determining strategies and as part of an effort to develop collaborative interventions between police and mental health professionals on behalf of children and families exposed to violence.

The convergence of principles of development and their application to policing strategies may be best illustrated in a description of a discussion that emerged in one of the seminar series about toddlerhood. Participants were asked to talk about their understanding of the salient features of the phase, and they responded with ideas about the "terrible twos," tantrums, toilet-training, and bossiness. These topics were elaborated in the discussion until participants began to make connections between how physical maturation, mastery, and the child's sense of omnipotence converge and at times clash with parental expectations and the notion of consequences. Issues regarding separation/individuation also entered into the discussion, as the behavioral assertion of strength, power, and well-being could be more broadly understood in terms of the child's developing sense of self-worth and capacity for regulating/expressing urges and feelings. Again, the emphasis of the discussion moved toward the common theme of articulating the relation between observable phenomena and underlying motivation. The central importance of feelings of power, control, and mastery, and the defenses employed when narcissism is injured, was discussed as it applies to toddlers, older children, and adults. Concepts regarding displacement, turning passive into active, and reaction formations were illustrated in material brought from the streets by the officers in the class (Marans et al., 1995).

One of the more powerful illustrations of the relation between anxiety and defense arose after a confrontation that occurred between police officers, a group of young drug dealers, and community members. Several of the officers, including the co-leader who had been involved, described the events. The day after the shooting death of a local drug dealer, a large group of teenagers gathered on a street corner. When two beat officers arrived, the group began jeering and moving toward them. The officers felt threatened and called for backup. Within minutes squad cars were speeding into the area; the arriving officers formed a line, holding billy clubs at the ready, as the crowd grew more vocal and insulting. Other members of the community joined the crowd and tensions continued to rise until supervisory officers intervened. They first ordered the line of officers to put their billy clubs away and return to their cars. Officers assigned to the neighborhood were asked to wade into the crowd and talk with the most vocal participants they knew—drug dealers and community leaders alike. This group was invited to attend a hastily convened meeting in a nearby church. As the group moved away, the crowd slowly dispersed. Over the next several days, community leaders accompanied officers on patrol as a way of supporting the peace.

Following the description of the events, the officers in the seminar were divided into two groups—cops and crowd members. After meeting separately for several minutes, the groups re-created the standoff. They easily assumed their roles. The "crowd" threw insults at the cops as they moved closer to the cops on the "line." While first remaining very calm, several of the cops broke verbal ranks and began responding to the taunts. While at first they appealed to the crowd to calm down, the replies grew increasingly combative and incendiary. One African American officer replayed with another African American cop on the line an interchange that had occurred when he had been at the original scene. He berated his fellow officer for being a "white man's nigger" and not knowing anything about what it is like to be a "real black man." True to the original scenario, the cop on the line argued that he had grown up in a similar neighborhood and that, unlike his tormentor, he had chosen to work hard and make a better life for himself, and so on. When the crowd member replied that the line cop was a "sellout," the mock pushing began, and the exercise was stopped.

In the discussion that followed officers spoke of intimidation, fear, humiliation, and the experience of being prejudged and insulted by people who do not even know them. In response to questions from the seminar leaders, "crowd members" spoke of their feelings of powerlessness in the face of unemployment and life in a blighted neighborhood—the sense of hopelessness and despair that finds some relief in the excitement and rage that gets targeted on a highly visible enemy. As the discussion continued, displacement and transference were addressed. The argument that developed around the issue of backing down in the face of a hostile crowd versus standing ground and demonstrating power and control were examined in relation to individual and group responses to various sources of anxiety, the degree of perceived danger, and the available capacities to defend against and diminish feelings of helplessness, fear, and humiliation. These themes and others are elaborated as the seminar moves through central concepts regarding the challenges and potential deviations of oedipal, latency, pubertal, and adolescent development.

As the seminars come to an end, officers increasingly refer to the scenes of violence and suffering they confront each day. Themes that commonly emerge in the discussions include sealing over—"getting used to it" and distancing them-selves as best they can—displacing their frustration onto family members or citizens with whom they interact, viewing the world dichotomously (that is, us versus them), and heightening the sense of vigilance. These responses are dis-cussed in terms of the defensive functions they serve—against feelings of fear, inadequacy, sadness, despair, and the like—as well as the interference they may pose in achieving the desired goals of their interventions.

Whereas the seminars on child development and human functioning are intended to develop a frame of reference for officers considering the relation between the child's inner life and manifest behavior, the consultation service provides direct support for officers in the field who are dealing with children and families exposed to violence and tragedy. The availability of immediate consulta-tion has often allowed officers in the field to feel more effective in the face of tragedy. By brokering clinical services and attending to the emotional needs of the children involved, officers have a new way of "taking control" and becoming active in the aftermath of violence rather than simply feeling overwhelmed by it, sealing over, and quickly turning away from the scene. For many of the children and families, the referrals may not only offer accessible and responsive clinical services for the first time but may also reflect a new and different experience of officers and mental health professionals. In many of these situations both police and clinicians are not simply viewed as aloof and disengaged, providing too little, too late, but as *benign* figures of authority who are able to play a role in reestablish-ing a semblance of stability in the midst of the emotional chaos that often follows children's and families' direct exposure to violence.

Integrating Perspectives and Interventions

In the first thirty-six months of operation, officers and clinicians together have seen more than 450 children through referrals to the consultation service made by community-based officers. The children, who range in age from two to seventeen, have been exposed to murders, stabbings, beatings, maiming by fire, death by drowning, and gunfire. They have been seen individually and as part of larger groups in their homes, in police substations, in emergency rooms, in schools, in community rooms of public housing projects, and at the Child Study Center. Because of the immediacy of the referrals, we have been able to observe children within minutes of a violent event. As each of these cases has been followed in the weekly Case Conference, we have been able to explore the effects of exposure to violence in terms of the specific characteristics of the event and its context within the family, the community, and the inner life of the child.

We have found, as have other investigators (Pynoos et al., 1987; Pynoos and Nader 1989; Terr, 1991; Martinez and Richters, 1993; Pynoos, Steinberg, and Wraith, 1994), that beyond the obvious factors of direct physical injury to chil-dren and their parents, the psychological toll that violence takes on children is determined by an interplay of factors within the child and between the child and his or her surroundings:

- the characteristics of the violence itself—that is, the child's relationship to the perpetrator and victim, proximity to the incident, response of the caregivers to the incident;
- the developmental phase of the child who is exposed—that is, the status of emotional and cognitive resources available for mediating anxiety associated with objective and fantasized dangers—including preexisting vulnerabilities;
- the familial and community context of the violent incident—that is, whether the incident is isolated and unusual or is part of a pattern of daily life; and
- the nature of responses to the possible effects of the child's exposure to violence by family members, school personnel, and community institutions.

In addition, while the configuration of these factors has varied, we have observed common immediate responses to violent events among the children seen through the consultation service. These include disbelief and denial of the outcome or even the occurrence of the violent event; intense longing for the presence of primary caregivers and concern about their safety (especially among children under age seven); concerns about bodily integrity and competence; revival of, and much talk about, previous losses, injuries, fights, and other episodes of violence; repetitive retelling of the events with ideas that might have altered the real outcome of the episode, described by Pynoos as "intervention fantasies" (1993); attribution of blame to those not directly involved in the violence; or, alternatively, reveling in the excitement of the action of the violence with talk of the weapons used—who got "capped," "smoked," or "aired" (Marans, 1994).

Discussions about referrals from the consultation service frequently focus on the extent to which children describe the violent events they have witnessed in terms of the developmental phase–specific anxieties that are aroused. By observing the acute reactions and by listening to the stories from the child exposed to violence, we are able to better see what constitutes the specific danger that overwhelms that child, or what aspects and meanings of the event are experienced as exceptional and overwhelming—and therefore "traumatizing." For clinicians, direct observation of and interaction with children in the community who have just been exposed to incidents of traumatic violence, as well as regular collaborative contact with community-based police officers, has enhanced our understanding of the realities of these children's traumatic experiences, the environmental background against which acute episodes of violence take place, and the potentially therapeutic use that many children can make from their contact with police officers and other adults in the community. Increased understanding of acute traumatic reactions and environmental variables has, in turn, led to greater flexibility in the delivery of clinical services to families that might not otherwise make use of these resources. For officers, exposure to developmental principles and clinical consultation has expanded the range and specificity of their observations of children with whom they come in contact and has led to an expanded range of possible policing interventions, including referrals for individual clinical services, direct supportive interactions between officers and individual children and parents, and police involvement in community efforts to address neighborhood problems regarding the physical and psychological safety of children and families.

As a result of the ongoing collaboration and the establishment of trusting relationships among police and mental health professionals, both clinical and policing responses are increasingly informed by shared assessments of an individual child's perspectives, needs, and resources, as well as those of the family and community in which the violent events have occurred. In direct response to our increasing understanding of the multiple and interrelated stresses confronting the children and families referred to the consultation service, collaborative responses to acute incidents of violence have increasingly involved the coordination of multiple resources that have impact on the lives of children and families—schools, protective services, medical care, housing, and the like. The following incidents illustrate these observations.

A Street Shooting

Acute responses. At noon on a late spring day, shots rang out. A school bus carrying eight children aged five and six was caught in the cross fire between rival drug dealers. The bus was hit by the gunfire, and a six-year-old boy was shot in the head. The bus went to a nearby middle school, where the children were met by police officers and emergency medical personnel. Officers trained in the CD-CP program were the first to greet the children; they contacted members of the consultation service, whom they asked to join them at the middle school. The boy who was shot was taken to the hospital. (He survived surgery and suffered neurological impairment for which he continues to receive rehabilitative services.) The remaining children were taken inside the middle school building by police officers, who immediately began coordinating efforts to get the parents to the middle school. The officers described their central aim as protecting the children from the excitement surrounding the shooting (camera crews arriving, multiple police personnel, onlookers) and reuniting them with parents. Children were *not* interviewed by officers about the shooting. Officers explained that while this practice used to be part of the standard approach in an investigation, the reality was that any information obtained from the children was not immediately necessary and, according to the sergeant in charge of the scene, would only retraumatize the children, especially when what they needed the most was to be with their parents.

The CD-CP clinicians arrived on the scene within ten minutes of the shooting. They were briefed by their police colleagues and were taken to the gym, where the children were sitting on the floor. Middle school personnel attempted to engage the children in a discussion about what they had seen, but the children remained quiet, clutching their knees and staring into the middle distance. The CD-CP clinicians were introduced to the school personnel, who moved to the background as the clinicians began to work with the children. The clinicians had brought paper and markers. They sat down with two children each and asked them whether they would like to draw pictures. Each child quietly declined, but when asked whether they would like the clinician to draw something, the response was unanimously positive as was the requested content of the pictures: "Draw my mommy." Each child was asked what sort of face the mommy should have and what words might fill the speech bubble that went along with the drawing of the face. The instructions for faces fell into two categories: happy and sad. The words alternated between "I'm so happy to see you!" and "I was so sad and worried about you!" After engaging in the drawings, the children grew more verbal, and each began to make inquiries about where their mothers were and when they would arrive. All of the children expressed concern that perhaps their mothers had been hurt and would not be coming for them. The senior police officer on the scene, a CD-CP fellow, told the children and clinicians that all of the parents had been located and were on their way to the school.

One of the children then asked a clinician to draw a picture of a head. Whose head? "Um, a boy's head . . . that just got shot with a bullet." The rest of the children overheard this question and immediately turned their attention to the picture. The clinician requested details in order to complete the picture and asked whether any of the children wished to add something themselves. Three children scribbled the same ingredient with a red marker—blood, which soon covered much of the page. There were some questions about what was happening to the friend who had been shot, but most of the questions and comments had to do with bodily functions—How much blood does the body have? Can parts of the body fall off?—and talk quickly turned to a more spirited group discussion about the physical feats each could perform. The discussion was punctuated by sidelong glances to the door as parents began to arrive to pick up their children. Each parent was seen briefly by the clinician, given a telephone number to call with questions regarding their child's experiences, and asked whether they could be contacted for follow-up assessments.

While the crime scene was secured and the criminal investigation was begun, similar attention was paid to the emotional needs of the children who were caught up in the experience of violence. All aspects of the response to the shooting—determining how to inform both the middle school and elementary school communities about the shooting; briefing parents and school personnel; consulting with teachers, school administrators, and parents about how to respond to children in the classroom and at home; and making additional clinical services available—were coordinated and carried out by the Child Development–Community Policing Program in conjunction with the school system. Officers trained in the program were able to communicate information about the shooting in formal briefing sessions with parents and school personnel and informally in their encounters with children who approached them in the streets. They delivered information about the circumstances and background of the shooting, and they communicated their understanding about the meanings of adult expressions of rage and feelings of helplessness in a manner that indicated their sophistication about the complexity of responses to violence. The CD-CP officers and clinicians were able to influence broader community responses to the shooting as well. They successfully argued that, while making some adults feel less helpless, using squad cars to escort school buses the day after the shooting would only exacerbate children's concerns about safety. In a similar vein, officers showed appreciation for children's anxiety and vulnerability by discussing their concerns about the children as they negotiated with the news people who gathered around the children's school. As a result, they helped to minimize the intrusiveness and associated excitement of cameras and the barrage of questions thrown at the children and families. Because of the CD-CP responses to the shooting, the police in this situation were seen not merely as harbingers of tragic news and violence but as sources of effective authority, concerned about the safety and emotional well-being of the children and families affected (Marans et al., 1995).

Clinical follow-up. Five of the seven children received follow-up psychoanalytic psychotherapy because of enduring post-traumatic stress symptoms—disruptions in sleeping and eating; increased separation anxiety; and hypervigilance, generalized anxiety, and avoidant behaviors—that were not part of the premorbid history. Two vignettes offer illustrations of how a child's developmental phase and life circumstances determine the context and specific meaning of a disturbing external event and illustrate the effectiveness of preventive intervention for longer-term emotional and social growth. Each case example is a condensation of material that emerged during two to four months of weekly and twice-weekly treatment.

Beverly, five and a half years old, was sitting across the aisle from her classmate when he was shot. Her previous school functioning was good, as was her adaptation in an intact family (mother, father, and ten-month-old brother). Her developmental history was unremarkable. After the shooting, Beverly had difficulties with sleeping and eating, multiple new fears, and a need to remain close to her mother. These symptoms continued for two weeks before her parents agreed with the clinician's recommendation for individual work with the child in conjunction with guidance for the parents.

In her individual sessions, Beverly repeatedly returned to the scene of the shooting, reviewing an increasing array of details both in play with toy figures and in her drawings. Each narrative ended with Beverly stating that she felt scared or bad. Over time, the therapist probed these feelings—either within the action of the play or within the narrative that accompanied the pictures. Beverly would elaborate that she felt scared that the bullet might have hit her and very bad because her friend had been hurt. In one session, she drew a picture of herself and her friend on the bus. She drew the bullet tracking around her head on an eventual path to the head of her classmate. She grew quiet and looked forlorn. With the suggestion that there was a connection between her feelings and the story that lay behind the picture, Beverly revealed a secret whose telling spanned many sessions and was accompanied by a dramatic reduction and final resolution of her presenting symptoms.

The first part of the secret was that for several days before the shooting Beverly had been reprimanded by the driver for her behavior on the bus. Beverly thought that perhaps the bullet had really been meant for her as punishment. Later she told the therapist that she had been teasing and poking at the very classmate who was shot. The third part of the secret was about her baby brother. With great anxiety Beverly reported that she teased the baby on numerous occasions and that, in fact, she often wished the brother were no longer around. With this confession, the cause of her worry and guilty feelings became more clear. She was able to articulate her fear that her bad wishes about her brother had come true in the shooting of her schoolmate and that her wishes would be discovered and severely punished. The therapist was able to point out that Beverly was behaving as if the reality of the scary events had somehow been under her magical control. Her hostile wishes toward a rival baby brother and their displacement onto a schoolmate were not unusual. However, for Beverly, the *realization* of these wishes—if only in the displacement—constituted the central source of her overwhelming anxiety and traumatization. In addition, her sense of magical control reflected both age-expectable phenomena augmented by reliance on magic for the purposes of restitution and recovery. That is, a belief in magical control would revise the original experience of traumatization or "absence of control" in the shooting, even if the belief in magic might also lead to a tremendous sense of responsibility for and guilt about the real and imagined events.

Another child, Miguel, age five, presented with multiple symptoms. Miguel was the youngest in a family of six. Both parents and a nineteen-year-old brother worked, one sister was in high school, and the other was in middle school. Prior to the shooting Miguel had no difficulties with sleeping or with leaving home for school or other activities. This changed dramatically after the shooting of his classmate. He insisted on sleeping with the light on throughout the night, departures from home were very upsetting for him, and in the remaining days of school he complained of sickness in order to avoid going. It took several weeks of treatment for Miguel to reveal in his play that he was terrified that the people responsible for the shooting of his classmate would come to shoot him and all of the members of his family. The fact that the shooters were in jail did nothing to alleviate Miguel's fears or symptoms. But his ability to express his central worry opened the door for further exploration, clarification of his thoughts, and greater mastery over a very frightening experience.

What lay behind Miguel's fear of being shot was his attempt to explain to himself why the shooting had happened and perhaps, with this explanation, to feel more able to predict similarly dangerous events. However, the explanation Miguel developed was limited by condensation and by the concrete thinking typical of his phase of development. Miguel was eventually able to explain to his therapist, and then to his parents, the following ideas: He had learned in school about how bad drugs are—that they do terrible things to the body, that they make people violent and are the cause of fights between drug dealers. When the shooting started and the bus was hit by gunfire, Miguel assumed that the shooting was about drugs and that if the school bus was being shot at, it must somehow be involved with drugs. If the school bus was involved in drugs and he was on the school bus, then he must somehow be connected with drugs, and if he was involved in drugs, then so must his family. If he and the family were involved in drugs, then they too would fall victim to gunfire. While there was no indication that the family was involved with drug use or dealings, the dangers were brought home to Miguel as a powerful response to being shot at and to seeing his friend bleeding. While generating considerable fear, Miguel's explanation relied on the cognitive resources available to him and provided the basis for altering the traumatic episode. In the version of *his* making, Miguel was able to anticipate the danger—he expected assailants to come after him—and he defended against the danger by staying up at night, staying close to home, keeping family nearby. Understanding Miguel's solution in the context of phase-specific concerns and capacities helped Miguel to clarify the distinction between his fantasy configurations and the factual information and led to a resolution of his developmental crisis and the attendant symptoms.

A Robbery at Gunpoint

Acute responses. Whereas phase-appropriate concerns associated with the body, sibling rivalry, and magical and concrete thinking played a crucial role in understanding and addressing the nature of trauma for Beverly and Miguel, another incident illustrated an adolescent version of overwhelming, disorganizing anxiety. Mark, age fifteen, was robbed at gunpoint on a Friday evening. He'd been walking with friends when two men put a reportedly large-caliber semiautomatic weapon in his face and demanded his money and gold jewelry. Mark had been walking behind several friends, and they were unaware of what occurred in an alley off of the main sidewalk. Mark later reported that men repeatedly shoved the weapon in his face and threatened to shoot him. After taking his valuables, the assailants fled, and Mark ran home. He ran into his room crying uncontrollably, hid on the floor of his closet and, in spite of his mother's urging, refused to come out. After a while, Mark told his mother through sobs what had occurred, and she phoned the police. Each of the three officers who arrived had been trained in the child development seminars, and the supervisory officer had completed the fellowship. As one of the officers approached the bedroom, Mark began to scream. The officer told him that he had heard what had happened to him and that he realized that the hold-up was terrifying. Mark would not look at the officer and yelled at him to leave the room. The officer was about to leave when the supervisor pointed to his gun and utility belt. The officer then removed his holster and weapon, explaining to Mark that he would leave them outside the room, as he understood how frightening guns might be to him. Mark continued to sob and shake uncontrollably, but he allowed the officer to help him out of the room, and he accepted the suggestion that he go to the emergency room for treatment. The consultation service clinician was called, and Mark was met at the hospital.

Clinical contact. During the interview, Mark was able to look at the clinician only after a comment was made about how fear could make a person feel small and helpless—a very undesirable feeling for a fifteen-year-old guy. Mark began to talk about the events, repeating the scene and the assailants' commands to him over and over. The repetition began to include slight alterations in the details, and Mark protested that he should have "grabbed the gun and kicked each of the [attackers] in the balls." He described the gun muzzle as huge and insisted that he thought the attackers meant to kill him. As his shaking, hyperventilating, and sobbing subsided, Mark began to talk about the earlier part of the evening. He explained that before being robbed he had been "hanging back from his home-boys because they were with their ladies" and he had wanted to "give them space." He shyly told the clinician that he didn't have a girlfriend, and then he exploded with rage and then broke into tears. He wanted to get a gun to kill the guys who "messed with him." He didn't deserve what had happened to him, he said—he was a good student and had just completed an important history paper. He explained that he had bought all of the thin gold chains he wore—emphasizing that he was not to be lumped with "low-life drug dealers." Mark began to cry again as he swore revenge. The clinician commented that it was humiliating to have to feel so terrified and suggested that Mark was wishing he could undo his experience. Mark replied that if he had had a gun or had disarmed his attackers he wouldn't have to feel as though he'd "wimped out." The clinician agreed that feeling powerful would certainly be the opposite of what he had experienced with a gun in his face. Mark brightened and looked up suddenly, exclaiming that now he remembered the gun more clearly—it wasn't a 9mm semiautomatic, it was a BB gun. As the acute terror diminished, he was also able to remember the make of the car in which the assailants drove off, as well as clear descriptions of the two men. His restitution fantasies of revenge began to take another form as Mark talked about helping the police make an arrest. At his request, Mark spoke with the detective involved in the case to offer the information he had recovered in the course of the interview. Two hours after admission to the emergency room, Mark was discharged.

Mark was seen in two follow-up sessions in which he continued to go over the events. The fantasies of what he should have done were intermingled with talk of the mortification of feeling helpless and of the increasing recognition that there actually was nothing he could have done to alter what had occurred. When his sleeping difficulties and hypervigilant feelings abated, Mark declined further clinical contact. However, over the following several weeks one of the three responding officers stopped in on him regularly for brief chats during the course of their usual patrol. In the last clinical follow-up, six months after the incident, Mark had still not bought a gun and, instead of reciting his numerous violent revenge fantasies, spoke of his latest academic demands and of his new friendships with the cops on his beat. While he had not forgotten the terror or rage associated with his experience, Mark added that his good memory had been instrumental in helping the police arrest the men who had attacked him. And, as he said, "that felt really good."

War, Communal Violence, and Therapeutic Implications

In our work with children exposed to communal violence in the American inner city, we hear frequent references in the popular press to "urban warfare" and to the notion that the experience of random, familial, and gang- or drug-related violence is analogous to the experience of violence associated with civil or international warfare. There are important similarities between the experiences of individuals exposed to warfare and to urban violence in terms of the range of acute and long-term physiological and psychological responses. Both in wartime and in violent city neighborhoods, children are vulnerable to the internal and external factors that place them at greater risk for developmental difficulties or, conversely, tend to protect them from the most adverse effects of their exposure to violence. Regardless of the arena of violence, children's healing and recovery are assisted by such internal attributes as cognitive competence, previously developed range of defensive mechanisms, self-esteem and secure attachments, as well as by external factors, including supportive parents and other adults, security of their physical environment, and continuity of interpersonal relationships and social institutions. Both in wartime and in the city, children can be helped to recover from their experiences of violence through prompt reestablishment of physical safety, family ties, and normal routines; through the provision of accurate information that promotes cognitive understanding; through the availability of opportunities to use imagination to take distance from upsetting memories and to try on different resolutions of the events to which they were exposed; and through the calm, sensitive attention of caring adults, particularly the child's parents.

Not only are there general similarities between children's exposure to warfare and to urban interpersonal violence, there are also important distinctions in the cultural context of children's experiences that can have a significant impact on their adaptation. In addition to the strengths that children and families may find within themselves for coping with exposure to communal violence, there are also protective factors built into cultures. These include a sense of purpose and a feeling of belonging to something greater than one's self. When they function well, ideology and the belief in a larger political or religious worldview justify terrible sacrifices and mediate suffering. In many wartime situations, at least where the fighting does not persist for generations, children are also protected by a sense of continuity with a community not torn by violence. In these circumstances, adults who remember a life of prewar stability can transmit to their children a sense that pervasive violence is not the only possible life experience, and that their own lives will return to normal.

Unfortunately for many poor children in urban America, it is precisely this sense of past stability, historical continuity, and hope for the future that is missing from the family and community environments in which their chronic exposure to communal violence takes place. In contrast with the experience of many children in wartime, children in the American inner city live in a world characterized not by consistent reminders of a more stable past but by multigenerational poverty, academic failure, political and economic disenfranchisement, and a pervasive absence of expectations that the future will be better than the present. In communities plagued by random rather than politically or ethnically driven violence, what is also missing is a sense that the suffering of individual children and families has meaning in relation to their belonging to a larger group. These limitations of socioeconomic security and family and community cohesion are likely to have placed inner-city children in developmental jeopardy before their exposure to violent events, and these same factors are likely to compound children's disadvantage in their efforts at restitution in the wake of violence. For these reasons, traditional modes of conceptualizing and delivering mental health and social services are likely to be inadequate to the psychological needs of the children and families who are most vulnerable to the effects of that violence. Professionals who hope to intervene successfully in these children's lives following their experience of traumatic violence must take extraordinary measures to create new external structures that can promote healing and recovery where existing family and community structure is so limited. We must be prepared to sustain these intensive efforts for a very long time if a new generation is to move beyond their traumatic experiences.

Extending Collaborations

Regardless of their shared concerns, no single group of professionals can address the multiple needs of the children and families subjected to massive environmental stress when the professionals attempt to intervene in isolation from one another. The collaboration between police and mental health professionals in New Haven provides one model of creative interdisciplinary action on behalf of children who are at great developmental risk owing to their exposure to violence and who would be unlikely to receive effective intervention through traditional models of social service delivery. Other collaborative projects around the country also engage mental health professionals in partnerships with other social service professionals and apply principles of child development to inter-disciplinary work with disadvantaged children in community settings. These integrative efforts offer possibilities for more efficient and effective service to vulnerable children and families in spite of the potentially overwhelming volume of children's psychological needs.

In one such project, a group of school administrators, teachers, pediatricians, and clinicians in New Haven developed a model for school-based crisis interven-tion to follow episodes of violence that affect large groups of children in a particular school, such as a death or serious injury to a student or teacher, or a shooting in the school building. By establishing crisis teams in advance, and by planning for possible crisis responses, schools are in a better position to provide children and their families with the stability and clear authority they need to reorganize in the wake of a frightening event; a sense of chaos can exacerbate feelings of fear and helplessness. School-based responses, utilizing personnel fa-miliar to the students and their families, can provide accurate information about the event, afford opportunities for many children to discuss their experience and reactions and to receive emotional support from peers and teachers, and identify those children who need more intensive mental health intervention (Schonfeld et al., 1994).

The work of Taylor et al. (1994) in Boston and Garbarino et al. (1992) in Chicago also link mental health and educational interventions by providing clini-cal support and consultation to day care centers, nurseries, and elementary schools in inner-city communities experiencing overwhelming levels of vio-lence. In these settings, thoughtful clinical support for teachers and other school personnel can enable school staff to understand and intervene in the symptomatic behavior of many young children suffering as a result of their exposure to the chronic violence around them. Clinically informed and well-supported teachers are also in a position to identify which of the many children exposed to violence are in most urgent need of direct clinical intervention.

Police, juvenile probation officers, and mental health professionals in New Haven have also begun to work together to address some of the inefficiencies and ineffectiveness of the juvenile justice system in attending to the needs of children and adolescents involved in violent activity. Many children arrested for delin-quent acts are known to multiple professionals before becoming involved in the juvenile justice system. Arrest therefore can represent an opportunity for collab-oration and interdisciplinary problem solving as an alternative to traditional ap-proaches, which emphasize the independence of the court and associated agen-cies and which often result in the duplication of efforts or in the assignment of court-ordered treatments that are mismatched to the needs of the child. In a pilot project, police and probation officers have begun to share supervision and moni-toring of juvenile offenders by relocating probation officers to community substations and by engaging neighborhood officers in supervising community service projects for youth on probation. In addition, the CD-CP Program is coordinating a collaboration among local probation, child welfare, and police and mental health services regarding the assessment, disposition, and case supervision of juvenile offenders.

Other collaborative approaches include home-based family support and preservation programs, in which child welfare professionals work to serve children who have been abused or neglected by their families, and children dealing with another war—that of AIDS affecting their caretakers (Adnopoz, 1993; Adnopoz, Grigsby, and Nagler, 1991)—or which coordinate clinical services for children with substance-abuse, psychiatric, or medical treatment for their disabled parents (Adnopoz and Nagler, 1992).

The specifics of these programs vary widely, but they all share a recognition that the volume of children whose psychological development is in jeopardy cannot be served through traditional clinic-based individual psychiatric approaches and that clinicians must move into community settings where the most vulnerable children and families are located and forge new partnerships with other professionals who share their concerns.

Conclusion

In this chapter we have considered the needs of children acutely and chronically exposed to communal violence, which has reached epidemic proportions in the United States. We have discussed some of the impediments that professionals face when responding with grave concern: they run the risk of becoming overwhelmed, much like the children they seek to help. Alternatively, we may face and tolerate the disturbing conflicts that are aroused in the areas of love and hate, empathy and sadism, bodily integrity and life-threatening injury, and the like. When this is possible we are in a much stronger position to admit our helplessness and renew our exploration of the phenomena associated with children's exposure to violence and the range of our potential responses. Recognizing both the complexity of human development and the multiple environmental factors that may impede that development, it is clear that our concerns require multifaceted and sustained responses. Those of us in the fields of mental health, law enforcement, and social and legal services do not have solutions for the multiple social problems that undermine the developmental potential of too many of our nation's children. But when we are able to share the burdens of our tasks, the wealth of our experiences, and the frustrating limitations of our knowledge, we can return together, again and again, to the question: What next? It is only then that the volume will not impede our abilities to listen and to attend to the needs of children and families whose present and future we aim to serve and protect.

REFERENCES

Adnopoz, J. 1993. Reaching out: The experiences of a family support agency. In E. Fenichel and S. Provence, eds., *Development in jeopardy: Clinical responses to infants and families,* 119–166. Madison, Conn.: International Universities Press.

Adnopoz, J., Grigsby, R. K., and Nagler, S. 1991. Multiproblem families and high-risk children and adolescents: Causes and management. In M. Lewis, ed., *Child and adolescent psychiatry: A comprehensive textbook,* 1059–1066. Baltimore: Williams and Wilkins.

Adnopoz, J., and Nagler, S. 1992. Supporting HIV infected children in their own families through family-centered practice. In R. Grigsby and S. Morton, eds., *Advancing family preservation practice,* 119–128. Newberry Park, Calif.: Sage.

American Psychiatric Association. 1994. *Diagnostic and statistical manual of mental disorders,* 4th ed. Washington, D.C.: American Psychiatric Press.

Freud, A. 1972. Comments on aggression. *International Review of Psycho-Analysis* 53:163–172.

Freud, S. 1926. Inhibitions, symptoms and anxiety. In J. Strachey, ed., *The standard edition of the complete works of Sigmund Freud,* vol. 20, 77–174. London: Hogarth Press.

Garbarino, J., Dubrow, N., Kostelny, K., and Pardo, C. 1992. *Children in danger: Coping with the consequences of community violence.* San Francisco: Jossey-Bass.

Kaufman, P., and Frase, M. J. 1990. *Dropout rates in the United States: 1989.* Washington, D.C.: U.S. Department of Education.

Marans, S. 1994. Community violence and children's development: Collaborative interventions. In C. Chiland and G. Young, eds., *Children and violence,* 109–124. Northvale, N.J.: Jason Aaronson.

Marans, S., and Cohen, D. J. 1993. Children and inner-city violence: Strategies for intervention. In L. Leavitt and N. Fox, eds., *Psychological effects of war and violence on children,* 218–301. Hillsdale, N.J.: Lawrence Erlbaum.

Marans, S., et al. 1995. *The police–mental health partnership: A community-based response to urban violence.* New Haven: Yale University Press.

Martinez, P., and Richters, J. E. 1993. The NIMH community violence project. II: Children's distress symptoms associated with violence. *Psychiatry* 56:22–35.

National Center for Health Statistics. 1988. *Vital statistics, natality.*

New Haven Public Schools. 1992. Report on the SAHA. *Social Development Project evaluation, 1991–92: Final Report,* 179–196.

Pynoos, R. 1993. Traumatic stress and developmental psychopathology in children and adolescents. In J. Oldham, M. Riba, and A. Tasman, eds., *American Psychiatric Press review of psychiatry,* vol. 12, 205–238. Washington, D.C.: American Psychiatric Press.

Pynoos, R., Frederick C., Nader, K., Arroyo, W., Steinberg, A., Spencer, E., Nuñez, F., and Fairbanks, L. 1987. Life threat and post-traumatic stress in school age children. *Archives of General Psychiatry* 44:1057–1063.

Pynoos, R., and Nader, K. 1989. Children's memory and proximity to violence. *Journal of the American Academy of Child and Adolescent Psychiatry* 28:236–241.

Pynoos, R. S., Steinberg, A. M., and Wraith, R. 1994. A developmental model of childhood traumatic stress. Unpublished manuscript.

Schonfeld, D., Kline, M., and members of the Crisis Intervention Committee. 1994. School-based crisis intervention: An organizational model. *Crisis Intervention and Time-Limited Treatment* 1(2):155–166.

Schorr, L. B. 1988. *Within our reach: Breaking the cycle of disadvantage.* New York: Double-day.

Surgeon General's Workshop on Violence and Public Health. 1991. In M. Rosenberg and M. Fenley, eds., *Violence in America: A public health approach.* Oxford: Oxford University Press.

Taylor, L., Zuckerman, B., Harik, V., and McAlister-Groves, B. 1992. Exposure to violence among inner-city parents and young children. *AJDC* 146:487–494.

———. 1994. Witnessing violence by young children and their mothers. *Developmental and Behavioral Pediatrics* 15(2):120–123.

Terr, L. 1991. Childhood traumas: An outline and overview. *American Journal of Psychiatry* 148:1, 10–20.

U.S. Congress, House of Representatives, Select Committee on Children, Youth and Families. 1989. *Children and their families: Current conditions and recent trends.* Washington, D.C.: U.S. Government Printing Office.

U.S. Department of Commerce, Bureau of the Census. 1990. *Current population reports,* ser. P-60, no. 168, *Money, income, and poverty status in the United States, 1989.* Washington, D.C.: U.S. Government Printing Office.

U.S. Department of Justice. 1994. *Crime in the United States: 1993 uniform crime reports.* Washington, D.C.: U.S. Government Printing Office.

Zill, N., and Schoenborn, C. A. 1988. *Developmental, learning, and emotional problems of our nation's children, United States, 1988.* Advance data from *Vital and Health Statistics,* no. 190. Hyattsville, Md.: U.S. Department of Health and Human Services, National Center for Health Statistics.

CHAPTER SEVEN

Youth and Violence

Trends, Principles, and Programmatic Interventions

MICHAEL B. GREENE

The author of this chapter continues some of the themes of the preceding chapter but centers on the problems of older children, especially older adolescents. Michael B. Greene's work in New York City has been found to have applications in other urban settings, including Hamburg, Germany, where Greene consults. He uses a public health framework, including a statistical overview and a clinical developmental framework, in arguing for the kinds of programs needed for adolescents—programs that mobilize progressive forces in development and that ultimately promote resourcefulness and resiliency.

Greene does not attempt to discuss principles of individual counseling and treatment, but he does include these interventions as components of or backup for group and organizational programs. We believe that the framework Greene has developed for devising and implementing these programs also enhances clinical work with individuals or small groups of adolescents. The emphasis on increasing autonomy and responsibility, encouraging a collective and collaborative perspective, can be quite salutary in dealing with teenagers who need to be carefully helped into psychotherapeutic modes that demand some regression and dependency, which can be quite frightening.

Greene does not shy away from the kind of frankness he espouses in dealing with adolescents; he deals explicitly with such charged and painful topics as the debates on violence within each minority community, the relation between poverty and violence, and the fact that many of the youths for whom these programs are designed are both victims and perpetrators of violence.

The literature on intentional interpersonal violence is growing at a pace matched only by the increasing frequency of fevered media reports on younger and

younger children committing ever more horrendous violent crimes. Some reports have characterized the expanding involvement of youths in serious violent
crimes as epidemic. Some have advocated a paradigmatic shift from a criminal
justice to a public health model in order to better understand and respond to this
so-called epidemic. The Centers for Disease Control in 1991 established the
National Center for Injury Prevention and Control and in 1993 issued a manual
entitled *The Prevention of Youth Violence: A Framework for Community Action*. The
American Psychological Association formed the high-level Commission on Violence and Youth to study and recommend a course of action in response to
increasing levels of violence among youths. It issued its summary report in 1993.
The National Research Council established the Panel on the Understanding and
Control of Violent Behavior and issued four volumes of findings and recommendations. Such prestigious journals as *Psychiatry* (vol. 56, February 1993) and
Health Affairs (Winter 1993) have devoted special issues to interpersonal violence,
with a major focus on youths. At least three important research and policy centers
have been established to focus exclusively on the topic of violence, devoting
special attention to youths and violence.[1] Finally, private and public foundations
have formed a national network through which to develop strategies to combat
youth violence (Metzger and Strand, 1993).

   In this chapter we selectively review the statistics on youths[2] and violence
and elucidate sound principles and practices of community-based intervention
programs. The sparse literature on program development is dispersed throughout
several professional disciplines. Nevertheless, significant progress has been made
in practice. Indeed, since 1990 a growing recognition has emerged among practitioners and some policy makers that older models of service provision based on a
deficits model are ineffective. Newer models based on "youth development" or
"youth participation" models are being embraced and articulated. Furthermore,
there is consensus among these practitioners that traditional evaluation research
techniques and measures must be reformulated to accommodate the methods,
content, and goals of youth development programs.

Youth Violence: Rates, Trends, and Relationships

   Three trends out of the vast array of statistics on intentional interpersonal
injury in the United States provide a backdrop for shaping and targeting intervention programs for youths.[3] First, older youths, in relation to other age groups,

---

   1. The three centers are the Center for the Study and Prevention of Violence at the University of Colorado at Boulder, the National Network of Violence Prevention Practitioners in
association with the Education Development Center in Newton, Massachusetts, and the Pa-
cific Center for Violence Prevention in San Francisco.
   2. Unless otherwise noted, *youths* refers to individuals aged twelve to twenty-one. Older
youths are individuals aged fifteen to nineteen or fifteen to twenty-four, depending on the data
source.
   3. Three other important trends are not addressed here: males commit and are victimized

are disproportionately and increasingly victimized by violent crimes. Second, older youths commit a disproportionate and increasing number of violent crimes, including homicide. And third, poverty-related variables, race, and neighborhood characteristics play powerful and entangled roles in accounting for the distribution of crime and victimization rates among youths. Factors that correlate with or predict rates of violent crime perpetration tend to predict rates of violent victimology with nearly equal strength (for a review of some of the empirical literature bearing on this relation, see Reiss and Roth, 1993, 32–33, and Sampson and Lauritsen, 1994, 30–34).

Victimization

Nationally, homicide has emerged since 1979 as the second leading cause of death among fourteen- to twenty-four-year-olds (Hammet et al., 1992; Hammond and Yung, 1993).[4] In 1991 an average of six youths under the age of eighteen were murdered every day in the United States. Furthermore, the number of adolescent victims of homicide has risen considerably during the past few years, a trend that shows no signs of abating. Homicide victim rates among fourteen- to seventeen-year-olds nearly tripled from 1984 to 1991 (Allen-Hagen and Sickmund, 1993). Lois Fingerhut (Fingerhut, Ingram, and Feldman, 1992; Fingerhut, 1993) has analyzed these data and has provided unequivocal evidence that the increasing use of guns accounts for nearly the entire increase in adolescent homicide fatalities from 1979 through 1990.[5] In 1990, 60 percent of all deaths and 91 percent of all homicide deaths among African American fifteen- to nineteen-year-olds resulted from gunshot wounds (in contrast with rates of 23 and 77 percent for their white counterparts); firearm homicide was the leading single cause of death within this population (Fingerhut, 1993).[6] These findings

---

by intentional interpersonal violence at much higher rates than women (except in the case of rape), drug and alcohol use seem to play an important role in violent crimes, and the media have become increasing filled with violent images and may have a significant effect on behavior. These issues are simply beyond the scope of this chapter.

4. Nearly all national statistics on homicide are drawn from the FBI's Uniform Crime Reports or the National Center for Health Statistics. See Reiss and Roth, 1993, 42–49, for a discussion of the strengths and limitations of these data sources, as well as those contained in the National Crime Survey, the primary national data base for for nonfatal crimes.

5. From 1979 to 1989 the firearm homicide fatality rate in the United States increased 61 percent among fifteen- to nineteen-year-olds. During this same period the nonfirearm homicide rate decreased by 29 percent (Fingerhut, Ingram, and Feldman, 1992, 3048). From 1985 to 1990 the overall firearm homicide fatality rate for ten- to fourteen-year-olds increased seventeenfold, while the nonfirearm homicide fatality rate did not change (Fingerhut, 1993). During this same period the firearm homicide fatality rate among fifteen- to nineteen-year-olds increased by 141 percent, while the nonfirearm fatality rate for this group increased by only 11 percent.

6. It is important to note that in *absolute* terms the percentage of adolescents in the population who die from homicide, even among African American youth, does not exceed 1 percent.

are consistent with surveys showing that older urban youths have easy access to guns (Sheley and Wright, 1993; McFadden, 1993; Pooley, 1991).

While these homicide rates are startling and dramatic, we also need to look more broadly at nonfatal victimization. Here, too, youths are disproportionately victimized. In 1992 more than 1.5 million violent crimes, or about one-quarter of all such crimes, were committed against twelve- to seventeen-year-olds. One in thirteen juveniles was a victim of a violent crime, a rate twice that found in the general population (Moone, 1994). The gun-related victimization rate among sixteen- to nineteen-year-olds (excluding homicide) is nearly three times the rate for the general population (Rand, 1994). Overall, the violent victimization rate peaks at ages sixteen to nineteen (Reiss and Roth, 1993).

A growing body of survey and anecdotal evidence has documented a high rate of chronic exposure to violence among children and youths residing in areas of concentrated urban poverty. For example, Bell (1987) reports that nearly one-third of a sample of fourth- , sixth- , and eighth-graders in an impoverished area of Chicago had seen someone shot or stabbed. In a similar survey of high-school-aged youths, Bell (1990) reports that nearly a quarter had seen someone killed and that 40 percent of the victims were family members, classmates, or neighbors. A snapshot survey of New York City's secure detention facility for juveniles revealed that 79 percent had seen someone stabbed or shot, 58 percent had a family member who had been stabbed or shot, and 38 percent had been stabbed or shot themselves (City of New York, 1993, 19). A 1993 survey of inner-city high school students revealed that 45 percent had been threatened with a gun or shot at and that one in three had been beaten up on their way to school (Sheley and Wright, 1993). Finally, Garbarino and his colleagues often observed children on Chicago's South Side playing "funeral," imitating the public ceremony with which they are most familiar (Garbarino, Kostelny, and Dubrow, 1991a).

Two studies of elementary school children reveal a disturbing rate of distress symptoms among witnesses to and victims of community violence (Richters and Martinez, 1993; Osofsky et al., 1993). Furthermore, Richters and Martinez documented an important and disturbing trend: parents tend to significantly underestimate their children's exposure to community violence, as well as the stress symptoms experienced by their children. Parents can play a critical role in helping their children cope with exposure to violence, but only if they understand the extent of their children's exposure. Indeed, the one demographic variable that tended to mediate the formation of stress symptoms was maternal education, a likely proxy variable for engaging children in verbal dialogue.

Perpetration of Crimes

In 1992, one in five of the people arrested for violent crimes were youths under the age of eighteen (Snyder, 1994).[7] Nonetheless, of all the serious crimes

7. The crime statistics listed here are based on Violent Crime Index offenses: murder,

for which juveniles are arrested, the vast majority are property crimes (Jones and Krisberg, 1994). Analyses of arrest data since the 1970s have focused almost exclusively on whether the rates of violent crimes perpetrated by juveniles are increasing. The answer to this question is unequivocally affirmative: between 1970 and 1980 the juvenile arrest rate for violent crimes increased by 82 percent, though the pace of increase from 1980 to 1990 slowed to 13 percent (Federal Bureau of Investigation, 1993). These increases, however, do not deviate significantly from the increase in violent crime among adults. That rate rose by 70 percent between 1970 and 1980 and by 28 percent from 1980 to 1990 (a rate of increase significantly higher than for youths). Throughout the past twenty years, age-distribution analyses based on Uniform Crime Reports data generally yield a bell-shaped curve from ages fifteen to twenty-four, with violent crime rates generally peaking at age eighteen (Federal Bureau of Investigation, 1993, 13–17).

Poverty, Race, and Neighborhood

Of all the statistics on youths and violence, perhaps the most frequently cited concern the persistent finding that African American youths are significantly overrepresented among the perpetrators and victims of violent crime (Reiss and Roth, 1993). In general, arrest rates of African Americans for violent crimes are five to six times greater than those of their white counterparts (Allen-Hagen and Sickmund, 1993, 1; Reiss and Roth, 1993, 71–72). African Americans, who constitute less than 15 percent of the U.S. population, in 1990 accounted for 45 percent of all arrests for violent crimes and 61 percent of all robbery arrests (Federal Bureau of Investigation, 1991).

Interpretations of these data are complicated by "minority overrepresentation."[8] We simply do not know to what extent bias in police practice rather than "objective" rates of crime commission account for the disproportionate representation of African American youths at every point within the juvenile justice system, particularly at the arrest stage, where the highest degree of decision-making discretion occurs (Smith, 1986; Pope and Feyerherm, 1993; see also Kempf, 1992, for an analysis of this question within the Pennsylvania juvenile justice system).

Data based on victim surveys—which are less prone to bias—reveal lower rates of violent crime perpetration by African Americans than do arrest data

---

forcible rape, robbery, and aggravated assault. Virtually all data on crime perpetration are based on arrest records, which are faulty as objective measures in two respects: (1) arrests are not made for the vast majority of crimes committed, and the arrests that are made may not reflect the pattern of actual crimes committed; and (2) arrests that are made are sensitive to varying trends in police enforcement policy, practice, and manpower.

8. These data are also limited by the fact that the Uniform Crime Reports figures are based on incidence rates of crime rather than prevalence; that is, repeat offenders are counted for each offense they commit, so that a group that contains a great number of repeat offenders will be overrepresented in these data.

(Sampson and Lauritsen, 1994, 20–21).[9] Minority overrepresentation within juvenile detention and correctional facilities has been so intractable and so troubling that the federal government in 1992, as part of its reauthorization of the Juvenile Justice and Delinquency Prevention Act, mandated states to collect data and formulate strategies to remedy bias-based overrepresentation in their juvenile justice systems (Roscoe and Morton, 1994).[10]

Neither victimization surveys nor homicide victim data are prone to bias-related distortions. Nonetheless, the data reveal that African American youths and adults are disproportionately victimized by violent crimes, including homicide. Since early in the twentieth century, the homicide victimization rate for African Americans has exceeded the rate for whites by a factor ranging from five to eleven (Allen-Hagen and Sickmund, 1993; Fingerhut, 1993; Reiss and Roth, 1993, 50). Indeed, half of the homicide victims in the United States in 1990 were African Americans (Federal Bureau of Investigation, 1992). Violent crimes other than homicide show similar though less dramatic differences. In 1992, African Americans were victims of robbery and aggravated assault at two to three times the rate of whites (Bastian, 1993).

The question of how to account for higher rates of crime perpetration and victimology among African American youths has not been resolved. There is, however, empirical and ethnographic support that poverty-related factors account for much of the observed patterns of racial disparity (see the comprehensive discussions by Reiss and Roth, 1993, 129–139; Sampson and Lauritsen, 1994, 9–29, 44–83; and the National Research Council, 1993, 151–174). In studies that examine the co-variation between race and income, racial differences in victimology rates generally disappear at all but the lowest income levels (see Reiss and Roth, 1993, 130). Differences in the patterns of poverty between African Americans and whites—such as the significantly greater persistency of long-term poverty among African Americans (Sawhill, 1992; see also Wilson, 1987)—may explain the finding of racial differences at low income levels. Within low-income and homogeneously African American communities, residence in high-density (households with two or more persons per room), low-income (less than $10,000 per year) census tracks appears to place children and adolescents at significantly greater risk for assaultive injury (Durkin et al., 1994)—that is, victimization rates within an African American population vary directly with the concentration levels of low-income families.

The literature on the relations between poverty-related variables and crime is vast and complex. Not the least of the problems in this literature is the confusion and variability over how to measure poverty. According to Sampson and Lauritsen (1994), poverty has been measured in at least twenty distinctive ways within the empirical literature. Though usually measured by some standard of

9. National Crime Survey data include only crimes perpetrated by a lone offender, which may account for some of the discrepancy.
  10. PL 102–586 42 U.SC. 5601 et seq.

income, poverty is a complex phenomenon that reaches the domains of child welfare, housing, education, family structure, and health care (Greene, 1993; National Research Council, 1993). In a comprehensive meta-analysis of the macro-level literature on the relation between crime and poverty, Land, McCall, and Cohen (1990) combined correlated predictor variables into statistically derived clusters. The cluster "resource deprivation/affluence," a commonsense proxy for poverty, was the most consistent and strongest predictor of homicide rates.[11]

Studies of the relation between poverty and crime are also complicated by the fact that results vary according to the unit of analysis—for example, individual versus metropolitan area versus census track. Generally, relations between specific poverty-related or community-related variables and crime have been most robust and illuminating when small neighborhoods, zip codes, or census tracks are chosen as the unit of analysis (see Sampson and Lauritsen, 1994, 45–50, and Reiss and Roth, 1993, 131–139). The power of such studies derives, in all likelihood, from the fact that small, geographically bounded neighborhoods reflect distinct patterns of relatively homogeneous socioeconomic dynamics. A study conducted by Furstenberg (1990) cited in Reiss and Roth (1993, 135) illustrates this point.

Furstenberg compared two distinct low-income neighborhoods in Baltimore. One was characterized by fragmented social ties among residents (due in part to the nature of the housing project in which they lived) and an "individualistic" child-rearing orientation. The other neighborhood was characterized by a high degree of social networks and neighborly support. Not surprisingly, the crime rate was significantly higher in the socially alienated neighborhood. Similarly, Taylor, Gottfredson, and Brower (1984) found that block-by-block measures of social ties and "near-home responsibilities" significantly accounted for the crime rate variance (as cited in Sampson and Lauritsen, 1994, 59). Other community-related factors that appear to underlie the distribution of crime rates include the availability of neighborhood-based supervision programs for adolescents and situations in which residents are economically isolated. Skogan (1986) has suggested that rising crime rates have a snowball effect in that crime breeds fear, which in turn inhibits social and public activities within the neighborhood (see also Garbarino, Kostelny, and Dubrow, 1991b). Thus, we need to learn about the particular economic and social relationships within a community in order to understand patterns of interpersonal violence. We can also learn much from ethnographies and biographic and autobiographic studies about subtle and powerful neighborhood dynamics (Anderson, 1990; McCall, 1994; Kotlowitz, 1991; Shakur, 1993; Williams, 1989). An understanding of these dynamics is essential in planning community-based violence-reduction programs.

11. The percentage of African Americans within each community was included in this cluster. Therefore, the question of the relative contribution of poverty and race could not be ascertained.

What are we left with? We know that youths, particularly older youths, are disproportionately represented among the perpetrators and victims of violent crime. We know that African American youths perpetrate and are victimized by violent crimes at rates far above the rates of their white counterparts. We know that concentrated poverty plays a vital but nongeneralizable role in accounting for differences in crime and victimology rates. We know that there is a great deal of regional and neighborhood variation in the social and economic dynamics underlying the statistics on youth violence. We know that the search for understanding how and in what context intentional interpersonal injuries are perpetrated requires a detailed understanding of each community.

Where do we go from here in developing programs for youths that can begin to address these dynamics? Several methods from the public health field and some principles from developmental clinical psychology can frame the data and serve as guideposts in developing responsive and effective programs for youths at risk.

Lessons from Public Health

A public health approach dictates a four-task process in program development. The first task consists of defining the problem and target population (Mercy et al., 1993). The problem, as articulated above, is embodied in the existence and consequences of an increasing rate of violent, intentional interpersonal injury among youths. The target population consists of youths. In order to maximize the impact of our interventions, we ought to direct our efforts toward those youths residing in urban communities characterized by concentrated poverty.[12]

The next task dictated by a public health approach entails a needs assessment, which systematically documents the risk factors that contribute to the problem, as well as the strengths and resources or protective factors that exist within and among the target population[13] (see Gonzalez et al., 1991; Able-Peterson and Bucy, 1992; National Center for Injury Prevention and Control, 1993). Two orienting questions must be answered regarding any needs assessment: What are the geographic boundaries of the target group, and who conducts the needs assessment? We know from the literature cited above that there are significant regional and neighborhood differences in the nature and extent of intentional

12. This is not to suggest that early intervention is not critically useful or that we should focus exclusively on youths in neighborhoods where interpersonal violence is most prevalent. Rather, it is a recognition that certain segments of our population are most at risk of intentional interpersonal injury and that intervention strategies need to be developed with and for these high-risk populations. Furthermore, the principles and strategies articulated herein are generally applicable for all youth in all communities. Early intervention will never mitigate the special needs of adolescents.

13. The focus on protective factors derives not so much within the public health field as within the developmental psychopathology literature (see Anthony, 1987; Garmezy, 1993; Smith et al., 1993).

interpersonal violence. Therefore, the answer to the question of geographic boundaries is reasonably straightforward: the needs assessment ought always to be done at the community or neighborhood level.[14]

The question of who conducts the needs assessments is not commonly asked because it is assumed that public health professionals are best suited to undertake this task. Nonetheless, community residents, including youths, are actually in the very best position to conduct detailed community needs assessments. Indeed, public health professionals commonly conduct focus groups with members of the so-called target population and typically use local informants or guides. They do this because community residents, particularly young people, simply know their communities better than anyone else.

With training, young people—including those who are commonly viewed as the source of the problem—can contribute significantly to solving that problem. In the process of conducting such needs assessment (either at the stage of initial program planning or as a part of an existing program), young people learn to work cooperatively with one another and with adults, barriers based on distrust and neighborhood fragmentation are gradually eroded, and they learn the math and reading skills required to conduct needs assessments. The process of conducting needs assessments is, in fact, an important violence reduction intervention. Community organizers have long known about these benefits, and the field of community organizing is gaining a new foothold as a critical methodology in violence reduction strategies (Greene, 1994; White, 1993; Delgado, 1994; Cohen and Lang, 1990).

Two examples illustrate this point. The first example derives from a component of a comprehensive neighborhood-based youth program called El Puente (The Bridge). The program is based in a Latino section of Brooklyn, New York. Young people were paid to identify and address problems in their community. One group of youths identified the need to increase the rate at which young children were being immunized. Many parents in the neighborhood were afraid to access public health services for fear of reprisals about their immigrant status. The young people went door to door speaking with parents about immunization and telling them that they could bring their children to El Puente to be immunized. El Puente had established credibility in the community, so the parents were willing to come. The youths who recruited the parents and their children were serious about their work and proud of what they had accomplished. Another group, which called itself the Toxic Avengers, did work that eventually led to the first-ever coalition between a Brooklyn community's Latinos and their Hasidic neighbors. These formerly antagonistic groups together fought a government proposal for a garbage incinerator and the continuing operation of a

---

14. The literature on what constitutes a community or neighborhood is vast. For our purposes, neighborhood is loosely defined as a group of people residing within a small geographic area who share similar social and economic characteristics and generally embrace a commonly held subjective sense of neighborhood identity.

radioactive waste storage operation in their shared neighborhood (Greider, 1993; Hevesi, 1994).

The second example derives from a program initiated by the City of New York. In 1991 the city's Department of Youth Services recruited young people in every neighborhood of the city to document on a block-by-block basis all services and programs for youths. Data on each program—including specifics on services offered, operating hours, contact persons, and catchment areas—were amassed and then geo-coded onto a software program. Young people were then trained to answer phone calls as "listeners" and information providers to young people and adults who called to find out about services or who "just wanted to talk to someone who would sympathetically listen." The "Youthline" data base also allows youths and youth workers in the field to provide feedback about the effectiveness and responsiveness of programs. The data base could be used to identify gaps in the youth service system, but this task has not yet been undertaken. The main point, however, is that youths played and play a central role in conducting needs assessment and in operating an invaluable service based on this work.

Following the needs assessment comes the determination of the kinds of programmatic interventions and strategies that can best address and ameliorate the problem. Public health has a tradition of developing innovative and creative multitiered strategies. A good example of such innovation is reflected in the highly successful designated driver campaign. Nevertheless, the transition from needs assessment to strategic intervention is guided not by scientific methodology but by trial and error and common sense. Furthermore, the philosophical base traditionally adopted within the field of public health rests on a medical model in which a specific "disease generating organism" is the direct cause of the "problem" (see Moore et al., 1994, 184–188). Risk factors, then, are those factors within the individual or in the environment that promote or enhance the process by which an individual is infected. As that definition applies here, risk factors induce or facilitate the likelihood of an individual intentionally harming another.

The overriding public health strategy for developing programmatic interventions rests on the reduction, elimination, or modification of risk factors within both the individual (temperament, attitudes, knowledge, and behavior) and the environment (social, physical, and legislative).[15] This philosophical orientation, however, limits the scope of interventions by implicitly placing the individual in a passive role (see McKnight, 1989).[16] This tendency is typically

15. In practice, however, violence prevention programs that have evolved out of a public health perspective tend to focus on the individual—for example, conflict resolution programs and mentoring.

16. There is also a tendency to decontextualize behavior from the particular subculture in which it exists (see Anderson, 1990; 1994) or to extrapolate "cultural" belief systems from individual behavior.

reflected in the language used to describe what we ought to do to reduce youth violence: "Youth can be taught skills. . . . They can be helped to develop. . . . They can be provided with . . . " (National Center for Injury Prevention, 1993, 4). Programs that evolve from this perspective give scant attention to the existing skills and talents among youths who are statistically categorized as high risk.

If the needs assessment includes, as it should, the strengths, talents, interests, and resources within the target population and the neighborhood, these aspects of the community can be utilized as a basis for program development (see Greene, 1993; McGillicuddy, 1991). Youths can play an important role in public health projects, such as lead-poison testing and hospital-based translation services. There is growing interest, as well, in utilizing the entrepreneurial skills of youths.

New York City has funded, through its federal appropriation of delinquency prevention monies, a community-based entrepreneurial skills program for adjudicated juvenile drug dealers who would have otherwise been placed in residential juvenile correctional facilities. During the course of developing legitimate micro-enterprises, these youths learn to work cooperatively with one another (that is, they learn conflict-resolution skills) and they acquire the math and reading skills that are an intrinsic part of developing a business.[17] Given the popularity of hip-hop music, clothing, and accessories in suburban America and throughout Europe, there are ample opportunities for urban youths to market and benefit from what they know best. Again, another caution: those with business experience are much better at developing entrepreneurial programs than are the typical youth workers.

Apart from these limitations of the public health approach, there is near-consensus within the public health field that violence is a complex phenomenon that requires collaboration from all sectors, including the schools, community leaders, community-based programs, government, religious sector, foundations, and professionals from the fields of mental health, criminology, and medicine. Notably absent in their recommendations, or mentioned only in passing, is the involvement of youths (and not only the so-called positive leaders) in all aspects of program development and operation (Carnegie Council on Adolescent Development, 1992a; Greene, 1993; McGillicuddy, 1991; Pittman, 1991). The voices of those to be served are, unfortunately, not considered. There is, however, unanimity that youth programs ought to be embraced, operated, and owned by community-based groups.

The final task in the public health process is program evaluation. The roles of the evaluator, program staff, and participants (often referred to as clients or subjects) traditionally are distinct and nonoverlapping. Given the emerging emphasis on the active participation of the program staff, community members, and youths in planning and implementation, we need to rethink the standard division of labor in the evaluation process. Traditionally, programs are evaluated in circumscribed domains—for example, pregnancy prevention, job training, reading.

---

17. In order to participate in this program, the juveniles must regularly attend school.

The outcome measures for such programs are reasonably straightforward. The orientation now favored emphasizes integrated services (within and among different programs) and holistic approaches in which a wide range of activities and interventions are offered and provided—that is, the process occurs through multiple channels and in multiple directions. Violence reduction is one outcome among many desired outcomes. In such programs, the identification of appropriate outcome measures, and, more important, the attribution of which intervention(s) generated the changes, become extraordinarily complex.

It is beyond the scope of this chapter to elaborate methodologies of program evaluation, but we offer four suggestions that begin to address the concerns of the new and evolving world of youth development programs (for further elaboration see O'Donnell, Cohen, and Hausman, 1990; Cohen and Wilson-Brewer, 1991; Carnegie Council on Adolescent Development, 1992b). First, every program ought to conduct ongoing process evaluations—that is, assess what is actually being done at the program. This is a complicated task for multilevel interventions and services, because selecting and integrating pertinent information require much time and reflection. We need to develop methods to record information on such subtle but important program features and processes as the establishment of peer friendships and youth–adult relationships. It is necessary to do this if we want to understand the mechanisms that underlie effective programs.

Second, before recommending that a program undergo a rigorous outcome evaluation, graduated levels of increasingly sophisticated program assessments ought to be undertaken. These assessments can and should lead to program modifications. If there is no indication of at least midlevel success from preliminary assessments, then there is no need to undertake full-fledged outcome evaluations.

Third, it is critically important to assess the range and application of skills learned. School-based conflict resolution programs typically examine only behavioral outcomes within the domain of the school, such as the number of school suspensions. Yet we need to know whether programs have an effect on the streets and at home. We also need to be careful about generalizing from knowledge and attitude measures to actual behavior.

Fourth, and most important, evaluators must work as active collaborators with program administrators and staff, with appropriately selected community members, with funders, and with the program participants. The purposes and uses of the evaluation should be discussed and elaborated in collaboration. Many program administrators and staff have come to fear evaluation because they believe that the results will be used exclusively for the purpose of making a funding decision. The evaluation ought to be discussed during the planning phase of program implementation. Evaluation methodologies can provide an important grounding for grandiose ideas. Cultural and ethical issues regarding test and outcome measures and research methodologies ought to be addressed in collaboration. Certainly, the user-friendly and richly evocative ethnographic methodologies ought to be utilized.

Lessons from Clinical Developmental Psychology

We know a great deal about adolescent development, yet much of what we have learned is overlooked in developing violence prevention programs for youths (Takanishi, 1993). First and foremost, we know that adolescents require opportunities to form positive and supportive relationships with adults in the community, among peers, and within their families. When young people are asked what it is that makes a good program work, they invariably cite the quality of relationships with staff (Carnegie Council on Adolescent Development, 1992a; Poplin and Weeres, 1992). Young people intuitively know who is, as they say, "real" with them. They overwhelmingly cite several characteristics that are important to them.[18]

Young people respond to staff who listen to, respect, and support them (Carnegie Council on Adolescent Development, 1992a). They need staff who understand what their lives are like—that is, they want at least some staff to live in their neighborhoods and to know and appreciate their brand of youth culture. They want staff who are willing to work with rather than dictate to them. Finally, staff need to like—if not love—the kids they work with. Youth work is often exasperating and frustrating and simply cannot be sustained by an interest in doing "good" work.[19]

Relationships among youths need to be supported and facilitated. Much of this support can come from group projects, such as those at El Puente. Much can also be derived from structured groups that are facilitated by an adult. What is essential for youths is an ongoing, structured setting in which the young people can talk to one another about their feelings and thoughts. Many young people feel extremely isolated. They rarely, if ever, talk about their vulnerabilities, fears, and hopes. Through participation in rap or discussion groups, young people come to realize that other young people share their insecurities and fears. This realization often relieves years of accumulated feelings of shame, during which they felt alone in their experience.

Finally, community-based groups and schools need to establish partnerships with entire families. Several ways to involve parents and guardians in community-based groups have been articulated (Carnegie Council on Adolescent Development, 1992a, 88; Kinney, Haapala, and Booth, 1990; Small, 1990). The importance of this work is underscored by the nearly universal research finding that family discord and conflict are key risk factors for a variety of negative outcomes among children and youths (Garmezy, 1993). Conversely, many writers and researchers, from Anna Freud (Burlingham and Freud, 1942) onward, have posed an "inoculation theory," which suggests that good parenting can buffer a child from the adverse consequences of exposure to poverty and violence (Anthony,

18. These qualities are derived from the author's work with youth programs and from discussions with and observations of young people over the past twenty-five years.
19. For an excellent discussion of staff training see the report on the professional development of youth workers by the Carnegie Council on Adolescent Development (1991).

1987; Garmezy, 1993). Further, the chronic trauma of poverty and violence can produce moments, if not regular patterns, of emotional upset in parents (mothers in particular), which diminishes or destroys their reserves for parenting (Garbarino, Kostelny, and Dubrow, 1991b). Sometimes staff working with parents focus exclusively on parenting issues. Although these are certainly very important, parents also need to discuss the everyday stresses, strivings, and successes that are not directly related to their roles as parents.

Beyond relationships, we know that adolescents require opportunities to pursue and develop their interests and competencies in positive and self-fulfilling directions. Under ideal circumstances, programs ought to offer a wide array of activities in the arts, sports, science, literature, neighborhood organizing, leadership training, education, and job preparedness and job placement. As noted earlier, youths should be centrally involved in choosing the activities offered and in structuring their implementation. Youths who are exposed to chronic conditions of poverty and violence typically are repeatedly told what they can't do. Too often, these youths are given options only about the kinds of treatment and services that can "help" them (for example, see Towberman, 1992). Over time, the message becomes clear: their desires and interests are simply unimportant. Young people need to be encouraged and supported in pursuing the activities they want to pursue and in which they have the potential to excel and enjoy themselves.

We know that adolescents require opportunities to develop a feeling of belonging and a positive sense of neighborhood. Like adults, they need to have a sense of belonging. Too often, all that is available is a gang or a drug posse. Belonging to a community-based organization can greatly enhance an adolescent's sense of being part of something positive and part of something beyond himself or herself. Membership cards and T-shirts with the organization's youth-designed logo can help (Carnegie Council on Adolescent Development, 1992a).

Within the community-based organization, a variety of neighborhood improvement projects are available to youths. New York City is filled with beautiful untagged (untouched by graffiti) murals painted by youths. Youth Force, a youth collaborative and leadership training program, pioneered the idea of reclaiming small urban parks that had been taken over by drug dealers. In the process, they worked with adult community leaders, with the local police precinct, and with the sanitation department. They also organized activities and events in the park such as storytelling by an African folk tale teller, and brought in singers, dancers, games, and films. Their sense of belonging and pride soared. For many it was the first time that they had truly been appreciated by adults for something positive they had done. Unfortunately, these types of activities are too often overlooked when violence reduction programs are being developed.

We know that children and adolescents evolve ways to adapt to their circumstances and that their adaptation occurs within a particular peer culture. Consistent with the literature on the relation between neighborhood and crime, we need to understand the circumstances and evolution of the individual and group adaptation processes utilized by young people before we attempt to intervene to change what they do. Anderson (1990; 1994), for example, has described a code of the streets that has evolved among African American youths residing in socially isolated and economically impoverished urban neighborhoods. Such codes, or "ecologically structured norms" (Sampson and Lauritsen, 1994, 63), prescribe specific forms of public behavior that garner respect, status, and power. They have evolved because access to mainstream symbols of status is simply unavailable to these young people (see Padilla, 1992, and Sullivan, 1989).

It is too easy to interpret these codes as a reflection of degraded and violence-oriented values that have to be changed. The most effective way to counter the negative aspects of these codes is to offer viable alternatives. Young people who know of these codes can provide useful insights on such efforts as reducing access to and availability of guns. In fact, a group of young people in New York City who had served time and who had "lived the code" led a provocative discussion on just this topic with experts in the fields of criminal justice and public health (G. I. I. F. T. Pack, 1994). Similarly, conflict resolution programs must use knowledge of the code if they are to affect behavior beyond the school. The youth "informants" in such forums and discussions can, in fact, gain status and satisfaction (and, ideally, stipends and part- or full-time jobs) through this process.

Children and adolescents must be given opportunities to express their thoughts and feelings about their exposure as victims of and witnesses to violence. With some notable exceptions (Garbarino, 1993; Marans and Cohen, 1993; Marans, 1994; Marans 1995), there have been few attempts to teach parents, teachers, and other community members how to help children and youths express their experience of acute and chronic exposure to violence. Most policy makers have mistakenly bypassed such efforts in favor of promulgating curricula—usually school-based—that teach children and youths how to resolve interpersonal conflicts.

Aside from expression, we know that the use of "corrective" or compensatory fantasies or actions by children and youths exposed to chronic violence can be extremely valuable to healing (Pynoos, 1994). Corrective fantasies and actions can impinge on the sense of hopelessness and vulnerability experienced by victims of and witnesses to violence. Such corrective actions are embodied in the orientation of securing the active participation of youths in all phases of program planning and implementation. Finally, the effects of trauma—and its treatment—must be examined within a developmental framework (Pynoos and Nader, 1988). For example, adolescents are particularly vulnerable to chronic exposure to violence because of their cognitive ability to generalize and deduce the consequences of such experiences (Macksoud, Dyregrov, and Raundalen, 1993).

We know that as the number of risk factors for "rotten outcomes" increases, the insulating power of protective factors diminishes (Smith et al., 1993; Garmezy, 1993). This means that those youths who are repeatedly and in various domains of their life exposed to risk factors—or reside in risky environments, such as socially isolated, economically impoverished, and violence-ridden neighborhoods—require the most intensive, integrated, sustained, coordinated, and comprehensive intervention. In fact, these program characteristics are just those recommended by a growing consensus of professionals in the field (Carnegie Council on Adolescent Development, 1992a; Citizens' Committee for Children, 1993; Greene, 1993; Palmer, 1983; Schorr, 1989).

Finally, we know that youths vary in their individual temperament and in their need and readiness to participate in activities. Three requirements emanate from this principle: the need to conduct active street outreach and recruitment, the need to set individualized objectives, and the need, as indicated earlier, to offer a wide range of activities and programs. Many youths, particularly those who have been treated like failures by their parents, their teachers, and their peers, are frighteningly cynical about their lives and about new programs. We cannot expect them to come rushing to our thoughtfully designed programs unless they can be convinced that "our" place is safe. The best way to attract young people is by word of mouth from other young people: actively recruiting young people on the street and encouraging friends and relatives to come to the program (see Able-Peterson and Bucy, 1992, for excellent elaboration of these and other techniques).

The initial point of entry into programs should be easy and attractive for youths. A friendly orientation tour is a good start. The range of services offered should be shown, not pushed. The intake interview should be conducted with respect and without judgment. The young person should be encouraged and guided to participate in services that pique his or her interest. Staff should listen and watch carefully: interests and needs are often expressed nonverbally.

Program leaders need to know what each youth needs and wants and, based on this assessment, to develop an *initial* structured plan to help the young person meet his or her needs and pursue his or her interests. *Preliminary* short- and long-terms goals ought to be established along with a schedule for reviewing accomplishments. We emphasize preliminary and initial because these goals and concerns will evolve. They will change because the young person will improve his or her ability to realistically assess what he or she can accomplish in a given time period, because the young person will come to know himself or herself better, and because the relationship with the adult who serves as his or her primary counselor will deepen, and formerly hidden vulnerabilities and concerns will emerge.

We cannot know in advance what every young person will respond to. We partly accommodate individual differences, as suggested above, by offering a range of activities that have been suggested by at least some of the youths we intend to serve. We also need to accommodate individual differences with a flexible stance regarding who is required to do what. Take the example of mentoring programs, a popular program component these days. Some youths will not like the idea and flatly refuse to be paired with a mentor. Some may change their minds (in both directions) about mentoring after a few weeks or months in the program. It is no one's fault if mentoring is simply not right for some young people. If a program rests entirely on the mentoring concept (contrary to the earlier recommendation of comprehensiveness), young people who do not want to be paired with a mentor should be helped to find a program that better fits their needs and interests.

Summary

Based on a review of the statistical evidence, we concluded that intervention programs are most efficient when they serve youths residing in neighborhoods characterized by a concentration of low-income families, social fragmentation, and minimal economic opportunities. They should be located in the communities they serve, staffed as much as feasible by local residents, and tailored to local conditions.

The first step in developing youth programs consists of a thorough needs assessment of the target population and neighborhood. This assessment should draw on the knowledge and understanding of neighborhood residents and youths. Programs should evolve from the strengths, interests, and desires of the youths and should build on the existing and potential resources in the neighborhoods. Program strategies and designs ought to be planned jointly by neighborhood youths and adults. Methods of program evaluation should be integrated into the initial planning phase and should include the active participation of youths, staff members, and other neighborhood residents. Minimally, project implementation ought to be documented in a thorough process evaluation, and quantitatively stated objectives should be set and assessed.

Program design should incorporate and reflect established principles from developmental clinical psychology. Six principles were articulated: (1) young people require opportunities to develop and enhance relationships among peers, family members, and other adult members of the neighborhood; (2) adolescents require opportunities to pursue their interests and areas of competencies; (3) adolescents require opportunities to develop and enhance a sense of belonging to a group and to their neighborhood; (4) the youth culture and mores in which young people grow must be appreciated, supported, and built upon; (5) youths require opportunities to speak about their feelings and thoughts, particularly in the areas of exposure to violence; and (6) individual differences in temperament, abilities, and interests must be accommodated and supported. In general, youth programs should be comprehensive, intensive, integrated, sustained, and coordinated.

Perhaps the philosophical orientation embodied in this chapter is best reflected in a Japanese proverb: *Tell me and I forget. Show me and I remember. Involve me and I understand.*

REFERENCES

Able-Peterson, T., and Bucy, J. 1992. *The streetwork outreach training manual.* Washington, D.C.: U.S. Department of Health and Human Services.

Allen-Hagen, B., and Sickmund, M. 1993. *Juveniles and violence: Juvenile offending and victimization.* Washington, D.C.: Office of Juvenile Justice and Delinquency Prevention, July.

American Psychological Association. 1993. *Violence and Youth.* Washington, D.C.: APA Public Interest Directorate.

Anderson, E. 1990. *Street wise.* Chicago: University of Chicago Press.

———. 1994. The code of the streets. *The Atlantic Monthly,* May, 80–94.

Anthony, E. J. 1987. Risk, vulnerability, and resilience: An overview. In E. J. Anthony and B. J. Cohler, eds., *The invulnerable child.* New York: Guilford, 3–48.

Bastian, L. D. 1993. *Criminal victimization 1992.* Washington, D.C.: U.S. Department of Justice, October.

Bell, C. C. 1987. Preventive strategies for dealing with violence among blacks. *Community Mental Health Journal* 23:217–228.

———. 1990. Preventing black homicide. In J. Dewart, ed., *The state of black America 1990.* New York: National Urban League.

Burlingham, D., and Freud, A. 1942. *Young children in wartime: A year's work in a residential war nursery.* London: Allen and Unwin.

Carnegie Council on Adolescent Development. 1991. *Report on the consultation of professional development of youth workers.* Washington, D.C., May.

———. 1992a. *A matter of time.* Woodlawn, Md.: Wolk Press.

———. 1992b. *Report on the consultation on evaluation of youth development programs.* Washington, D.C., January 15, 1992.

Citizens' Committee for Children. 1993. *Keeping track of New York's children.* New York: Citizens' Committee for Children.

City of New York. 1993. *Juvenile detention alternatives initiative.* August.

Cohen, S., and Lang, C. 1990. *Application of principles of community-based programs.* Newton, Mass.: Educational Development Center.

Cohen, S., and Wilson-Brewer, R. 1993. *Violence prevention for young adolescents: The state of the art of program evaluation.* Washington, D.C.: Carnegie Council on Adolescent Development, September 1991.

Delgado, G. 1994. *Beyond the politics of place.* Oakland, Calif.: Applied Research Center.

Durkin, M. S., Davidson, L. L., Kuhn, L., O'Connor, P., and Barlow, B. 1994. Low-income neighborhoods and the risk of severe pediatric injury: A small-area analysis in northern Manhattan. *American Journal of Public Health* 88(4):587–592.

Federal Bureau of Investigation. 1991. *Crime in the United States: 1990.* Washington, D.C., Uniform Crime Reports.

———. 1992. *Uniform Crime Rates, 1991.* Washington, D.C.: Government Printing Office.

———. 1993. *Age-specific arrest rates and race-specific arrest rates for selected offences, 1965–1992.* Washington, D.C., Uniform Crime Reports, December.

Fingerhut, L. A. 1993. Firearm mortality among children, youth, and young adults 1–34 years of age, trends and current status: United States, 1985–90. *Advance Data,* March 23, no. 231, National Center for Health Statistics.

Fingerhut, L. A., Ingram, D. D., and Feldman, J. J. 1992. Firearm and nonfirearm homicide among persons 15–19 years of age: Differences by level of urbanization, United States, 1979–1989. *Journal of the American Medical Association* 267(22):3048–3053.

Furstenberg, F. 1990. "How families manage risk and opportunity in dangerous neighborhoods." Paper presented at the annual meeting of the American Sociological Association, Washington, D.C.

Garbarino, J. 1993. *Let's talk about living in a world with violence.* Chicago: Erikson Institute.

Garbarino, J., Kostelny, K., and Dubrow, N. 1991a. *No place to be a child.* Lexington, Mass.: Lexington Books.

———. 1991b. What children can tell us about living in danger. *American Psychologist* 46:376–383.

Garmezy, N. 1993. Children in poverty: Resilience despite risk. *Psychiatry* 56:127–136.

G. I. I. F. T. Pack. 1994. "Ideas related to gun control." Unpublished manuscript.

Gonzalez, V. M., Gonzalez, J. T., Freeman, V., and Howard-Pitney, B. 1991. *Health promotion in diverse cultural communities.* Palo Alto, Calif.: Health Promotion Resource Center.

Greene, M. B. 1993. Chronic exposure to violence and poverty: Interventions that work for youth. *Crime and Delinquency* 39(1):106–124.

———. 1994. "Community organizing as a program model for working with youth exposed to chronic violence and urban poverty." Paper presented at the 13th international Congress of the International Association for Child and Adolescent Psychiatry and Allied Professions, San Francisco, July 27.

Greider, K. 1993. Against all odds. *City Limits,* August/September, 34–39.

Hammet, M., Powell, K. E., O'Carroll, P. W., and Clanton, S. T. 1992. Homicide surveillance—United States, 1979–1988. *Morbidity and Mortality Weekly Report: CDC Surveillance Summaries* 43(3):1–33.

Hammond, R. W., and Yung, B. 1993. Psychology's role in the public health response to assaultive violence among young African-American men. *American Psychologist* 48(2):142–154.

Hevesi, D. 1994. Hasidic and Hispanic residents in Williamsburg try to forge a new unity. *New York Times,* September 18, 1994, p. 47.

Jones, M. A., and Krisberg, B. 1994. *Images and reality: Juvenile crime, youth violence and public policy.* National Council on Crime and Delinquency, San Francisco, June.

Kempf, K. L. 1992. *The role of race in juvenile justice processing in Pennsylvania.* Shippensburg, Pa.: Center for Juvenile Justice Training and Research.

Kinney, J., Haapala, D., and Booth, C. 1990. *Keeping families together: The HOMEBUILDERS model.* Hawthorne, N.Y.: Aldine de Gruyter.

Kotlowitz, Alex. 1991. *There are no children here.* New York: Doubleday.

Land, K. C., McCall, P. L., and Cohen, L. E. 1990. Structural covariates of homicide rates: Are there any invariances across time and space? *American Journal of Sociology* 95:922–963.

McCall, N. 1994. *Makes me wanna holler.* New York: Random House.

McFadden, R. D. 1993. Report finds 20% of students in New York City carry arms. *New York Times,* October 15, p. B-3.

McGillicuddy, K. 1991. Response to Karen Pittman. *Future Choices Toward a National Youth Policy* 3(2):95–99.

McKnight, J. L. 1989. Do no harm: Policy options that meet human needs. *Social Policy* (Summer 1989):5–14.

Macksoud, M., Dyregrov, A., and Raundalen. 1993. Traumatic war experiences and their effects on children. In J. P. Wilson and B. Raphael, eds., *International handbook of traumatic stress syndromes.* New York: Plenum.

Marans, S. 1994. Community violence and children's development. In C. Chiland and J. G. Young, eds., *Children and violence.* Northvale, N.J.: Jason Aronson.

Marans, S., and Cohen, D. J. 1993. Children and inner-city violence: Strategies for intervention. In L. Leavitt and N. Fox, eds., *Psychological effects of war and violence on children,* 218–301. Hillsdale, N.J.: Lawrence Erlbaum.

Marans, S., et al. 1995. *The police–mental health partnership: A community-based response to urban violence.* New Haven: Yale University Press.

Mercy, J. A., Rosenberg, M. L., Powell, K. E., Broome, C. V., and Roper, W. L. 1993. Public health policy for preventing violence. *Health Affairs* (Winter):7–29.

Metzger, D., and Strand, V. C. 1993. Violence prevention: Trends in foundation funding. *Health Affairs* (Winter):209–220.

Moone, J. 1994. *Juvenile victimization: 1987–1992.* Washington, D.C.: U.S. Department of Justice, June.

Moore, M. H., Prothrow-Stith, D., Guyer, B., and Spivak, H. 1994. Violence and intentional injuries: Criminal justice and public health perspectives on an urgent national problem. In A. J. Reiss and J. A. Roth, eds., *Understanding and preventing violence.* Vol. 4: *Consequences and control.* Washington, D.C.: National Academy Press.

National Center for Injury Prevention and Control. 1993. *The prevention of youth violence: A framework for community action.* Atlanta: Centers for Disease Control and Prevention.

National Research Council. 1993. *Losing generations: Adolescents in high-risk settings.* Washington, D.C.: National Academy Press.

O'Donnell, L., Cohen, S., and Hausman, A. 1990. *The evaluation of community-based violence prevention programs.* Newton, Mass.: Education Development Center.

Osofsky, J. D., Wewers, S., Hann, D. M., and Fick, A. C. 1993. Chronic community violence: What is happening to our children? *Psychiatry* 56 (February):36–45.

Padilla, F. 1992. *The gang as an American enterprise.* New Brunswick, N.J.: Rutgers University Press.

Palmer, Ted. 1983. The 'effectiveness' issue today: An overview. *Federal Probation* 47 (1983):3–10.

Pittman, K. 1991. A framework for defining and promoting youth participation. *Future Choices Toward a National Youth Policy* 3(2):85–90.

Pooley, Eric. 1991. Kids with guns. *New York Magazine,* August 5, 20–29.

Pope, C. E., and Feyerherm, W. 1993. *Minorities in the juvenile justice system.* Washington, D.C.: Office of Juvenile Justice and Delinquency Prevention, December.

Poplin, M., and Weeres, J. 1992. *Voices from the inside: A report on schooling from inside the classroom.* Claremont, Calif.: Institute for Education in Transformation.

Pynoos, R. S. 1994. *Trauma and development in children exposed to catastrophic violence and disaster.* Paper presented at the 13th international Congress of the International Association for Child and Adolescent Psychiatry and Allied Professions, San Francisco, July 25.

Pynoos, R. S., and Nader, K. 1988. Psychological first aid and treatment approach to children exposed to community violence: Research implications. *Journal of Traumatic Stress* 1(4):445–473.

Rand, M. R. 1994. Guns and crime. *Crime Data Brief.* Washington, D.C.: U.S. Department of Justice, April.

Reiss, A. J., and Roth, J. A. 1993. *Understanding and preventing violence.* Washington, D.C.: National Academy Press.

Richters, J. E., and Martinez, P. 1993. Children as victims and witnesses to violence in a Washington, D.C., neighborhood. In L. Leavitt and N. Fox, eds., *Psychological effects of war and violence on children,* 243–278. Hillsdale, N.J.: Lawrence Erlbaum.

Roscoe, M., and Morton, R. 1994. *Disproportionate minority confinement.* Washington, D.C.: U.S. Department of Justice, Fact Sheet No. 11, April.

Sampson, R. J., and Lauritsen, J. L. 1994. Violent victimization and offending: Individual-, situational-, and community-level risk factors. In A. J. Reiss and J. A. Roth, eds., *Understanding and preventing violence.* Vol. 3: *Social influences.* Washington, D.C.: National Academy Press.

Sawhill, I. 1992. Young children and families. In H. J. Aaron and C. L. Schultze, eds., *Setting domestic priorities: What can governments do.* Washington, D.C.: Brookings Institution.

Schorr, Lisbeth B. 1989. *Within our reach.* New York: Doubleday.

Shakur, S. 1993. *Monster: The autobiography of an L. A. gang member.* New York: Penguin.

Sheley, J. F., and Wright, J. D. 1993. *Gun acquisition and possession in selected juvenile samples.* Washington, D.C.: U.S. Department of Justice, December.

Skogan, W. 1986. Fear of crime and neighborhood change. In A. J. Reiss and M. Tonry, eds., *Communities and crime.* Chicago: University of Chicago Press.

Small, S. A. 1990. Preventive programs that support families with adolescents. Washington, D.C.: Carnegie Council on Adolescence, February.

Smith, C., Lizotte, A. J., Thornberry, T. P., and Krohn, M. D. 1993. Resilient youth: Identifying factors that prevent high-risk youth from engaging in serious delinquency and drug use. Unpublished manuscript. August.

Smith, D. R. 1986. The neighborhood context of police behavior. In A. J. Reiss and M. Tonry, eds., *Communities and crime.* Chicago: University of Chicago Press.

Snyder, H. 1994. *Juvenile violent crime arrest rates, 1972–1992.* Washington, D.C.: U.S. Department of Justice, Fact Sheet No. 14, May.

Sullivan, M. 1989. *Getting paid: Economy, culture, and youth crime in the inner city.* Ithaca, N.Y.: Cornell University Press.

Takanishi, R. 1993. Changing views of adolescence in contemporary society. In R. Takanishi, ed., *Adolescence in the 1990s.* New York: Teachers College Press.

Taylor, R., Gottfredson, S., and Brower, S. 1984. Black crime and fear: Defensible space, local social ties, and territorial functioning. *Journal of Research in Crime and Delinquency* 21:303–331.

Towberman, D. B. 1992. National survey of juvenile needs assessment. *Crime and Delinquency* 38:230–238.

U.S. Department of Health and Human Services. 1991. *The third national injury control conference,* 16–241. Atlanta: Centers for Disease Control.

White, A. 1993. As far as the people will go. *City Limits,* August–September, 6–11.

Williams, T. 1989. *The cocaine kids.* Reading, Mass.: Addison-Wesley.

Wilson, W. J. 1987. *The truly disadvantaged: The inner city, the underclass, and public policy.* Chicago: University of Chicago.

CHAPTER EIGHT

Mobilizing Communities to Meet the Psychosocial Needs of Children in War and Refugee Crises

NEIL BOOTHBY

In this chapter Neil Boothby presents another perspective on community mobilization with the goal of rehabilitating children and optimizing their emotional well-being. Boothby is a psychologist and a practitioner of psychologically informed policies. He is now in an academic position at Duke University, and he has spent many years in the field—indeed, in the killing fields of Cambodia and Mozambique, and most recently in Rwanda. He writes from a perspective derived from working with communities devastated by war. These communities lack the infrastructure described in the previous chapters in connection with programs in New York or New Haven, where community resources could be mobilized for the benefit of children traumatized by violence.

The author discusses the plight of children living without adult supervision in large anomic metropolises. The topic is covered in a recent UNICEF *book (Blanc, 1994), but little has yet been written about the inner mental life of these street children. The most profound psychological portraits have been in such films as the 1988* Salaam Bombay, *the heart-rending tale of a preteen boy, parentless, and a preteen girl, sold by her parents as a prostitute. Many of the ideas and programs discussed in this chapter may also have relevance for these prematurely independent children living in squalor. Boothby, after all, has worked with children who were taken to war and required to participate in acts of violence. Does what he writes extrapolate to other children, such as those taken for prostitution? We cannot be certain.*

Boothby does point the way to the need for informed caring programs for rehabilitation of children who seem very far gone. In mobilizing to meet the psychosocial needs of children, communities can reclaim their children and their future, and the children can regain some semblance of childhood.

Wars, large and small, are raging all over the world, afflicting millions of civilians. Most armed conflicts are taking place in developing countries, where children are already the most numerous casualties of multiple breakdowns between people and environmental support systems. War, in turn, can drain a society's limited resources by redirecting the society toward death and destruction and by feeding misguided myths of national, ethnic, or religious glory. Five out of six nations on the U.N. list of countries most seriously affected by hunger are also racked by civil war (Timberlake, 1986).

In earlier wars, military personnel constituted most of the casualties, but that trend has been reversed. In today's wars, with their emphasis on "ethnic and religious conflict," "national liberation," "counterinsurgency," and "guerrilla warfare," most of the victims are women and children. The changing technology of warfare has contributed to this trend. Automatic weapons, antipersonnel mines, carpet bombing, and other modern weapons make the carnage difficult to contain. Armed conflicts destroy a country's infrastructure and lead to deforestation, landlessness, drought, and famine. Increased infant and child mortality rates are but two of the fatal results of the failure to get development back on track.

War also makes children vulnerable to social and emotional traumas. Indeed, research indicates that large percentages of children in countries afflicted by armed conflict are being exposed to violence, torture, hunger, loss of family, displacement from communities, and forced recruitment into military and paramilitary groups. A recent study of the health of refugee children who immigrated to Sweden from a dozen war-affected nations found that more than 60 percent of them had been exposed to violence in their countries of origin, either as immediate witnesses or as participants (Leyens and Mahjoub, 1989). The situation of internally displaced children often is worse. In war-torn Mozambique, a survey of more than five hundred children revealed that 77 percent of them had witnessed civilian murders, often in mass killings (Boothby, Upton, and Sultan, 1991). An additional 28 percent had been abducted from their families, trained as combatants, and forced to kill other human beings.

A Policy Perspective

The dangerous circumstances faced by children in war zones point to an urgent need to develop strategies to prevent or ameliorate the negative psychosocial effects of exposure to violence and other war-related traumas. But psychosocial programs for war-affected children are still relatively scarce, and only a handful of these efforts have been developed as integral components of broader relief and development systems. Instead, most psychosocial programs piloted in recent years have remained marginalized, with little or no relevance to larger assistance efforts.

Part of the problem is that armed conflicts and refugee crises are delimited as situations requiring emergency responses. Emergency responses, in turn, tend to be defined in logistical terms: how many tons of food, tents, medicines, and clothing can be delivered in the shortest period of time (Forbes-Martin, 1994). Failure to respond to these immediate needs quickly and efficiently can result in thousands of deaths. Nonmaterial needs are much more difficult to quantify. The logistical challenges of preventing family separations and helping children cope with the loss of parents or come to terms with the aftermath of witnessing murder simply have not been worked out.

Paradoxically, the fact that war-related trauma is widespread among civilian populations also works against serious commitments to mental health assistance. At a time when donor agencies are asking major international organizations to economize—to assist more war victims and refugees with fewer resources—the trauma statistics appear to be overwhelming. Instead of identifying a significant but containable problem with clear solutions, the numbers point to something that affects vast numbers of people but has no clear-cut remedies. From a policy perspective, increasing the funds for mental health programs at a time when food and other material resources are critically scarce may not be perceived by donor agencies and international relief and development organizations as an appropriate allocation of resources.

Even when funds have been available to address these difficult problems, conventional mental health approaches have proved too narrow and too expensive to effectively respond to large numbers of war-traumatized people. In recent years, center-based mental health programs have managed to treat only an average of two hundred war-affected individuals per year. Moreover, the cost of center-based mental health services has been ten times higher than the costs of life-sustaining (food, shelter, basic medical care) supplies. Center-based programs have not, in other words, provided a viable, cost-effective model for mental health assistance in situations where tens of thousands of men, women, and children have suffered war-related traumas.

In the final analysis, both the individual and the society are hurt by failures to integrate mental health assistance into mainstream relief and development systems. The physical, mental health, and social needs of war-affected populations are, of course, intertwined. On the one hand, basic needs assistance is crucial to psychosocial well-being: families that do not have food or shelter or security, for instance, will not be able to care for their children adequately. Economic redevelopment, increased employment opportunities, housing, and education are also services that benefit the social and mental health of entire populations. On the other hand, the affective state and motivation level of any given population is a fundamental underpinning of social and economic progress. Children who have been traumatized by war may not be able to concentrate in school, and youths may be unable to take hold of employment opportunities when their minds are preoccupied with the past.

Going to Scale

Given the scale of need associated with war and refugee crises, and the severe lack of financial and professional resources, a primary mental health approach may be a more effective way of mounting sustainable responses to the social and psychological needs of children and their families. Primary mental health is not well defined: there are no "standardized" methodologies or "model" programs. Nonetheless, a number of innovative mental health initiatives have been developed to mobilize communities to respond to large numbers of war-affected children in cost-effective ways. While these programs emerged out of the particular history of a given country and the philosophies of staff members and implementing organizations, their basic design structures and activities can be categorized and described.

Community-Based Programs

Community-based programs utilize paraprofessionals, relief workers, social workers, teachers, nurses, or clerics who provide services through community agencies, religious groups, or international nongovernmental organizations. In the past, these people and organizations have assisted in reestablishing social support networks, enhancing parental coping skills, responding to the needs of especially vulnerable groups, mobilizing public awareness, and organizing self-help groups of women and single parents.

The West Bank and Jerusalem Counseling and Health Program is one effort to make mental health services accessible to children in communities, as well as to sensitize the community itself to mental health concerns. The program works to bridge the gap between psychosocial care offered in counseling rooms and education in the wider community because it sees individual dysfunction as linked to social problems. Indeed, a basic assumption of the program is that psychosocial care for children exposed to violence cannot occur in a therapeutic vacuum but must take into account the values, perspectives, and beliefs of the surrounding community.

The program began by placing lay counselors in primary health care clinics accessible to the local populations. It then provided these paraprofessionals with training on counseling techniques and intervention and prevention strategies for children and mothers. In the community, a number of different projects have been devised, including lectures, community awareness and educational programs, and plays about the effects of emotional stress and psychological disorders. The program also has a school counseling project designed to reach children affected by violence. School counselors, teachers, and mental health paraprofessionals are trained in some of the practical skills needed in working with children, and in the problems children face living in dangerous environments.

One of the advantages of linking mental health services to existing health services is that intake procedures can take place at the health clinic rather than at another location and on another day. The clients do not have to go to a clearly demarcated counseling center and thus do not have to carry some of the stigma associated with it. At the same time, doctors and health professionals can be trained to identify emotionally based problems and conditions, and also have an option for referring them to other specialists. Health care, in turn, is more holistic and cost-effective.

Radda Barnen's Save the Children, a Swedish community-based program for Afghan refugee children in Pakistan, has an even stronger communal self-action orientation. Radda Barnen began this work by establishing a training unit for community action that has facilitated the development of "child support groups" in twenty-six refugee communities. Each support group is composed of adult refugees who engage in a range of activities in support of children with special needs. These include stimulation, rehabilitation, emotional support, and assistance to children with psychological and behavioral problems.

One of the biggest obstacles the project had to overcome was the way that women were controlled by Islamic fundamentalists in the Afghan camps. Women were not allowed outside their homes, and visitors were restricted to relatives. Employment was out of the question. Because women and children made up almost 80 percent of Afghan refugees, women's seclusion limited community mobilization in the camps. Because of war losses, many of these women were widows. A typical refugee widow might be fifteen years old with two or three children. In camps, the extended family no longer operated well enough to care for widows, who found themselves alone, with no idea of how to survive. For many widows the only means of support was sending their sons to party schools or to the military forces for recruitment. A poor diet, combined with the cultural practice of women eating after men and children, left most women under-nourished and weak.

Direct efforts by international organizations to help the women failed. Female teachers and outreach workers were harassed by Afghan extremists. In one camp, where only widows and their children lived, community projects were destroyed and the inhabitants chased away. Political and religious leaders did not approve of community participation for Afghan women.

Radda Barnen's project tried another approach, one that was less direct and ultimately more effective: community workers recruited men to form social welfare committees that were put in charge of all community-based action. Ideas to help children surfaced, and playgrounds and schools were set up. Libraries were built where the group could meet and where the children could hear traditional stories. Eventually the men saw that their wives needed to be involved in the work to support and help their children. The women saw the value of the committees and wanted similar committees to deal with female matters. Men, in turn, selected the women who could participate. Women became teachers in schools, child-care and preschool workers, trainers in sewing and soap making projects, and community health workers.

Informal networks of related women devised a system for going visiting one another without entering the streets; they used ladders to connect their homes. Mobile medical teams with women health promoters and women-only clinics helped to surmount the cultural barriers that had limited women's access to health and psychological care. Elderly women, who had more freedom to move around and to express their opinions, proved to be valuable resources as health and mental health promoters. Some of these groups and associations have continued to play vital roles in their villages after their members repatriated to Afghanistan.

Comprehensive-Integrated Programs

Comprehensive-integrated programs implement a package of services apart from purely psychosocial ones and are based on a broader consideration of the children's and the community's multiple needs. Psychosocial components have been integrated into broad-based economic development and employment initiatives, housing and agricultural programs, and education and job training projects. Programs such as these usually are coordinated by various groups within and outside the community.

In Mozambique, the Project on Children and War has evolved from a center-based program into a more comprehensive and integrated response to the estimated 200,000 children who either "do not know the whereabouts of their parents or have suffered the terrible trauma of watching their execution or their death" (UNICEF, 1989). Since there were no trained mental health specialists in Mozambique, the Project on Children and War began its work by finding and training individuals within the Ministries of Health and Education and the Organization of Mozambican Women (OMM), who seemed to have an aptitude for work with war-affected children. After a series of training workshops, national participants were assigned to twenty-five war-affected districts of Mozambique, where they taught an additional five hundred paraprofessionals and local volunteers how to use sociodrama, dance, oral history, and art to help children cope with the consequences of trauma.

The Project on Children and War also brought together representatives of government agencies and nongovernmental organizations (NGOs) to examine how to mount an effective family tracing and reunification program. The object was to use members of community associations as core components of a national tracing program that would be linked through the National Directorate of Social Action (DNAS) tracing teams and a computerized information system. Procedures also were developed to identify, document, search for, reunite, and provide follow-up services for unaccompanied children and lost family members.

As the project extended its activities throughout Mozambique and into refugee settlements in Malawi and Zimbabwe, its staff identified additional ways to locate unaccompanied children and search for lost family members. The tracing networks were expanded to include people who had escaped from zones controlled by RENAMO (the guerrilla force fighting the government) and who had assumed responsibility for seeking out relatives of other kidnapped or impressed people. They also added chiefs and traditional healers, because they are often the first to be consulted when family members are separated.

Central to this response to war-affected children is a broader package of support to help stabilize *deslocado* (displaced) communities and promote family and foster family care. Preschools, vocational training, mentor and skills-for-life programs, and water and agricultural projects have been initiated in communities that have been willing to absorb large numbers of orphans and unaccompanied children. Today, more than 15,000 community leaders and volunteers supported by 700 national and international organizations have helped to locate and reintegrate more than 30,000 unaccompanied children with their families and communities. Many local volunteers also are the primary implementers of community-based foster care, primary mental health care, and vocational training programs.

How One Child Soldier Was Helped

> Every morning I wake up and remember the dreams from the night before. I always see my mother's face and it is looking at me. When I think about these dreams I get sad. Then I get angry. Then I start to fight with the other boys.

Tomas was six when his ordeal began. He was at the river. He was grabbed and shoved up the path toward his village. First, he was forced to set his family's hut afire. Then he watched as guerrilla soldiers cut off his parents' heads and impaled them on stakes. Around the staring head of Tomas' mother, the soldier wrapped a Mozambican flag. "This," he was told, "is what the government buys you."

During the Lhanguene training, participants learned how Tomas and most of the other children had retained frightening images or memories of their worst moments as former combatants. Each child remembered a particular event—the cutting of a throat, the scream of a brother, the burning of one's home—that was especially traumatic. Encouraging the child to speak about this almost unspeakable moment was one of the first steps toward recovery.

Tomas' worst moment was the sight of his mother's head stuck on a post, an image that fueled his aggressive behavior. By the time he had reached Lhanguene, Tomas had stopped talking. Through drawing and quiet conversation with a gifted Mozambican social worker, Tomas managed to share his "worst moment." By recalling dreams of his mother's face, Tomas began to understand how his past was affecting his fighting with other boys.

The training of the Lhanguene caregivers incorporated traditional Mozambican practices as well as Western psychological techniques. Storytelling, dance, theater or sociodrama, and art were adapted for therapeutic purposes. They were used to encourage children to express and come to terms with the terrible events

they had experienced. Folk healers, who had been excluded from the government's health care efforts, also played an essential role in the healing. Through
bereavement ceremonies, children were able to process the horrific events morally and psychologically.

Tomas' treatment involved a sociodrama, in which the events of his ordeal
were reenacted by children at the center, each assuming the role of an assailant,
victim, or liberator. Another child played the role of Tomas so that Tomas himself
had an opportunity to view the events through the eyes of someone else. The
child also articulated two troubling refrains that preoccupied Tomas: his guilt
over failing to protect his parents and his fear and anger over having been abandoned in such an awful world. After the drama, the children talked about their
experiences. In this way Tomas' peers were able to help him understand that he
was not responsible for what had happened.

But the most important factor in Tomas' recovery was a slowly formed
relationship with a Mozambican woman who volunteered to work with him. At
first he screamed at her, then he was willing to sit in her lap and let her comb his
hair. A relationship of trust grew, in which the woman continued to care for
Tomas and gave him the chance to experience once again a constructive relationship with an adult. Staff members encouraged caretakers in group meetings to
understand that Tomas and many other children would become symptomatic at
the point of attachment to them. That is, as trust in and attachment to the
caretaker grew, the overtly aggressive behavior diminished and the child manifested signs of anxiety, guilt, and sadness, including such symptoms as phobias,
compulsions, and bed-wetting. Such a shift signals an increased ability on the part
of the child to tolerate and experience painful feelings, instead of exhibiting
destructive actions as a way of warding off pain—a pathway toward a better
resolution of the child's conflicts. Most caretakers, in turn, were able to weather
what was typically two to three months of problematic behavior.

Community-Managed Programs

Community-managed and -directed programs are based on a model of a
self-reliant community where residents of a local area identify their own problems, select their own project workers, evaluate their programs, and make their
own decisions about the program's future. They are the most participatory of
intervention types: all of the actors involved in projects are also recipients. No
one is employed just to provide services or to reach others.

The UNICEF-supported Triangulo Ixchil Program in Guatemala is a response
to a specific context and way of life (Richenberg, 1994). The program focuses on
enhancing the self-esteem of parents and other community members in an effort
to address racism and oppression against an indigenous people. The decision to
promote self-esteem through a range of program components was reached because the indigenous population in Guatemala has been subjected to extreme

racism and, as a group, was targeted during the war. According to local leaders, this resulted in negative individual and communal self-images that have kept indigenous people from moving forward. It was deemed necessary to change self-esteem in order to enable indigenous people to progress socially and econom-ically.

In spite of the constraints of war and the suppression of democratic initia-tives, the program works to connect self-esteem to both empowerment and community mobilization. The program also encourages teachers, youth workers, and other community actors to develop the self-confidence needed to monitor and make decisions about their respective programs.

The Triangulo Ixchil Program operates in sixty-four communities in three municipalities of Ixchil in Guatemala. It provides training to 160 community youth promoters and 215 primary school teachers who, together, work with more than 12,000 children. The main components of the program include psy-chosocial rehabilitation, education, vocational training, educational scholarships, and income-generating activities. Empowerment is a core element of all training inputs for primary school teachers and community youth promoters. "I can, I count, I am worthy" is a refrain integrated into the combination of indigenous and Western traditions that provide content for training modules.

Project workers also targeted the main actor in the recovery effort—the teenagers themselves—who were recruited as community youth promoters (CYPs). They received training that improved their skills, rehabilitation services that fostered psychological healing, and support in organizing activities for younger children and families. Clear goals were set so that the community could judge progress. Goal one was to improve the quality of life and the educational opportunities for teenagers. The second goal was to increase school enrollment and improve development opportunities for younger children. Goal three was to rebuild the community's cultural identity and members' self-esteem.

The teenagers' action plan was to:

- work with younger out-of-school children to organize recreation and solve problems that prevented school attendance;
- help parents increase their participation in children's activities, assess their children's school attendance, and create opportunities to foster self-worth in both children and parents.
- solve their peer group's problems related to working conditions, educa-tional opportunities, and self-worth;
- reconstruct the history of the area to help inhabitants heal through re-claiming personal and collective identities (teenagers collected demo-graphic and personal data through oral recollection, storytelling, and map drawing);
- participate in training workshops to improve skills and performance.

The three-day training sessions, led by a psychologist and one or two full-time social promoters and held every five weeks, were critical to the success of the project. Content was driven by the CYPs based on previous sessions and on problems encountered during the five weeks of community action. One day of training was devoted to healing. The CYPs shared their thoughts and feelings, desires and disappointments, needs and hopes. In addition to discussion, such activities as role-playing, drawing, and plays contributed to healing. At first, CYPs expressed shame. They thought that something must be wrong with them, their parents, and the Ixiles in general to have been the target of such violence. Slowly they came to understand that genocide is never deserved.

The other two days of training were spent developing skills. The CYPs learned how to ask questions, draw maps, collect and organize information, plan group activities, motivate young children to learn, make decisions, solve problems, and lead. Problems that arose out of the prior five weeks of community work were addressed; in this way the teenagers conducted their own ongoing assessment and used it to improve their work.

Among the Ixiles, school attendance has shot up. While none of the CYPs was in school when the project began, 40 percent are now attending either primary or secondary grades. The remainder are involved in a variety of vocational and informal educational programs. Of the younger children, 400 (or 10 percent) more attend school. Self-image among the teenagers has improved as the community now seeks their help. Village leaders have invited CYPs to join development councils, and new villages are requesting their services. Parents committees have been formed in one-third of the schools, and three new schools were set up. Cultural identity has been strengthened. The collection of oral histories and traditional legends has spurred some CYPs to learn to read and write in their own language, even though Ixil has been used traditionally only for oral communication. Traditional musical instruments can be heard at village festivals, where before none were played.

A Comparative Perspective

Although the programs described above differ in conceptualization, approach, and activities, two common premises undergird their development. First, the leaders of these programs see the psychosocial needs of children as intrinsic to human growth and development. Factors such as loving relationships with primary caretakers, the possibility of developing meaningful peer relationships, the opportunity to derive both cognitive and affective stimulation from the immediate environment, and a chance to identify with and absorb elements of one's culture are needs of primary importance. They must be investigated, understood, and responded to within larger efforts to provide food, shelter, and medical care.

Second, the leaders of these programs believe that assisting war-affected and displaced people requires recognizing them as active and capable, both individually and as communities. It means understanding that they can, and do, work to solve their own problems and meet their own needs. Yet within war-affected, displaced populations there are "vulnerable" individuals who are less able to meet their own needs and who may benefit least from assistance aimed at the at-large group. Still, it is important to realize that this vulnerability often results from the weakening or absence of family, community, and other social support systems. Effective assistance to vulnerable individuals—unaccompanied children, rape victims, child soldiers, marginalized youth—needs to be based on thoughtful initiatives that maximize the participation not only of indigenous project staff but of truly grassroots social networks and institutions as well. Along with increasing community capacities to respond to the scale of problems, grassroots participation also appears to enhance normal coping processes among "victims," build self-esteem, decrease programmatic costs, and promote self-sufficiency.

Identifying Community Resources

How did nongovernmental and international organizations help to catalyze or support this community action strategy? What did they have to offer? How did they train staff, develop programs, and evaluate the results of these initiatives? How can lessons learned at the micro level be translated into programmatic guidelines at the macro level?

The staff of these organizations worked hard to identify and build upon existing community resources. For example, they distinguished between indigenous organizations that *draw* upon community resources and those that are merely *in* the community. Some community clinics, for instance, provide the same services in pretty much the same way as traditional clinics and hospitals. What need to be identified are groups that are rooted in the communities they serve, organizations that rely on the residents of a local area to identify their own problems, select their own project workers, evaluate programs, and make decisions about the program's future.

The staff members also learn to build on community resources by identifying individuals who are already involved in specific interventions and by documenting what they did and how they did it. Natural networks are not overlooked. Schools are used for many preventive, emergency, and rehabilitation actions. Universities also are encouraged to incorporate practical uses of psychology, social work, anthropology, and education into their programs and courses. Religious institutions are used to promote conflict negotiation and other humanitarian efforts because in indigenous communities healing often takes place through rituals, prayer, meditation, cultural activities, drama, song, and games. Thus a focus on spiritual healing is more relevant to many communities than Western psychotherapy or "talk it out" interventions.

Enhancing Participation

Several programs have activities that encourage the communities they work with to identify their own needs, make decisions, and establish mechanisms to meet those needs—commitments that are built into many project activities. Community members, for example, are involved in initial needs assessments, and in some cases, the needs assessment itself is envisioned as a means of recruiting mothers, fathers, single parents, and other community members into collective examinations of how to protect and promote the psychosocial well-being of children.

Some programs also are designed to examine community leadership issues. Whom does the leadership represent, and how does it do so? Is the leadership paternalistic or solely professional, limiting the prospects of wider participation of various groups in the community? How does leadership respond to the needs of children, families, single-parent families, and orphans? What changes have taken place in existing structures since the crisis, and do these changes benefit only professionals, or do they extend to the wider community? An understanding of local leadership dynamics is important to the development of child-focused, gender-sensitive initiatives.

Another benchmark of community mobilization is the emergence of hidden resources within the community. Traditional leaders, spiritual healers, midwives, village court systems, educators, and others have often come forward to create and carry out child-focused solutions. In Mozambique, for instance, healers helped to exorcise harmful spirits from former combatants, and local groups organized to locate the families of unaccompanied children. The absence of emergent local leaders and volunteers may mean that a project has failed to create a shared vision within the community itself.

The Role of Specialists and Training

All of these programs employ professionals with solid child development or mental health backgrounds. Several programs also benefit from individuals with training or practical experience in the broader domestic and international concerns that affect policy formation in their respective contexts. But what distinguishes the principal leaders of these programs as a group is their perception of themselves as facilitators of community action rather than as professionals who develop discrete programs.

This perspective is evident in the training modules developed by these individuals. The basic premise of these training modules is the need to impart knowledge and task-related skills for interventions among groups and communities without specialist psychotherapeutic or child development backgrounds. This knowledge contains sophisticated content related to (1) the needs of children, childhood development, and the skills necessary for empathetic communication with children, their families, and their communities; (2) provisions for adaptive responses to the care of children; (3) identification of and care for high-risk groups; and (4) necessary skills for working with other agencies and networks involved in the lives of children. But the basic mental and social health messages are delivered in simple and practical ways.

Program staff and community members also work together to identify local participants and define specific training objectives. Clear definitions of skills to be acquired and specific tasks to be performed are related to concrete, child-focused, or family-focused outcomes. Training sessions, in turn, are participatory rather than didactic. The training task is not only to impart new information but also to draw on the experiences of participants in ways that foster their problem-solving skills. Experiential learning exercises and field experiences are important to the application of problem-solving skills. Training is thus envisioned as yet another mechanism to promote community strengths and to avoid dependency on the mental health specialists.

The Role of Evaluation and Research

Evaluation and research also are viewed in practical terms—as forms of social communication among helpers and the communities they seek to help. Comparative studies of what works, with whom, how, and why are critical to efforts to improve collective responses for children and families. The establishment of organizational infrastructures for evaluation and research that promotes better communication among practitioners, policy makers, and researchers is thus a high priority.

Evaluations are explicit about program objectives, activities, and results. This means that each program has a theory about how it is supposed to work. This theory-driven approach does not mean adopting a top-down evaluation strategy. On the contrary, the changes in processes and outcomes desired and, ultimately, the goals and objectives of the program are arrived at through a participatory process with the community. By focusing on questions—What are we trying to achieve? and Is there evidence that we are achieving our objectives?—we are able to attend to the basic and fundamental realities faced by children, families, and communities. Training programs, for example, are evaluated from three interrelated perspectives: (1) Do they increase helpers' skills? (2) Do helpers apply these skills in their communities? (3) Does the application of these skills make a measurable difference in the lives of children and families? In this way, the relationship between activities (training), change in process (new skills and strategies), and change in outcome (children / families) is examined.

The staff members of several programs have found a worldview to be crucial to the development of relevant individual assessments and diagnostic outcomes. They note that indigenous healers and spiritualists have taxonomies of illness that differ from those of Western mental health specialists and that health-seeking behavior is based on culture-specific symptoms, not post-traumatic stress disorder symptoms. This is why the staff members and consultants of these programs have shifted away from the conventions of Western diagnosis in favor of social adaptation and functioning models.

From this vantage point, symptoms are not the focus of assessment or outcome measures. Instead, the principal interest is: Can the child or caretaker function? Can a child go to school and learn? How is the child getting along with friends? How is the child's physical health? A child's descriptions of suffering, physical illness, feeling well or sick, for example, are also employed to gauge adaptation that, over time, has led to important information and insights about the work that is being done.

The workers behind many of these projects believe that the major responsibility for data collection should lie with community members. Conventional evaluation reports often use professional terms and statistics that community members cannot understand. In a participatory approach, evaluation findings should emerge in terms understandable to the community; in this way, evaluation increases the community abilities to make decisions and manage their lives.

The Guatemala program, for instance, used focus groups for collecting information about project impact. These groups set goals that were appropriate for this particular culture and for the developmental stages of their children. In the beginning, program staff asked parents about the kinds of problems they were having with their children and what changes they would like to see. Because parents set the criteria, they were culturally appropriate. The parents also were involved in monitoring and evaluating what had been made.

Leadership and Interagency Cooperation

Identifying and building on community networks are difficult. In many conflicts, there is a polarization of the civilian population that reaches into governmental, nongovernmental, and religious institutions. Different political agendas and goals among actual or potential political counterparts pose serious but not insurmountable problems. In these contexts, the staff members of the community programs we have discussed support reconciliation and cooperation by identifying shared goals among community groups and encouraging members of these groups to first work together in limited ways on selected points of agreement. Such efforts are needed to forge the multi-institutional coalitions required to address complex problems in complex situations.

Several programs also have become leaders in forging broader coalitions of governmental, nongovernmental, and international organizations to examine and collectively act on important policy, human rights, and programmatic concerns in their respective situations. In southern Africa, for example, the Project on Children and War has been instrumental in establishing the Sub-Regional Child Policy and Advocacy Group, consisting of senior staff members, policy makers, and researchers from forty organizations, including universities and child welfare agencies in Mozambique, Malawi, and Zimbabwe. The group meets quarterly to identify and prioritize key issues, recommendations, actions, and contingency plans for children inside Mozambique as well as in neighboring countries. Assumption of this responsibility has facilitated both interagency and cross-border relationships, training programs, and interventions that have proved to be especially important during the post-conflict and repatriation period.

Conclusion

There are many ways to promote the psychological and social well-being of children. The projects reviewed in this chapter range from helping especially vulnerable groups, such as child soldiers and unaccompanied children, to initiating community development, such as locally managed credit unions and vocational training. None of them represents a comprehensive response to children in war and refugee crises. While some communities and groups of children have benefited from these pioneering efforts, many more have gone wanting. The many responsibilities involved in the protection and care of war-affected and displaced children need to be shared among many more relief and development organizations than are involved in any of today's war or refugee situations.

Nonetheless, all these programs can be adapted to local and changing realities. For example, what began as a center-based effort in Mozambique evolved into grassroots development. In the West Bank and Jerusalem, workers shifted from delivering traditional clinical services to developing human capacities.

In this sense, all these projects began with preconceptions rather than a shared community vision. Their ultimate effectiveness was the result of shedding the preconceptions and engaging the community. It is hoped that new programs will start far beyond where these began.

REFERENCES

Blanc, C. S. 1994. *Urban children in distress: Global predicaments and innovative strategies.* Florence: United Nations Children's Fund.

Boothby, N., Upton, P., and Sultan, A. 1991. *Children of Mozambique: The cost of survival.* Washington, D.C.: U.S. Committee for Refugees.

Forbes-Martin, S. 1994. Policy perspective on mental health assistance to refugees. In A. Marsella, T. Borneman, and E. Ekblad, eds., *Amidst peril and pain: The mental health and well-being of the world's refugees.* Washington, D.C.: American Psychological Association.

Leyens, J. P., and Mahjoub, A. 1989. The mental health of refugee children exposed to violent environments. Unpublished project proposal by the Refugee Studies Programme, Oxford University.

Ortiz, R. 1994. Building a holistic safety net for CSAC: How the Kapatrian Programme mobilizes Filipino communities for psychosocial care. Case study prepared for the Southern African Training and Research Initiative, available through SATARI at the Terry Sanford Institute of Public Policy, Duke University.

Richenberg, D. 1994. The Triangulo Ixchil Program for war-affected children in Guatemala. Case study prepared for SATARI.

Ronstrom, A. 1994. Afghan children: Invisible, forgotten, traumatized. Case study prepared for SATARI.

SATARI. 1993. Repatriation of vulnerable groups: Field based planning and coordination workshop.

Timberlake, L. 1986. *Africa in crisis.* London: Earthscan.

UNICEF. 1989. *Children on the front line—1989 Update.* New York: UNICEF Annual Report—Mozambique.

CHAPTER NINE

Attempting to Overcome the Intergenerational Transmission of Trauma

Dialogue Between Descendants of Victims and of Perpetrators

DAN BAR-ON

The preceding chapters are all premised on the continuous interdependence of the fate of the traumatized child and that of the family and society. This chapter extends the awareness of "horizontal" interdependence—that is, interdependence at any given point in time—to "vertical" interdependence of the generations, both those antecedent to the child and those that the child will beget. Dan Bar-On, a psychologist whose family left Germany for Israel in the early Hitler years, has devoted much of his professional energy to studying the transgenerational impact of trauma and the attempts to heal the trauma. He is thus among a cadre of mental health professionals who have studied these issues in relation to Holocaust survivors and their descendants. By far the majority of work on the intergenerational effects of war has been done in relation to survivors of the Nazi Holocaust. (Notable exceptions are Legaretta's 1985 study of the Basque children sent abroad during the Spanish Civil War and Dalianis' 1994 study of Greek children imprisoned as infants with their mothers during the Greek civil war.) One explanation for the relative paucity of such studies lies in the all-too-human wish to forget. But unless one tries to work through the experience, there is no incentive to make profound changes in the regulation of aggression and hatred.

Bar-On's contribution is important not only because of the depth and detail of the data he has collected but also because he has researched both the "downward" transmission of trauma and the "upward" transmission of healing and transformation from the younger to the older generations. His work has helped to delineate the complex ways that parental suffering and parental crimes affect children. No simple formulation accounts for the variety of outcomes in subsequent generations. But Bar-On's data are based not only on interviews but also on attempts to intervene—to interrupt and repair the process of intergenerational transmission. His detailed study of dialogue groups of children of Nazi perpetrators and children of Nazi victims provides major insights into processes that have hitherto been subsumed under such rubrics as "guilt of the survivor" or the assumption that children have incorporated the unspeakable burdens of their damaged parents. His work forces us to confront terms that are unusual in psychological and psychotherapeutic discourse, such as forgiveness and reconciliation, and to come to terms not only with one's own enemies but also with those who have been enemies of loved ones, perhaps for many generations. The enormous psychic pain in these dialogues, and the enormous psychic gains that can be achieved through them, should encourage us to attempt such meetings elsewhere.

In many ways, Bar-On's work is part of a movement in psychology and development that emphasizes studying salutogenic as well as pathogenic elements in experience, and understanding their interplay. Thus, we are left with the distinct impression that in studying the intergenerational transmission of trauma we are dealing with the most terrifyingly pessimistic aspects of human psychology and with some of the most astonishingly affirmative and reparative capacities of the human psyche.

Many readers will be reminded of the recent studies growing out of attachment theory and psychoanalytic theory on the transmission from mother to child of patterns of attachment, including pathological and destructive forms (Fonagy et al., 1993; Main, 1993). The pioneering experimental work of John Bowlby and Mary Ainsworth on attachment and of Selma Fraiberg on mothers at risk for battering their infants— "the ghosts in the nursery"—stimulated these researchers (see Fonagy et al., 1993). Thus, there is a growing body of thought and data that can in time unify studies of intrafamilial trauma with studies of the massive trauma of war, persecution, and chronic murderous violence.

The psychological literature on the transgenerational aftereffects of trauma relates mostly to the lot of the descendants of survivors (Krystal, 1968; Barocas and Barocas, 1979; Kestenberg, 1972; Davidson, 1980; Danieli, 1988; Vardi, 1990).[1]

1. I am grateful to the Board of Education of NordRhein Westfalia and the German Federal Foreign Ministry for their generous support and to Professor David Greenwood and the Center for International Studies at Cornell University for their donation, which supported the first encounter. I use the term *descendants* instead of *children* because these people are grownups in their own right. The term *offspring* sounded too biological to me; in this context one should be wary of biological connotations.

Many of these reports reveal that the "survivors' syndrome" was transmitted to the children mainly through a "conspiracy of silence." Children of survivors had to fill the emotional vacuum left by their parents' difficulty in confronting their Holocaust past. Many of these reports rely heavily on clinical samples, though we know that most of the families of survivors did not seek therapy (Reick and Eitinger, 1983). Also, psychopathological conceptualizations have been used to account for post-traumatic effects without clarifying the differences between these effects and the usual pathologies and normal reactions to traumatic events (Albeck, 1994).

Lately, these somewhat mechanical conclusions have been replaced by more sophisticated models, which assume a diversification of reactions (Danieli, 1983), predicaments rather than disorder (Albeck, 1994), and "shattered assumptions" (Janoff-Bulman, 1992). For example, Janoff-Bulman has suggested that most people grow up with positive assumptions about the benevolence of the world and with positive self-esteem. The trauma shatters these assumptions, breaking the relationship to oneself and the world. Only through a social or therapeutic process that enables the traumatized person to reestablish positive assumptions can he or she find a way to live with the traumatic event (Lehman, Wortman, and Williams, 1987).

In a study my students and I tried to identify transgenerational transmission of trauma through narrative-analysis of the life stories of three generations of Holocaust survivors' families in Israel (Bar-On, 1995). We found that the third generation introduced a new dimension in many of these families. The grandchildren created a healing effect by developing an independent dialogue with the aging survivors, and the untold traumatic fear was reframed into a told story by grandparents. Also, the second generation was found to play a much more active and innovative role than was described in earlier publications, navigating their family life between their survivor-parents and their own children.

There is little professional literature so far on the aftereffects of these events on the descendants of the Nazi perpetrators. Have they been traumatized by their parents' atrocities during the Nazi era? Has this trauma been transmitted to them through a "conspiracy of silence"? How and to what extent did they confront and work through this burden (Hardtmann, 1996; Sichrovsky, 1988; Rosenthal, 1989; Bar-On, 1989, 1990, 1992)? What happens to people who learn that a beloved father was a mass murderer during the Nazi era? How do they live with and work through such unbearable discrepancies within their identity?

Interestingly, the family past of both survivors and perpetrators has been silenced by the therapeutic community (Heimannsberg and Schmidt, 1993; Danieli, 1988). It took this community some time to identify the transgenerational transmission of trauma and to try to help individuals and collectivities work through it (Kestenberg, 1972; Davidson, 1980; Vardi, 1990; Hardtmann, 1996). The "double wall" phenomenon (Bar-On, 1995) could be identified not only between the survivor-parents and their children but also between patients and therapists.[2] In both cases there was difficulty in accepting the "others" who survived and their descendants as part of oneself.

For emotional and political reasons, few attempts have been made to find similarities or differences in transgenerational aftereffects experienced by the two sides of this man-made catastrophe. Until 1990 one could not even imagine a discourse between these two, and the idea of trying to create a process of reconciliation would simply have been rejected as a "sin" (Bar-On, 1989).

In this chapter I attempt to move beyond that point. My work is based on the assumption that reconciliation of the first generation is not possible (Dorff, 1992): the perpetrators and survivors of the Holocaust cannot confront each other genuinely, especially as so few people survived the extermination. The descendants of the victims and the victimizers, however, who had faced this traumatic part of their family biography, could now test the possibility of a "secondary reconciliation," or at least an open dialogue between the two sides. Their encounter may enhance the prospects for a genuine discourse necessary for establishing a bond between their people, as part of their own moral, emotional, and psychological growth.

Before presenting the three encounters of our group, I will address three general issues: (1) the question of normalization versus normalcy after the Holocaust; (2) the transgenerational psychological literature of the Holocaust; and (3) the issue of asymmetry and reconciliation between Germans and Jews.

Normalization versus Normalcy

Immediately after the Holocaust, survivors, perpetrators, and bystanders all tried to normalize life by repressing the horrors of the event and their psychological aftermath. In this context, normalization actually meant that the meaning of psychological normalcy was blurred. Who was more "normal" after surviving Auschwitz: the person who could not sleep at night, who heard voices of Nazis everywhere, or the person who went back to business as usual? On the perpetrators' side, what did normalcy mean—adjusting to postwar German society, or breaking down under the load of memories of the atrocities perpetrated (Bar-On, 1994)? Normalization and its pseudo-discourse became functional in the immediate sense: people could function in the postwar society without constantly relating to the past. But normalization also implied that the less immediate psychological processes—mourning the dead, working through the helplessness and the aggression, redefining one's moral self, reestablishing trust and faith in

2. The double wall phenomenon suggests that silencing in the family is supported mutually: parents do not tell, and children do not ask. And when one side does open a window in this wall, it is usually confronted with the other's wall. We have found almost no spontaneous incidents of both parties opening windows simultaneously, allowing the feelings of both parents or children to be mutually presented and accepted.

oneself and others—all had to be postponed for better times. In the unfavorable social conditions of postwar society, this meant deferring the working-through to the following generations.

The failure to deal with such basic issues means that the Holocaust, aside from causing the death of millions and pain and suffering for many more, broke a basic human bond: the possibility of human beings' having faith in each other, having faith in their right to exist (Janoff-Bulman, 1992). The breaking of this bond meant that no genuine discourse could develop between these groups (Bar-On, 1994). To rebuild such trust is far more difficult than to reestablish the separate physical existence of both groups, though that effort in itself consumed the energy of the first generation of survivors. However, the descendants of the survivors and perpetrators of the Holocaust may have reached a stage of physical security that enables them to work through their parents' survivor psychology, thereby entering the deeper and more difficult domain of going beyond their "tribal identity," of bridging the broken human bond.

The Transgenerational Aftereffects of the Holocaust: An Overview of the Literature

Most of the psychological studies on the long-range effects of the Holocaust focus on the second generation, which is perceived as having been influenced and activated by events experienced by their parents many years earlier. This focus was a breakthrough, for earlier research and therapies ignored the possibility of such long-range effects (Danieli, 1980). But the results were not as clear as one would expect (Albeck, 1994), and the argument developed mainly along two partially overlapping dimensions: the clinical-research dimension and the dimension of "negative" versus "positive" effects.

The discussion concerning the first dimension derived from clinical studies that identified long-range effects on the second generation. For example, children of Holocaust survivors were described as having difficulties with individuation (emotional independence), suffering from identification with the aggressor or from psychic numbing, or showing a stronger achievement need (Kestenberg, 1972; Krystal, 1968). These findings, based primarily on clinical reports, were not confirmed when random sampling was used, including control groups (Reick and Eitinger, 1983). It is unclear whether the instruments used in the controlled studies were sensitive enough to test the effects found in the therapy, or whether the results found in clinical self-selected samples were not valid for the population at large (Albeck, 1994).

Regarding the second dimension, clinicians tended to assert that the second generation suffered from the burden of the Holocaust that their parents had transmitted. In spite or because of their parents' silence, the children grew up with a fearful, cautious stance toward the world, which they viewed as hostile. One study shows that children of Holocaust survivors who suffered from battle shock in the war with Lebanon did not adjust to daily life as well as did a control group (Solomon, 1983). Other researchers pointed out the positive achievement-oriented response and suggested that the descendants had a better ability to cope with current problems precisely because they were children of Holocaust survivors. Studies show that members of the second generation achieve higher economic and educational accomplishments than those of western origin whose parents were not involved in the Holocaust (Reick and Eitinger, 1983). This argument overlaps with the argument in the first dimension. As a rule, clinicians present more data about negative aftereffects. Researchers who conducted controlled studies usually showed a lack of effect, or even a relative advantage of having a Holocaust-survivor parent.

Another line of studies, which is based on more complex assertions and on trying to overcome the contradiction between clinicians and researchers, suggests interpersonal differences. For example, Danieli (1988) categorized the second-generation's reactions according to their parents' objective experiences during the Holocaust (camp survivors as opposed to partisans) and their own subjective type of coping (fighting versus resignation). In another study, Vardi (1990) stated that families of Holocaust survivors "chose" one child to fulfill the role of a memorial candle. It is this child who carried the emotional burden that the parents had not worked through. According to Vardi, the child designated as the memorial candle is the one who generally seeks therapy because he or she is more burdened than the other children.

These categorizations and diagnoses helped clinicians to choose effective forms of therapy for their work with families of Holocaust survivors and to evaluate the prognosis. However, the categories did not always help us to understand the phenomenon of intergenerational transmission in the shadow of the Holocaust (Albeck, 1994). Indeed, as we have noted, most Holocaust survivors and their families did not seek therapy. How did they deal with similar traumatic burdens? If one assumes that they succeeded in developing a normalization of these emotional burdens (Rosenthal, 1987), the question then is posed: When is normalization a proof of competent functioning, and when does it indicate malfunctioning that is passed from generation to generation? Did working-through processes develop spontaneously, outside the frame of therapy? How are they similar to or different from the working-through patterns initiated by therapists?

It may have been the primary wish of most survivors to quickly attain normalization after the Holocaust. One could call this wish both functional and dysfunctional. It helped the survivors to return to normal life, to avoid the burdens and frightful memories of the past as they performed everyday functions in the present. But normalization could become dysfunctional, as the survivors avoided a psychological mourning process and thereby became fixated in the past (Davidson, 1980). Adherents to this approach accept that normalization is a "normal" reaction to an abnormal, extreme life event but assume that survivors or their descendants *should* be able to go beyond normalization by developing a genuine strategy, working through the past (Vardi, 1990). This is still a strong normative approach. But how can we actually know how survivors developed normalization strategies differently (or more extensively) than did other émigrés to Israel or the United States? Did immigrants from Asian countries not use normalization strategies in order to overcome the emotional burden of being uprooted? Did people born in Israel not have to develop normalization strategies while fighting in the 1948 war of independence? What was the unique quality of the normalization processes of Holocaust survivors and their families?

Second, how do we know whether normalization implied hope for a better future or was mainly a way to control the fears and memories of the past? Perhaps we should look for better answers to these questions by softer conceptualizations, analyzing the narrations of survivors, describing their life stories.[3] For example, can traces of fear and hope be recognized in the biographical reconstructions of these interviewees? Did their descendants internalize the parents' normalization strategies? Will those descendants express in their own biographical reconstructions the same feelings of burden or relief, fear or hope? I believe that if we can find answers to some of these questions we may better understand the link between normalization strategies and the working-through of traumatic events like the Holocaust and its intergenerational effects (Bar-On, 1994).

The reason for moving toward softer concepts is derived principally from our inability to isolate processes and study them separately. In fact, every researcher into intergenerational transmission has to deal with four interwoven processes that affected their interviewees simultaneously. These processes, which are part of the burden that survivors carry with them from the Holocaust, are the uprooting brought on by emigration, the immigration into a new culture, specific family processes, and personal processes. I will show how these processes are interwoven.

To begin with, most of the Holocaust survivors left their homeland. Emigration takes a psychological toll: separation from family, tradition, culture, language, and childhood home. Rarely does it allow gradual parting—moving back and forth between the émigré's imagination and reality, testing the old and new until the final choice matures—to suit the dynamics of the psychological working-through. For example, Aronian (1990) showed that Poles who immigrated to the United States acclimated better to their new culture only after they had revisited their homeland. In Israel this type of emigration is called "luxurious."

But most emigration is characterized by a final, onetime severance, without the objective possibility or subjective desire to reexamine life in the original context. Psychologists suggest that in such cases, difficulties in the working-

3. The use of "strong" and "soft" conceptualization relates to the assumptions underlying research methods (Schon, 1983). Under strong assumptions one can expect to find answers concerning the ultimate truth. Under softer assumptions one will tend to rely heavily on the meaning-making of the subjects themselves, as no single ultimate truth can be defined (Bar-On, in preparation).

through process arise. The abruptness of the severance makes the separation more difficult to accept. And even though the émigrés become involved in their new reality, the old one persists in their repressed or unconscious thoughts (Bar-On, 1986). We differentiate between compulsive severance and severance by choice, and the essence of *aliyah* (literally *ascent,* the word used for immigration to Israel) reflects the atmosphere that surrounds severance by choice.

For survivors of the Holocaust, compulsive severance did not begin with emigration but rather ended with it. Most were compelled to sever ties with their points of origin violently and unexpectedly, while they were still within their home context. This severance usually caught them unprepared for emigration and in life-threatening danger, so it became extremely traumatic. Keilson (1992) refers to three stages of traumatization that Holocaust orphans experienced: separation from their family (parents, children, spouses, wider family network), survival during the war, and return to "what no longer existed" at the end of the war. He asserts that the final stage was the most traumatic, because by then many of the orphans understood the irreversibility of what had happened: everything dear to them was lost forever.

For many survivors, emigration from Europe became not just an act of severance (that had already occurred) or of leave-taking (most people did not have anything to part from) but also a *corrective act,* an attempt at "rebuilding life," making a new start, erasing or forgetting what had happened. Emigration was, in fact, an expression of strength. At this stage the survivors did not concern themselves with how and when they would deal with taking leave of what had been lost. They had to prove to themselves and to others that they were capable of living, and not just by physical and technical standards.

The familial process has to be added both to emigration and to the process of adapting to the new values of the absorbing society. Families have patterns of confronting external and internal family pressures (Cohler and Grunebaum, 1981). This is especially apparent in relation to emigration and changes in social values. According to Bar-Semech (1990), a pattern involves four central axes: continuation of the family's origin as opposed to inventiveness based on the changing norms of the environment, closeness and intimacy as opposed to independence and loneliness, investment in personal growth as opposed to investment in group cohesiveness, and symmetry, which may turn into competition between the spouses as opposed to complementary relations between them.

Each family has its own timetable: the progression of births, weddings, old age, death—all the events that bind families together. The family has been defined as a unique system that one can join only through birth and marriage and leave only through death or divorce (Carter and McGoldrick, 1988; Chang, 1991). The Holocaust caught families at various stages, speeding up some timetables and disrupting others, usually irreversibly. It wiped out the possibility of a full life cycle of multigenerational families, in which daughters learn to become mothers from their own mothers, and grandchildren hear stories and get a sense of continuity from their grandparents (Cohler and Grunebaum, 1981). This happened in addition to the distortion of family timetables because of emigration, which was painful in itself.

One may hypothesize that the Holocaust caused more of the same patterns identified among other families of émigrés. But it had a qualitative influence in that it disrupted the continuity of the family context. Within a softer conceptualization, one could hypothesize that the historical events flooded the frame of the personal life story far beyond its family-bounded context (Rosenthal, 1987).

The descendants of the perpetrators usually did not go through similar acts of physical severance. But they describe the effect of their psychological uprooting, saying that they have been "poisoned" by the atrocious acts of their parents. They also were not given the chance of the corrective act of immigrating to rebuild life, but they did undergo a severe contextual value change that is imposed by the "winning" culture. The hero of the Nazi era became the criminal of the postwar era (Zizek, 1989). German identity became a disgrace rather than a source of pride. Most Germans tried to normalize their past by putting all their energies into building their postwar society (Mitscherlich and Mitscherlich, 1967).

Reconciliation and Asymmetry Between Jews and Germans

Although Jews and Germans had met on a personal basis for years and Israel and Germany had signed a reparation agreement as early as 1954, for many years no one could imagine a planned encounter between descendants of survivors and descendants of perpetrators of the Holocaust. Dorff (1992) addresses the question of whether, according to Jewish tradition and law, there is a possibility of reconciliation or forgiveness between Jews and Germans after the Holocaust. Dorff does not accept the position that such forgiveness is an act the Gentiles have to accomplish all by themselves, nor does he believe that the descendants of the victims have no right to be part of a process of reconciliation on behalf of their parents: "If we see ourselves as part of an extended corporate entity known as the Jewish people, then we, as its present members, do have the right (indeed, the responsibility) to act on behalf of the group—past, present and future—in this issue as in all others" (209). He suggests that the quality of the acts and feelings of the German people and the Catholic and Protestant churches will determine the willingness of Jews to get involved in a secondary reconciliation[4]—"specifically, evidence of recognition of the act as a violation, admission of guilt, remorse, efforts to seek forgiveness and steps to insure that the act will not happen again" (208). Dorff does not specify how one can act so that it "will not happen again." Nor does he address the question of whether it is important for the German

---

4. Primary forgiveness, according to the Talmud, can occur only between the perpetrator and the victim. Because this could not be achieved between Germans and Jews after the Holocaust, there will, according to Dorff, be a greater burden on the German people because of the nature and extent of the past violence.

people to work through the past so that they will become emotionally healthier for their own sake (Bar-On, 1990).

Dorff summarizes his argument: "Shall we forgive? That is a matter the Jewish community must still discuss. It will depend, in large measure, upon continued evidence of a Catholic (German) desire to repent. A positive Jewish response to this will probably not take place in one single moment or be universally offered by the Jews. Forgiveness will rather be achieved little by little, through joint word and action, just as personal forgiveness usually is" (214).

Dorff's discussion may account for the fact that it took me four years, after I had finished my interviews in Germany and my interviewees had established their own self-help group, to decide to offer these descendants of perpetrators the opportunity to meet a group of descendants of survivors.[5] During these four years I followed their difficult and courageous work and became convinced of the depth of their commitment (Bar-On, 1993). One might wonder what one could expect from a combined group that would be more fruitful for its members than working separately. Previous discussions showed clearly that such a combined group would have to face strong resistance, especially from the Jewish side, from people who believe that one should not forget or forgive—people who would regard such encounters as acts of recognition, especially when the descendants of the perpetrators are involved.

One answer would be the pragmatic one. Both groups very much wanted such an encounter.[6] The German self-help group showed interest in the proposal, and it was easy to find descendants of survivors in the United States and Israel who were equally eager to meet descendants of the other side. The danger was that one could get engaged in a group dynamic, creating an as-if discourse ("We feel good with each other: let's forget the past") that would put aside rather than address the discomfort of the prolonged tension between Germans and Jews and the paradoxical nature of the discourse through which undiscussable facts were transmitted from one generation to the next (Bar-On, 1994). One group might

5. The idea of bringing together children of perpetrators and children of survivors was suggested to me by Dr. Mona Weissmark in a letter written in April 1991 after she read my book *Legacy of Silence* (Harvard University Press, 1989). We could not agree on how to do this, however, and therefore went our separate ways. I had already had experience with a few of my interviewees meeting children of survivors during two conferences at the University of Wuppertal in 1988 and 1989. Also, in the German self-help group there was a Jewish member, the wife of a son of a perpetrator. In addition, I learned from Gonda Scheffel-Baars of her experience with a Dutch therapy group made up of children of collaborators and survivors, in 1989–90 (Kombi). In 1991 a group of my Israeli students studying the effects of the Holocaust met with a group of German students interested in the same subject (Bar-On, 1992). During my 1992 sabbatical in Boston I became acquainted with a German-Jewish dialogue group that had been meeting for four years. Two Jewish members of this group decided to join our group.

6. There is growing evidence that this is becoming the rule rather than the exception (Toll, 1992). My hunch is that as the survivors are dying out, their descendants are starting to express their own voice. Many of them feel a need to meet the other side as part of their own "healing process" (Work, 1993) in contrast with the ultimate demand "not to reconciliate."

fear that by sharing the other's struggle with the past, by recognizing the paradox-ical discourse on each side, a symmetry would emerge, placing the burden for the Holocaust equally on descendants of both sides and ignoring the Germans' responsibility for the atrocities. This suggests that the German members of the group might misuse the Jewish members to enable themselves to forget how the extermination process had actually happened. I will define this as the reconcilia-tion issue. Alternatively, one could envision a process in which the descendants of the survivors become the center of the group, owing to their parents' fate, and enslave descendants of the perpetrators to their own needs. This possibility had to be considered, particularly because I, a Jew, was going to facilitate these encoun-ters. I call this the asymmetry issue.

A process had to be planned to address personal, interpersonal, and inter-group issues, which are difficult to discuss in front of the "other." One could assume that members of both groups were engaged in a dialogue with a fan-tasized, idealized other. An encounter would give them an opportunity to exam-ine these fantasies and let go of some of the less realistic aspects. But could such an encounter help members of both groups in their working-through processes? It could be argued that such personal therapy does not justify an encounter like this one, which breaks the vow of the survivors that there will be no reconciliation.

Personal help may be a necessary outcome, but it is not a sufficient one. I believe that we should learn from such a group process about the issues that have to be addressed in the wider social context. Can such encounters help people on both sides who were not personally involved in the encounters? If a generalizing effect can be shown, these encounters may become relevant for a variety of other social contexts in which a violent regime broke the fragile social contract, impos-ing control by using extreme violence and humiliation against another group. Replacing that regime with a new, quasidemocratic one (Dahl, 1989) could not repair the broken social bond because the collective memory did not work through past atrocities and the implied asymmetry. Only by bringing together descendants of the perpetrators and victims, addressing how the atrocities had taken place, and mutually working through the betrayed trust can a new social contract be established—if at all.

The Group Process: Wuppertal, Nveh Shalom, and Brandeis

Dr. Konrad Brendler, of the University of Wuppertal, and I designed the first four-day workshop carefully, choosing people who we felt had worked through their own lot to the extent that they were ready to face people of the other side. The German participants were mostly members of a self-help group of descendants of perpetrators who had met regularly since 1988, as an offshoot of my interviews in Germany (Bar-On, 1989) and of a conference in Wuppertal (Brendler and Rexilius, 1991). During the Wuppertal conference the inter-viewees met for the first time with their fellows to share their experiences. They were exposed to the Dutch experience with self-help groups made up of children of collaborators with the Nazis. The Dutch groups had met regularly since 1981 (Scheffel–Baars, 1988).

The German group was composed of Bernd,[7] the son of a high-ranking Nazi official; Monika, daughter of a high SS commander; Hiltrud, daughter of a physician who had been in charge of the euthanasia program in his district (and her daughter, Antonia, who came only to the second encounter in Israel); Renate, daughter of an Einsatzgruppen commander; Fritz, the son of a Gestapo commander, and Maya, his Jewish wife; and Helga, daughter of a railway worker who was stationed in Lamberg during the war. Kurt's parents were not involved in the extermination process. Igmar was the daughter of an engineer at an ammunition factory; she lived in the United States and was the only one who had not participated in the German self-help group. They ranged in age from forty-four to sixty-two. They were older, on average, than the Jewish group, whose ages ranged from twenty-six to fifty-three.

The Jewish group was composed of five descendants of survivors from the United States, three of whom were members of One Generation After, a Boston support group, and three of my students from Israel (only one of whom was a child of survivors) who had taken a course on the psychosocial aftereffects of the Holocaust on the second and third generations. During that course they had met twice with a parallel German student group (Bar-On, 1992).

Two members of the Jewish group (Jean and Chaim) had at least one parent who had survived Auschwitz, Buchenwald, or Bergen-Belsen. The parents of two other members of the group (Jonathan and Chava) had survived work camps and had hidden from the Nazis. Sarah's parents had survived the Nazi era by fleeing into Russia, and Danya's mother also had fled Germany. In all these families most of the other members had been murdered in the Holocaust. Tamar's parents were born in Israel, and Nathan's in Argentina. Still, quite a few members of their families also perished in the Holocaust.

Before the first encounter some members of the German group became quite anxious, wondering whether I planned to bring in the media. They had experienced such interventions before that had been sensationalized. They had opposed an earlier plan to use a professional facilitator at the encounters. One of the group members said, "There are no objective people in relation to the Holocaust. Those who try to be objective have a problem with it themselves." Some even resisted the idea of having the workshop documented, fearing that they would become part of a research plan that would be manipulated by outside persons or ideas.

Videotaping was allowed only after we promised that the documented material would not be used without the group's consent and that those who wished not to be photographed could sit in the camera's blind spots. Finally, shortly before the workshop, some of the Germans asked that we exclude any additional

7. Some of these pseudonyms appeared in *Legacy of Silence*.

German applicants who had not taken part in their earlier self-help group. After the workshop started they did agree to include a German-born person who arrived from the United States, but only after making sure that she did not come as an observer or a researcher and that she was willing to tell her own story as well. These conditions, mostly from the German group's side, showed members' sensitivities and willingness to share in structuring the encounters so that they could be open and successful.

The Wuppertal Encounter

We started the process by getting acquainted.[8] We proposed that the group get acquainted either in couples, reporting later to the whole group, or in the presence of the whole group. The group chose the second way, and the process took up almost the whole first workshop. In the last morning session, a few group members who had spoken first felt an urge to supply details they had left out of their brief introductions. Clearly, many other things happened during this round of getting acquainted. More and more people reacted emotionally to the stories, asking clarifying questions, coming up with their own associations, providing emotional support in difficult moments, sharing their feelings, anxieties, and apprehensions.

I started the workshop by noting that our spoken language would be English, though it was not the mother tongue for any of us. It was symbolic of our situation, as we might have difficulty finding words to express what we wanted to share. Perhaps not by coincidence, Maya started by telling the story of being trapped in a ghetto in Ukraine and being rescued by her gentile grandmother with the assistance of the local Gestapo commander—the same officer who, the night before, had ordered the execution of all the Jews in the ghetto. Maya was a kind of living bridge between the two groups. As a Jew living in Germany for more than twenty years, and as the wife of the son of a Gestapo commander, she had long experienced the unusual convergence of her own and her husband's struggles with the aftereffects of the Holocaust.

Soon the room was filled with stories: Bernd grew up amid the Nazi leadership and did not know about the atrocities his father was part of until after the war, when he was about fifteen. He reacted by converting to Catholicism and entering the priesthood (which his father despised and fought against) after living for two years with a family of Austrian farmers who were genuine believers in God. He cited dates and detailed events, as if these could help calm his still overt anxiety. Though he had left the priesthood and married, Bernd had no children, like a few of the other children of perpetrators in the group. One even spoke of the feeling that she carried a "bad seed" within herself. For many years she did not know why she did not want to have children, but once she started to question

8. A detailed description of this first encounter appears in Bar-On, 1993.

the role of her father during the war, with the help of her husband, it became clear that her father's ideas about the pure Aryan blood had hindered her. She was afraid to transmit such ideas to future generations.

One by one, the stories of the children of survivors unfolded. A few spoke of their own protected childhood, in which the devastating details of their parents' experiences were not revealed until they, the children, were willing and able to face that part of their family's history. Jean, for example, grew up in Germany but was raised with gentile Germans, among whom the unpleasant past was never mentioned. She went to a boarding school in England, married, and later went to the United States. Only when she had joined a group of children of survivors and heard their stories did she return to Germany with a tape-recorder to interview her own parents. Her father had arrived in Auschwitz with his younger sister, who was torn away from him and never seen again. Her mother was also in Auschwitz, where both of her parents (Jean's grandparents) were murdered. Jean's parents met after the war, in a displaced persons' camp near Braunschweig, while her father was searching for his sister and other members of his family.

Jean mentioned an incident that occurred when she visited a friend from school days and decided to raise the topic of the Holocaust. Her friend's mother asked her politely how her parents were doing. Jean responded by saying, "Considering what they went through, they're doing fine." Her friend's mother replied, "Yes, the war was difficult for all of us," to which Jean's prompt response was, "There is still a big difference between going through the war and surviving Auschwitz." Stunned, the mother changed the subject and left the room. Jean's friend, frozen by her mother's reaction, exclaimed, "This how it always ends. I never succeeded in bringing up this subject in my family and getting any response." For Jean this was a small healing experience—to be able to confront and break through the German silence.

We needed breaks not only to drink and rest but also to hug each other, to cry, to reflect on the stories that had been told inside the room. Still, we all felt committed to continuing the process. At that stage we could not socialize with people outside the discussion group. But soon the two original groups could no longer be distinguished. People intermingled, both in their stories and in informal encounters. Telling the stories and relating to each other openly allowed them to walk a hidden path between the pitfalls of the asymmetry and reconciliation issues.

One learned from the stories how members of both groups were burdened by the Holocaust and their parents' actual or possible involvement in it. They were trying to figure out, breaking through silence or paradoxical discourse,[9] what impact it had on their lives. For some members the issue was: How did I figure it out all by myself, and what impact has it had in terms of my (and my family's) self-estrangement and social estrangement? Members of both groups

9. Paradoxical discourse is defined as discourse in which narrated stories cover up untold stories or silenced facts (Bar-On, 1993).

mentioned being uprooted in their own social context. This was acceptable for the children of survivors, who had to recover from physical uprooting as well, but it was difficult to understand in relation to the Germans, who were physically located in their families, with their mother language and home country. Nevertheless, the Germans felt psychologically uprooted from elementary feelings of trust and dignity. They felt that their roots still existed but were poisoned and no longer could nourish them. This psychological uprooting was difficult to identify because it had no physical entity. The Germans felt that it might take generations to get over this kind of poisoning.

The group decided to meet again in the spring in Israel. I encouraged the members to write their impressions of the group process. A few weeks later I received this poem from Sarah; it later became part of the group's collective memory.

The Circle
Like a magnet
the center holds us there
compelled,

Poised on the edge of
A well
      of stories
      of details
      of torrents

An enormity
so vast.

We all know it.
We drink from it
We cry in it.

It is always there.

This is the place where the
whirlpools freely swirl.

This is the place where the
torrents are contained.
We reach around full circle
Hands join.

The waters start to calm.

From Nveh Shalom to Brandeis

Nveh Shalom was our second choice for a site at which to hold the Israel encounter. Nathan's kibbutz would have been cheaper, but when he asked,

"How will our kibbutz's Holocaust survivors react if they find out who is taking part in this workshop?" it was clear that we were now in a far different social context—one that would have an impact on our encounter. On top of that, the Holocaust memorial day happened to be the last day of our planned workshop. Nveh Shalom ("Oasis of Peace") has a special quality: it is the only settlement in Israel where Arabs and Jews choose to live together and to conduct seminars related to the Arab-Israeli conflict.

Everyone who was in Wuppertal decided to come to Nveh Shalom, which was significant in terms of motivation and continuity. Antonia, Hiltrud's daughter, was the only new admission accepted by the group. Hiltrud was unhappy after the meeting in June, attributing her feelings to her poor English. First she wrote me that she would not come to Israel, but after Kurt proposed that Antonia join the group to translate for her, she changed her mind.

It was obvious that the euphoric atmosphere of Wuppertal created a problem for the coming sessions: What now? How were we going to proceed? I decided against a prestructured agenda; this group had to develop its own agenda, even if that might be difficult at times, because none of us had ever experienced such a group. The warm atmosphere of the first encounter created an opportunity to go further, but it was not yet clear whether the group could handle aggression, conflicts, and despair. These difficult issues surfaced at the outset of our Nveh Shalom encounter and occupied most of the meetings at Brandeis.

The first question that came up at Nveh Shalom was, "How are we going to relate the group process to the reality outside the group?" A few people told about their efforts to share the warm feelings of the first group encounter with friends and others. They elicited curiosity and interest but also a lot of estrangement, even hostility: "What for? Why you? Don't you have problems of your own; why deal with 'their' problems?" It was a conflict between becoming an isolated group, disconnected from the rest of the world, or accepting the external norms while keeping positive experiences in the group to oneself. Was there a way to be open with each other and be open to the world around us? If not, what will the price be? This became one of the central issues of the following meetings.

The next morning this issue came up again in a different form: What do we regard as "effective time"? Specifically, is the time devoted to our group processes wasted? Jean felt that we should undertake some common tasks outside the group, specifically in Germany. She described the fear and disillusionment of her parents, Holocaust survivors still living in Germany, who were going through the new wave of anti-Semitism and xenophobia in Germany. She felt that if we continued to deal only with ourselves she would be disappointed. Jonathan presented the opposite point of view: if we try to concentrate on external activities we will be running away from the group process, from learning about our real problems with ourselves and with each other. Most of the German participants shared his view. Many of the Jewish participants shared Jean's. This was the first sharp division in our group, but it was not strictly according to the original groups. It had to do with our individual limits and strengths: What, if anything, can we change in ourselves or in the world around us?

I suggested another interpretation of Jean's concern: Are we allowed to start to live our own lives, independent (neither dependent nor counterdependent) of the expectations of our parents or of their social context? Can Jean go on working within this group regardless of what her parents have to go through in Munich? It was Helga who reacted spontaneously to this question, and with rage. She felt she had lived her own life for a long time, independent of her parents, who had never understood her interest in the Holocaust. Her father never answered her questions about what he had done or seen in Lamberg during the deportations. He died after our June meeting and left her with no way to find out. Her mother also did not satisfy her eagerness to know. I tried to test with Helga the possibility that she had developed a counterdependent relationship with her parents rather than an independent one, an issue difficult to work through now, after her father's death. But Helga refused to accept my proposition; she felt good about her independence and did not want to test anything in this respect.

Soon there surfaced other aspects of the limits of our capacities to change things around us. Danya was excited. In June, on her first trip to Germany, she came across an exhibition in Düsseldorf of paintings from the 1930s by Jewish children who had been taught by a teacher who died in Auschwitz. She bought the album and found out that her own mother's paintings were part of that exhibition. She showed the album to her mother, who looked at the pictures quietly. Finally she looked at Danya and said: "Until I saw these paintings *I thought I had made it all up.*" Still, she refused to contact the other people whose paintings and addresses appeared in the album. And now, here at Nveh Shalom, a BBC producer had brought Danya color photocopies of her mother's paintings from the museum. I felt we had been taken back and forth in time with Danya and her mother.

I invited the German participants to share their feelings about being in Israel for the first time. Now Renate was crying. She did not come to the party at Bernd's place last night because she had felt awful since arriving in Israel. She believed, especially after last June, that she would feel relaxed in Israel and could even take a holiday before the workshop. But she was not at ease. For example, she and her husband had rented a room near Tiberias, and one evening an Israeli family living in the same house ate all their food, which was stored in the common refrigerator. She did not protest because her accent would betray her German origin. "What if they were survivors of the Holocaust?" She could not stand it when people were nice to her and wanted to speak German. She had fantasies before she came that if she got killed by Arabs, this would be a small expiation for what her father had done.

Monika and Fritz also had archaic fantasies of sacrificing their lives in expiation for what their fathers had done. However, Monika told Renate that she felt better in Israel than she had expected. Somehow she had put her father aside, after all she had worked on during the past few years, and was able to see the Israeli side, even in the Arab-Israeli conflict. I saw this as a very interesting link. As long as one was still struggling with the atrocious deeds of one's own father, one can be either pro- or anti-Israeli in the current conflict with the Palestinians. As soon as one has come to terms with one's father, one can see both sides of the conflict.

Chava responded to Renate, "I feel I belong here." Nathan added, "I feel I have now very short roots, but they are a beginning of something I never had before." Danya responded, emotionally, "I envy you, as these 'short roots' you have are more than we American Jews have. I feel we have no roots at all." Bernd said: "I came from Sinai, in the footsteps of the ancient Israelites. I am fascinated by what I saw was accomplished here, and I love Israel." I cried quietly. Was it in response to Bernd's warm words, to Nathan's sensitive expression, or was I responding to my own feelings?

But these difficult moments also helped us develop our own humor, our refined discourse. The next morning at breakfast Renate told me that a mosquito bothered her the whole night. I smiled and said, "An Israeli mosquito." Renate laughed, at ease: "Yes, but if I could, I would have killed him anyway." After a few hours, during one of those serious sessions, Renate suddenly slapped her arm and we both burst into loud laughter. "I killed an Israeli mosquito!" she announced proudly to the astonished group. The discussion in the group made things easier for Renate later on, as she enjoyed the rest of her three weeks' stay in Israel much more.

Then the asymmetry issue was raised in the group: some of the German participants felt that the group was being controlled by the Jewish members—by the issues they raised and the language they used. The focus of our discussions suddenly became, "Who is more important?" Some people mentioned that among Jewish survivors there is a hidden hierarchy of who suffered more. Then an old tension within the German group surfaced. Kurt and Hiltrud were angry at Renate and Monika because "whatever conditions they put down, the group will have to accept them. They are prima donnas because of their fathers' role in the Nazi regime." Monika got furious. "This is bullshit. How can you dare to think this way, after all we have gone through in relation to this issue?" She cried, pointing at Kurt, Helga, and Hiltrud: "You don't understand how terrible it is to have such a father, how difficult it is to live with. What is happening now here is perverse."

I provided my interpretation: some of the German participants were disappointed because they had hoped that the problems they had not resolved within their own group would be resolved automatically when they joined with the Jewish group, and now they have found that the unresolved conflicts are still there. Also, it may be that Renate, Monika, and to some extent Bernd play major roles in the group not so much because of what their fathers had done but because of what they had worked through to be able to survive emotionally in the shadow of these fathers. The hierarchy to which Hiltrud and Kurt referred was an artifact of the society and the media outside the group, which were running after sensationalism. One should dismiss these values rather than accept them. However, Kurt and Hiltrud rejected this interpretation. They felt that I was trying to "help" Renate and Monika and that I "preferred" them in some sense. One could also interpret the tension within the German group as a result of the members' common history, which the Jewish group members did not have. This implied that internal tensions would arise among the Jewish participants at a later stage. But the history of a self-help group strongly suggested that the members of that group simply did not have the necessary support or facilitation within the group to work out the problems each of them had as children of Nazis.

Toward the end of the second encounter at Nveh Shalom, Renate tried to explain why she will never be able to talk about her father in public: "I always start to cry when I talk about my father. I still mourn his loss as a father. How can I manage this in public?" Two days later, during a public meeting at the Goethe Institute, she stood up without any warning, talked about her father, cried, and then felt she had conquered something in herself. Even when a woman survivor attacked Renate: "If your mother knew what your father had done, how could she give birth to you?" Renate handled the situation eloquently, answering very quietly, not at all intimidated. Later Renate told us that in Germany she is slowly "coming out of the closet," speaking about her father with friends and at work.

Nathan brought up the issue of the perpetrators within us: Can we identify them? Can they talk to the victims within us? What do they say to each other? This was Nathan's reaction to a video shown by Igmar at Nveh Shalom, in which she tried, in the framework of her psychodrama studies, to work on this issue with an Israeli colleague. Nathan felt that they were overdoing it, creating an inauthentic effect in their role-playing. During his latest military reserve service in the occupied territories he had experienced the dialogue between the two sides within himself. Through his experience in our group, he could for the first time also talk with a Palestinian terrorist who had been captured by the Israel Defense Force (IDF).

This story related to a question posed by some of the German members of the group: "We know what we gain from these encounters; the recognition and legitimacy of our own problems." Igmar, for example, said she felt for the first time that she belonged somewhere. "But what do you, the Jews, gain from our sessions?" Danya answered first: "I still want the world to be divided between the good and the bad guys, me being on the right side. This group helps me confront this too-simple division." Tamar described in detail her encounter the week before with two aunts who had been in Auschwitz, whom she had met in New York. It was a difficult meeting because they were totally uprooted and estranged from their surroundings. Tamar felt that she would not have had the patience to see them had she not been part of the group.

Jean and Chava agreed. They stressed the external pressure to maintain a clear–cut division between evil and good. This discussion relates to the recon–ciliation issue; the concept was being reexamined. If behind reconciliation there is an assumption of equality and mutuality, we need another word that will express the asymmetry as well: the perpetrators', not the victims', responsibility for what had happened in the Holocaust. Jean summarized, telling how she had given a talk about our encounters. A religious member of her congregation had responded in a moving way. He said that, despite the evil that exists as a potential in all of us, we must strive to diminish the possibility of its spread, to look at people beyond our "tribal ego." The concept of the tribal ego became one of the group's metaphors. We found ourselves reconstructing our biographies on a new common ground, beyond the prevalent tribal ego of each side.

My way of helping the process along was to introduce questions that helped reframe delicate issues and overcome moments of destructive guilt or helpless–ness. For example, by asking Jean, "Are you allowed to start to live your own life, independent of your parents' context?" I reframed the discussion of undertaking external projects versus internal group processes (which was also important but too early for the group to resolve). By proposing that the hierarchy issue was externally imposed and that for us the importance was not what the parents had done during the Nazi time but what the descendants had confronted and worked through, a positive meaning was offered to an initially negative definition. How–ever, not all of my proposals were welcomed, and I never tried to impose them on the group. I found myself wanting more and more to become a member of the group rather than its facilitator.

There was a need to meet again to continue working on individual processes while undertaking external projects. Monika and Chaim planned to start a group of Austrian descendants of perpetrators and survivors. Kurt, Tamar, and Dan planned to work with a group of Israeli and German students in 1994. A few of the members were to come to a conference in Hamburg, and we planned to meet in the summer of 1994 in Berlin.

The Personal and Societal Working-Through Process

We started our encounters by asking whether a meeting between descen–dants of Holocaust survivors and perpetrators could be justified. Would it assist those involved in their own working-through processes? Would it enable the reconstruction of a social bonding of faith and trust in oneself, in others, for Jews and Germans? We learned that personal growth went beyond what members of both groups had achieved on their own, in their own personal or prior group's frameworks.

From the three public meetings held after every encounter one could sense that this group had an impact on wider circles of Jews and Germans. This was more true for the American public than the Israeli one, especially for people who felt involved and interested. The German members of the group still feared being exposed to the public in Germany, which, they felt, was not ripe for such an open encounter.[10] In the Israeli public we could sense hostility and apprehension.

The encounters of this group illustrate the obstacles to reestablishing the social bonds of faith and trust. These obstacles were especially evident when the group was threading its way through the major issues of reconciliation, particularly the issue of asymmetry between the descendants of Holocaust survivors and the descendants of Nazis. Similarly, difficulties in reestablishing the bonds of faith and trust emerged whenever tension arose in the group, owing to conflicts within the group or between members of the group and the outside world. Still, its record was remarkable: this small group was willing to try to rebuild a little of what was destroyed during the Nazi era.

Finally, the group made an art of telling stories and reading poems, and it developed its own refined humor and gestures. Telling stories helped release tension, elicit warm support from other members, and reconstruct a more genuine discourse, in comparison to the external, as-if discourse, which supported tribal identities based on silencing the past and its effects on the present. This was the beginning of reconstructing a common biography, based on acknowledging what had happened in the Holocaust and reflecting on it but also trying to envision and strive for a different future. This probably could not have been achieved within the original tribal identities.

We assume that the process presented here is alternative and complementary to other political, juridical, and ethical processes. It is complementary because during those processes, a few perpetrators had been brought to trial and punished for their deeds, and the loss and suffering of the victims and the survivors had been acknowledged and compensated for. However, the break of the social contract between the two collectives has never been acknowledged or worked through (Dahl, 1989). Paradoxically, in order to initiate such a process, one has to move out of the simple schema that one side represents "total good" and the other "total evil" (Hadar, 1991). The process is alternative in that it makes possible an open confrontation and dialogue and thereby starts to heal the social and psychological pain of broken bonds and shattered assumptions that have been transmitted to the following generations. The possibility of accomplishing this goal so many years after the catastrophe gives hope to those of us who are still experiencing man-made violent conflicts and the traumas, shattered assumptions, and broken social bonds that accompany them.

The questions this group tried to work through can become relevant for a much wider social context. Issues like internal group processes versus external pressures, internal ratings and external hierarchies, physical and psychological uprootedness, the ability to reconstruct a common perspective beyond the prevalent tribal ego, the legitimacy of developing one's own life story, independent of

10. In February 1994, I participated in an encounter of a similar group with a wider public in Berlin. These meetings, held during a conference at an Epiphanic church, clearly showed the generalizing effect of the group process.

the heritage of the past, the capacity to address both sides of current conflicts—all these are central issues with which every society has to struggle, especially when its social contract has been broken by the violent acts of the former regime. The capacity to handle these issues, addressing the differences within each group as well as those between the groups, became one of this group's most important accomplishments.

REFERENCES

Albeck, H. J. 1994. *Intergenerational consequences of trauma: Reframing traps in treatment theory . . . A second generation perspective.* Westport, Conn.: Greenwood.

Aronian, K. J. 1990. A model of psychological adaptation to migration and resettlement. *Nursing Research* 39:1.

Barocas, H. A., and Barocas, C. B. 1979. Wounds of the fathers: The next generation of Holocaust victims. *International Review of Psycho-analysis* 6:1–10.

Bar-On, D. 1986. *The pantomime's stick.* Tel Aviv: Meirav (in Hebrew).

——. 1989. *Legacy of silence: Encounters with children of the Third Reich.* Cambridge, Mass.: Harvard University Press.

——. 1990. Children of perpetrators of the Holocaust: Working through one's moral self. *Psychiatry* 53:229–245.

——. 1992. Israeli students encounter the Holocaust through a group process: "Partial relevance" and "working through." *International Journal of Group Tensions* 22:2, 81–118.

——. 1993. First encounter between children of survivors and children of perpetrators of the Holocaust. *Journal of Humanistic Psychology* 33:4, 6–14.

——. 1994. Normalcy after Auschwitz: Problems in the definition of abnormalcy when we move between pure and impure ideological contexts. In H. F. Fulda and R. P. Hortsmann, eds., *Vernunftebegriffe in der Moderne: Proceedings at the International Hegel Conference.* Vol. 20. Stuttgart: Klett-Cotta, 484–514.

——. 1995. *Fear and hope: Three generations of five Israeli families of Holocaust survivors.* Tel Aviv: Hakibbutz Hameuchad (in Hebrew); Cambridge, Mass.: Harvard University Press (in press).

Bar-On, D., and Charny, I. W. 1992. The logic of moral argumentation of children of the Nazi era in Germany. *International Journal of Group Tensions* 22(1): 3–20.

Bar-Semech, M. 1990. Partnership and complementarity in the Kibbutz family. *Igeret Lachinuch* 88: 47–51 (in Hebrew).

Brendler, K., and Rexilius, G. 1991. *Drei Generationen im Schatten der NS-Vergangenheit.* Wuppertal: University of Wuppertal.

Browning, C. R. 1992. *Ordinary men.* New York: HarperCollins.

Carter, B., and McGoldrick, M. 1988. *Changing family life-cycle: Framework for family therapy.* New York: Gardner Press.

Chang, J. 1991. *Wild swans: Three daughters of China.* New York: Simon and Schuster.

Cohler, B. J., and Grunebaum, H. U. 1981. *Mothers, grandmothers and daughters: Personality and child care in three-generation families.* New York: Wiley-Interscience.

Dahl, R. A. 1989. *Democracy and its critics.* New Haven: Yale University Press.

Dalianis, A. 1994. *Children in turmoil during the Greek Civil War, 1946–1949: Today's adults: Follow-up of Greek children imprisoned with their mothers during the Civil War.* Stockholm: Karolinska University.

Danieli, Y. 1980. Countertransference in the treatment and study of Nazi Holocaust survivors and their children. *Victimology* 5: 3–4.

———. 1983. Families and survivors of the Nazi Holocaust: Some long- and short-term effects. In N. Milgram, ed., *Psychological stress and adjustment in time of war and peace.* Washington, D.C.: Hemisphere.

———. 1988. Confronting the unimaginable: Psychotherapists' reactions to victims of the Holocaust. In J. P. Wilson, Z. Harel, and B. Kahana, eds., *Human adaptation to extreme stress,* 219–238. New York: Plenum.

Davidson, S. 1980. The clinical effect of massive psychic trauma in families of Holocaust survivors. *Journal of Marital and Family Therapy* 1:11–21.

Dorff, E. N. 1992. Individual and communal forgiveness. In D. Frank, ed., *Autonomy and Judaism,* 193–217. New York: State University of New York Press.

Fonagy, P., Steele, M., Moran, G. S., Steele, H., and Higgit, A. 1993. Measuring the ghost in the nursery: An empirical study of the relation between parents' mental representations of childhood experiences and their infants' security of attachment. *Journal of the American Psychoanalytic Association* 41:957–989.

Grossman, D. 1989. *See under love.* Trans. B. Rosenberg. New York: Farrar, Straus, and Giroux.

Gutman, I. 1990. *The Holocaust encyclopedia.* Tel Aviv: Yediot Achronot (in Hebrew).

Hadar, Y. 1991. The absolute good and bad in the eyes of Holocaust survivors and their descendants. Paper presented at eighth Family Therapy Conference, Bat-Yam.

Hardtmann, G. 1996. "Partial relevance" of the Holocaust: Comparing interviews of German and Israeli students. In D. Bar-On and A. P. Hare, eds., *Reconstruction of the past.* Frankfurt: Campus Verlag (in German).

Heimannsberg, B., and Schmidt, C. 1993. *The collective silence: German identity and the legacy of shame.* San Francisco: Jossey-Bass.

Janoff-Bulman, R. 1992. *Shattered assumptions.* New York: Free Press.

Keilson, H. 1992. *Sequential traumatization.* Jerusalem: Magness.

Kestenberg, J. S. 1972. Psychoanalytic contributions to the problem of children of survivors from Nazi persecution. *Israeli Annals of Psychiatry and Related Sciences* 10:311–325.

Krystal, H., ed. 1968. *Massive psychic trauma.* New York: International Universities Press.

Lehman, D. R., Wortman, C. B., and Williams, A. F. 1987. Long-term effects of losing a spouse or child in a motor vehicle crash. *Journal of Personality and Social Psychology* 52:218–231.

Legaretta, D. 1985. *The Guernica generation: Basque refugee children of the Spanish Civil War.* Reno, Nev.: University of Nevada Press.

Main, M. 1993. Discourse, prediction, and recent studies in attachment: Implications for psychoanalysis. *Research in Psychoanalysis* 41 (supp.):209–244.

Mitscherlich, A., and Mitscherlich, M. 1967. *The inability to mourn.* Munich.

Novey, S. 1962. The principal of "working through" in psychoanalysis. *Journal of the American Psychoanalytic Association* 10:658–676.

Reick, M., and Eitinger, L. 1983. Controlled psychodiagnostic studies of survivors of the Holocaust and their children. *Israeli Journal of Psychiatry* 20:312–324.

Rosenthal, G. 1987. "Wenn alles in Scherben fällt . . . " Von Leben und Sinnwelt der Kriegsgeneration. Opladen: Leske und Budrich (in German).

——. 1989. Leben mit der NS-Vergangenheit heute. Zur Reparatur einer fragwürdigen Vergangenheit im bundesrepublikanischen Alltag. In Vorgänge. Zeitschrift für Bürgerrechte und Gesellschaftspolitik, Heft 3, S. 87–101 (in German).

Scheffel-Baars, G. 1988. Self-help groups for children of collaborators in Holland. In D. Bar-On, F. Beiner, and M. Brusten, eds., *Der Holocaust—Familiale und gesellschaftliche Folgen—Aufarbeitung in Wissenschaft und Erziehung?* 80–94. Wuppertal: University of Wuppertal.

Schon, D. 1983. *The reflective practitioner.* New York: Basic Books.

Sichrovsky, P. 1988. *Born guilty.* New York: Basic Books.

Solomon, Z. 1983. *Combat stress reactions: The enduring toll of war.* New York: Plenum.

Toll, T. 1992. Personal communication.

Vardi, D. 1990. *Memorial candles.* Jerusalem: Keter.

von Westernhagen, D. 1988. *Die Kinder der Täter: Das Dritte Reich und die Generation Danach.* Munich: Kosel.

Work, V. 1993. Personal communication.

Zizek, S. 1989. *The sublime object of ideology.* London: Verso.

CHAPTER TEN

Who Takes Care of the Caretakers?

The Emotional Consequences of Working with Children
Traumatized by War and Communal Violence

YAEL DANIELI

*Yael Danieli pioneered the systematic study of the reactions of therapists treating survivors
of the Holocaust. Her work in this area has been generalized to include therapists' reactions to treating a wide variety of trauma victims. This chapter represents an extension of
her research to the array of difficulties and resistances experienced by those who undertake
to work with children traumatized by violence.*

*The work presented here continues the thesis of the previous chapter, on the intergenera-
tional transmission of trauma, but Danieli describes the reverse situation, of the child
transmitting trauma to the adult. The material applies to adults who work closely with
traumatized children, whether as parents, teachers, or therapists.*

*The heart of the chapter is a description of one mode of training in countertransference, a
powerful but manageable set of exercises usable in a group or individual setting. These exercises can be modified for specific settings, and they serve as a springboard for further exploration of how we can best work with such children.*

*Earlier studies on mourning in childhood suggested how much parental response to the
child's distress around death and separation can facilitate or suppress expressions of grief
(Wolfenstein, 1966; Wolfenstein and Kliman, 1965; Furman, 1974). These studies
also have important implications for how therapists hear children's reactions to loss and
other forms of trauma.*

In his monumental *Song of the Murdered Jewish People,* describing the suffering,
struggle, and slaughter of the Jews of Warsaw, Yitzhak Katzenelson, who per-

ished in the gas chambers of Auschwitz in 1944, devoted the sixth poem, "The First Ones," written in November 1943, to the children. He writes:

4. The first to perish were the children, abandoned orphans,
The world's best, the black earth's brightest.
These children from the orphanages might have been our comfort.
From these sad, mute, bleak voices our new dawn might have risen. . . .

6. I watched the two-year-old grandmother,
The tiny Jewish girl, a hundred years old in her seriousness and grief.
What her grandmother could not dream she had seen in reality.
I wept and said to myself: Don't cry, grief disappears, seriousness remains. . . .

14. They, the Jewish children, were the first to perish, all of them,
Almost all without father or mother, eaten by cold, hunger and vermin,
Saintly messiahs, sanctified by pain. . . . O why such punishment?
Why were they first to pay so high a price to evil in the days of slaughter?

15. They were the first taken to die, the first in the wagon.
They were flung into the big wagons like heaps of dung
And were carried off, killed, exterminated,
Not a trace remained of my precious ones! Woe unto me, woe.

More than a million Jewish children were murdered during the Holocaust. One of the perspectives Katzenelson so poignantly highlights is the anguish of the witnessing caregivers who shared their fate.

Elie Wiesel (1960), who survived as an adolescent, writes in *Night:* "Not far from us, flames were leaping up from a ditch, gigantic flames. They were burning something. A lorry drew up at the pit and delivered its load—little children. Babies! Yes, I saw it—saw it with my own eyes . . . those children in the flames. (Is it surprising that I could not sleep after that? Sleep had fled from my eyes)" (42). Later, describing the hanging of two adults and a child: "The two adults were no longer alive. . . . But the third rope was still moving; being so light, the child was still alive. . . . For more than half an hour he stayed there, struggling between life and death, dying in slow agony under our eyes. And we had to look him full in the face. . . . Behind me, I heard [a] man asking: 'Where is God now?' And I heard a voice within me answer him: 'Where is He? Here He is—He is hanging here on this gallows.' " (76).

Judith Hemmendinger (Robinson and Hemmendinger, 1982) describes the reactions of the staff members of Taverny, a rehabilitation center in France, to the 120 male survivors of Buchenwald, ages five to seventeen, who were brought to Taverny immediately after the war: "Communication with these children was extremely difficult at first. They looked alike, had the same short haircut and a serial number tattooed on their forearm, and wore discarded German army uniforms. They were completely apathetic and indifferent to what was going on around them. They avoided contact with the educational personnel in the rehabilitation home; attempts to reestablish communication with them only met with hostility and tension. The superintendent and counselors found it difficult to tolerate their behavior and considered them psychotic or psychopathic. Some staff gave up in despair, and the superintendent quit" (398).

Hemmendinger took over and stayed with the children until 1948, when the center was closed. Thirty years later she located fourteen of "her children," now adults living in Israel and France. She found that they do not talk about their past. All were married, one divorced, and all work. None of the fourteen had had psychiatric treatment, although "several acknowledged psychological problems associated with depression, insomnia and nightmares about their past" (398) and admitted that "intense underlying feelings about their concentration camp experiences are easily triggered by contemporary events" (399).

The authors note that "given the bizarre behavior patterns these people showed when they left Buchenwald, it is unlikely that any foster home could have tolerated their presence, and the typical civilian psychiatrist would have diagnosed them as severely, if not irreversibly, disturbed and have recommended hospitalization. Taverny functioned as a self-help group with all of the therapeutic characteristics associated with such groups" (399). Most child survivors were not as fortunate as the children of Taverny.

In truth, after liberation, as during the war, most survivors were victims of a pervasive societal reaction comprising indifference, avoidance, repression, and denial of their experiences. Shunned, abandoned, and betrayed by society, the survivors could share the most horrifying period of their lives and their immense losses only with their children or with fellow survivors. The most common consequence of the conspiracy of silence for survivors and their children has been a profound sense of isolation, loneliness, and alienation that exacerbated their mistrust of humanity and made their task of mourning and integration impossible.

Indeed, Krell (1993) writes that the majority of child survivors have never told their stories to anyone. As children they were encouraged not to tell but to try to lead normal lives and forget the past. They desperately wanted to be like everybody else. They were preoccupied with normality, with belonging, with coping, with not being identified as different. As adults, they tend to feel that their stories are unimportant because they were "only children" during the war, and most of them were not in concentration camps. Krell (1985) further comments that it is a relatively recent phenomenon to hear them identify themselves as among the children who were destined to be murdered, had fate not intervened (see also Valent, 1994). Kestenberg has frequently noted (1985, for example) how the child survivors, despite their good adjustment, often felt excluded or shy. Some parents could rationalize that their children did not suffer because children so young do not understand.

Keilson (1992) delineated three traumatic sequences in the Netherlands: the occupation, with its terror; direct persecution, with deportations; and the postwar period. Having followed up two thousand child survivors, he noted that "approximately twenty-five years later, children who experienced a favorable second but adverse third traumatic sequence will display development features which are less favorable than those of children presenting an adverse second but favorable third traumatic sequence" (440). That is, a poor postwar environment could intensify the preceding traumatic events and, conversely, a good environment could mitigate some of the traumatic effects.

In her report on family functioning and children's psychological adaptation among Yugoslavian refugees in a camp near Stockholm, Sweden, Ekblad (1993) concluded that the buffers against mental ill health in children were an optimistic mother and the perception of social support. She recommended that "family members should not be separated during the asylum" (159) to ensure that the sense of continuity would be maintained over time, despite their refugee status.

Yule and Williams (1990) attribute the relative paucity of knowledge about post-traumatic stress reactions in children in part to the adults' protectiveness, unwillingness to acknowledge what children may have suffered, and denial that children have major psychological sequelae that warrant investigation. Reporting their study of families of children who survived the 1970 capsize of the *Herald of Free Enterprise* in Zeebrugge Harbor, Belgium, they relate their surprise at the failure of teachers to note the problems these children were experiencing at school. They suggest that "in part, this must be because they did not wish to acknowledge the horrors the children experienced and did not know how to respond to their needs" (292). Similarly, after the 1985 fire disaster at Bradford city football stadium in England, many schools refused to acknowledge that the children who had been at the stadium but were not burned could have psychological aftereffects (Yule and Williams, 1990). McFarlane (1988) was thwarted in his attempt to study the children who saw the 1983 bush fires in southeastern Australia because the schools would not cooperate, saying that it was best to let past things remain in the past. "Thus, there is a consensus in recent literature that teachers report less psychopathology among child survivors than do parents, and that both report far less than the children themselves" (Yule and Williams, 1990, 292–293).

The phrase conspiracy of silence has been used to describe the typical interaction between Holocaust survivors and their children and psychotherapists when Holocaust experiences are mentioned or recounted (for example, Barocas and Barocas, 1979; Krystal and Niederland, 1968). Whereas society has a moral obligation to share its members' pain, psychotherapists and researchers have, in addition, a professional contractual obligation to do so. When they fail to listen, explore, understand, and help, they too inflict the "trauma after the trauma" (Rappaport, 1968) or the "'second injury' to victims" (Symonds, 1980) by maintaining and perpetuating the conspiracy of silence.

Elsewhere, I have reviewed in detail the literature on the conspiracy of silence (Danieli, 1982a), described its harmful long-term impact on the survivors (Danieli, 1981b, 1989a), their families (Danieli, 1981a, 1985), and their psychotherapies (Danieli, 1984, 1988a, 1988b, 1992), and reported my research on therapists' difficulties in treating survivors and their children (Danieli, 1980, 1984, 1988a). In my later research I identified and examined forty-nine countertransference reactions and attitudes reported in the literature by sixty-one psychotherapists working with Holocaust survivors and children of survivors. Although the in-depth interviews I conducted did not focus on participants' reactions to child survivors, many of them spontaneously volunteered that their most intense reactions were to stories of the murder and brutal treatment of children—the ultimate symbol of innocence and vulnerability.

Some of the major categories of countertransference phenomena systematically examined in my study follow. They are listed in order of frequency.

- Various modes of defense against listening to Holocaust experiences and against the therapists' inability to contain their intense emotional reactions (for example, numbing, denial, avoidance, distancing, clinging to professional role, focus on method or theory).
- Affective reactions, such as bystander's guilt; rage with its variety of objects; dread, horror, shame, and related emotions (for example, disgust and loathing); grief and mourning; "me too"; sense of bond; privileged voyeurism.
- Specific relational context issues, such as those between parent and child, and victim and liberator; viewing the survivor as hero; and attention and attitudes toward Jewish identity.

These themes are described and illustrated in detail in a series of articles (Danieli, 1980, 1982a, 1984, 1988a, 1993).

Similar themes have been reported by Dyregrov and Mitchell (1992), primarily in the context of acute trauma, with particular sensitivity to the assumptions shattered in working with traumatized children (see also Nader, 1994).

Because my original study focused on working with survivors and children of survivors in general, rather than on child survivors themselves, for the purpose of this chapter I sought the help of twelve leading therapists and researchers who work or supervise work with children traumatized by war and communal violence. I asked them to review in detail the themes in my original research and to evaluate whether they apply to working with children. Nearly all participants stated that there were no differences except in degree and intensity. For example, one participant said, "At the core of it is that adults feel that children fundamentally should not be threatened or exposed to danger, to this level of violence. . . . Children should be protected by adults, and when you cannot protect them, it rocks your sense of a protected childhood. It's very frustrating for an adult not to be able to protect a child. It makes you feel that you don't have any control. You believe that adults have certain [cognitive] capacities to deal with trauma whereas young children do not, so that the adults should provide that safety for them."

Another psychotherapist commented, "When you see a battered woman you may ask, 'Why didn't you get yourself out of that situation?' When you see a battered child you think very differently, because you can't think that children should have [left]. Someone should protect them, come to take them, rescue them. The emotions, . . . moral outrage, are greater because you know they had no chance to get out." Similarly, a therapist stated:

> When you deal with adult victims of torture it comes across to me so clearly that experience of torture was very much part of the equation in these people's decision to engage in political violence, to engage in the movement. When you are confronted with child victims it's not so clear that the situation the child is in is of his own making and is a result of clear mature judgment and decision making. As a therapist I am forced to share the blame and the guilt of putting this child in his/her situation because I am part of the system, perhaps even a contributor to the system that breeds oppression and that has exposed this child to a life of poverty and violence.

A caregiver in the midst of war proclaimed, "Face the facts. Adults have the capability to face war and do something for themselves and children do not. When you face that dimension of war you are astonished." Garbarino (1993) describes difficulties experienced by researchers attempting to study children systematically in situations of war. See also Parson's (1994) descriptions in the context of urban violence.

Telling of finding a pair of red shoes after a fire, a policeman burst into tears as he said, "My daughter has red shoes too."

The innocence, helplessness, and vulnerability of children may evoke sadism and abuse of power in the adult, as in the case of police freely killing street children in Rio de Janeiro, or armies recruiting children who become cannon fodder.

But what participants experienced as most painful is children as perpetrators—killers, torturers, combatants, rapists. One therapist said, "My countertransference problem started when patients stopped being only war victims and became torturers too. One said to me, 'I can kill you now if I wish.' "

A therapist treating children in a refugee camp reported feeling "very anxious"; she preferred to co-lead the therapy groups because the children were "very aggressive, uttering terrible noises and using terrible words, very threatening." She added, "When you work with an adult saying he can kill somebody, it's more bearable than a child, because somehow we are not used to having such aggression in children. It took me time to realize how to make my knowledge help me to accept such aggression in children. My image of childhood was not appropriate to the situation when a child said, 'I will kill you the same way my mother was killed.' "

The fact that eighteen of the sixty-one psychotherapists in my original study were themselves Holocaust survivors or children of survivors permitted a comparison between their reactions and those of the participants who were not (see Danieli, 1982a and 1988a.) Similarly, the responses of the participants interviewed for this chapter can be differentiated according to the reactions of caregivers who are members of the communities that are at war or in other violent situations and those that are not. These membership similarities may be seen in therapists who are sympathizers with the political underground versus those who are part of the regime (Danieli, in preparation).

Countertransference in Training Professionals Working with Trauma

Traditional training generally has not prepared professionals to deal with massive trauma and its long-term effects. This lack of training is underscored in situations of war and community violence, in which many of the caregivers working directly with children may not be professionals and may themselves be unpredictably and chronically in danger and traumatized. They may not be trained to help traumatized children—those most in need. This is evident in war zones in developing countries as well as in poor neighborhoods in the United States.

The Group Project for Holocaust Survivors and Their Children has offered short- and long-term training seminars and individual supervision to professionals since 1975.[1] In-house, on-the-job training and supervision have been offered by other agencies. The International Society for Traumatic Stress Studies, for example, has begun to ameliorate this lack of training by issuing its *Initial Report* from the (1989) Presidential Task Force on Curriculum, Education, and Training (see Danieli and Krystal, 1989). This report contains model curricula formulated by international specialists in the field, representing such technical specialties or interests as psychiatry, psychology, social work, nursing, creative art therapy, clergy, media, and public health. The need to recognize, cope with, work through, and therapeutically utilize countertransference difficulties was uniformly seen as imperative for optimal training in this field.

As early as 1980, when I published the preliminary thematic overview of this study, I stated, "While this cluster [of countertransference reactions] was reported by professionals working with Jewish Holocaust survivors and their offspring, I believe that other victim/survivors populations may be responded to similarly and may suffer . . . similar [consequences]. . . . Defining the[se] reaction-clusters . . . will lead therapists and investigators to be better able to [recognize them so that they can monitor,] contain and use them preventively and therapeutically" (Danieli, 1980, 366). In 1981 I noted that these reactions "seem very similar to alexithymia, anhedonia, and their concomitants and components which, accord-

---

1. The Group Project for Holocaust Survivors and Their Children was established in 1975 in the New York City area to counteract survivors' profound sense of isolation and alienation, compensate for their neglect by the mental health profession, and attempt to respond to pessimism about helping survivors (Krystal, 1981; Chodoff, 1980). It provides individual, family, group, and intergenerational community assistance in a variety of noninstitutional settings, training for professionals working with traumatized populations, and consultation with and for relevant resources and institutions (hospitals, synagogues) in the community.

ing to Krystal, characterize survivors" (Danieli, 1981b, 201). In 1989, in the context of training I referred to these phenomena as the "vicarious victimization of the care-giver" (Danieli, 1989b).

These insights and hypotheses about the ubiquity of countertransference reactions in other victim populations have now moved to the forefront of our concern in the preparation and training of professionals who work with trauma victims and trauma survivors. Indeed, the literature reflects a growing realization of the need for professionals working with other victims or survivors to describe, understand, and organize various aspects of the conspiracy of silence (see Herman, 1992; Danieli, 1994a; Wilson and Lindy, 1994). Countertransference reactions are integral to and expected in our work, which calls on us to confront, with our patients and within ourselves, extraordinary human experiences. This confrontation is profoundly humbling in that at all times it tries our view of the world and challenges the limits of our humanity.

In reality, countertransference reactions are the building blocks of the societal as well as professional conspiracy of silence. They inhibit professionals from studying, correctly diagnosing, and treating the effects of trauma. They also tend to perpetuate traditional training, which ignores the need for professionals to cope with massive real trauma and its long-term effects.

Although information cannot undo unconscious reactions, knowledge about trauma in its historic context does provide the therapist with perspectives that help him or her know what to look for and determine what may be missing in the survivor's account and what types of questions to ask. But countertransference reactions interfere in the acquisition of knowledge about the trauma as well (Danieli, 1994a).

Familiarity with the growing body of literature on the long-term psychological sequelae of trauma on survivors and their offspring also helps prepare mental health professionals. Nonetheless, they should guard against simply grouping individuals as "survivors," all of whom are expected to exhibit the same "survivor syndrome" (Krystal and Niederland, 1968) or PTSD, and the expectation that children of survivors will manifest a single child-of-survivor syndrome (see, for example, Phillips, 1978).

Many of the countertransference phenomena examined in my study were found to be reactions to patients' Holocaust stories rather than to their behavior. The unusual uniformity of psychotherapists' reactions suggests that they are responses to the Holocaust—the one fact that all the otherwise different patients have in common. Because the Holocaust seems to be the source of these reactions, I suggest that it is appropriate to call them countertransference reactions to the Holocaust rather than to the patients themselves. Therapists' difficulties in treating other victim-survivor populations may be rooted in the nature of their victimization; I therefore term them event countertransference.

Processing Event Countertransference

Regarding event countertransferences as dimensions of one's inner, or intrapsychic, conspiracy of silence about the trauma allows us the possibility of exploring and confronting these reactions to the trauma events independent of the therapeutic encounter with the victim-survivor patient, in a variety of training and supervisory settings.[2] I have developed the exercise presented below over the past two decades; it has proved helpful in working through event countertransference in numerous workshops and training institutes, in the debriefing of "front liners," in short- and long-term seminars, and in consultative and supervisory relationships around the world.[3] While it originally evolved—and is still done optimally—as part of a group experience, it can also be done alone by the clinician working privately. As one veteran traumatologist stated, "It is like taking an inner shower when I am stuck with . . . [a] patient."

Instructions for Participants

I ask participants in a group setting to arrange the chairs in a circle. After everyone is seated, I immediately say, "Take a large piece of paper, a pen or a pencil. Create space for yourself. The first phase of the process will be private, totally between you and yourself. Please don't talk with each other during this first phase."

"Choose the victimization-trauma experience most meaningful to you. Let yourself focus on it." When I lead this exercise, I always begin with the Holocaust, and only after completing the process described below do I ask the participants to take another large piece of paper and to choose the victimization-trauma experience most meaningful to them.

1. Imaging: "Draw everything and anything, any image that comes to mind when you think about the experience you chose. Take your time. We have a lot of time. Take all the time you need."
2. Word association: "When you have completed this task, turn the page, and please, write down every word that comes to mind when you focus on this experience."
3. Added reflection and affective associations: "When you finish this, draw a line underneath the words. Please look through and reflect on the words you wrote. Is there is any affect or feeling word that you did not include? Please add it or them now. Roam freely around your mind and add any other word that comes to mind now."

2. Portions of this section appeared in Williams and Sommer, 1994, and in Wilson and Lindy, 1994. While event countertransference and personal countertransference (that is, reactions to the patient's behaviors) are not mutually exclusive, for training purposes it is useful to differentiate the two.

3. The word *event* was chosen to specify the source of these therapists' reactions, not to imply that it was just one event.

4. First memory: "When was the very *first time* you ever heard of the experience you chose? How did you hear about it? What was it like for you? Whom or what did you hear it from? Go back and explore that situation in your mind in as much detail as you can. What was it like? How old were you? Where are you in the memory? Are you in the kitchen, in the bedroom, living room, in class, at the movies, in the park? Are you watching TV? Are you alone or with other people? Who are you with—your parents, family, friends? What are you feeling? Do you remember any particular physical sensations? What are you thinking?"

5. Choices and beliefs: "Are you making any *choices* about life, about people, about yourself at the time? Decisions like 'Because this happened, therefore . . . ,' or 'This means that life is . . . , that people are . . . , that the world is . . . ' What are you telling yourself? Are you coming to any conclusions? This is very important. Stay with that."

6. Continuity and discontinuity of self: "Think of yourself today, look at that earlier situation—are you still holding those choices? Do you still believe what you concluded then? Would you say 'This is still me' or 'This is not me any more'? What is the difference? What changed and why?"

7. Sharing with others: "Have you *talked with other people* about it? Whom did you talk to, both in the past and now? What was their reaction? What was your reaction to their reaction?"

8. Secrets—not sharing with others: "Is there anything about this that you haven't told anyone, that you decided is not to be talked about, is 'unspeakable'? Is there any area in it that you feel is totally your *secret,* that you dealt with all alone and kept to yourself? If there is, please put it into words such as, 'I haven't shared it because . . . ,' or, 'I am very hesitant to share it because . . . ' Please mention the particular people with whom you won't share it, and why."

9. Personal knowledge of survivors: "Moving to another aspect of the *interpersonal realm,* do you personally know survivors of the experience you chose or their family members as friends, neighbors, or colleagues?"

10. Self secrets: "There are secrets we keep from others to protect either ourselves or them, and there are *self secrets.* Take your time. This is very important. Imagine the very first time you ever heard anything about it. Roam inside your mind. Is there anything about it that you have never talked to yourself about, a secret you have kept from yourself? An area that you have sort of pushed away or kept at arm's length from yourself? Or about which you say to yourself, 'I can't handle that?' Why is it the one thing that was too much for you? What is still lurking in the corner of your mind that you haven't put into words or looked into yet?"

11. Personal relationship to the trauma: "What is your *personal relationship* to

the trauma? Please write the answers down, because even the way you write makes a difference. Did your place of birth figure in your relationship to the trauma? Does your age figure?"

12. Identity dimensions: "What is your *religious, ethnic, cultural, political, class, racial,* and *gender* identity? Do these parts of your identity figure in the choices you made, influence your relationship to the experience? How? You can answer these one by one."

13. Professional relationship to the trauma: "Let us move to your *professional* self. What is your professional discipline? How long have you been working in your discipline? What is your professional relationship to the experience you chose? Within your professional practice, have you seen survivors of the experience or their children? How many?"

14. Therapeutic orientation: "If you have worked with trauma survivors professionally, what therapeutic modality did you employ—emergency-crisis intervention, short- or long-term, individual, family, or group therapy? Was it on an inpatient or outpatient basis? What modality have you found most useful, and why?"

15. Victim and trauma survivor populations: "Was this the only victim-survivor population you have worked with professionally?"

16. Training in trauma work: "Have you ever been trained to work with victims or survivors of trauma, either in school or on the job? If you were, what have you found to be the elements of your training without which you won't feel prepared to do the job?"

The sequence of the first phase of processing event countertransference is from the immediate visual imagery through free associations to the more verbal-cognitive material. It then moves to articulate how the trauma fits within the therapist's experience, personal and interpersonal development, and the gender, racial, ethnic, religious, cultural, and political areas of her or his life. It begins with one's private world of trauma and proceeds through the context of one's interpersonal life to one's professional work.

While the material can be analyzed privately, the second phase of the process, the sharing and exploring phase, works best in a group setting (Danieli, 1982b; 1988b; 1989a). Similarly, therapists can explore with each other the trauma they have experienced directly or indirectly, as well as the conspiracy of silence that frequently follows these events. Sharing helps therapists to understand the consequences in their lives and to express their feelings and concerns. The group modality thus serves to counteract their sense of isolation and alienation about working with trauma.

Elsewhere, in discussing the value of the group modality for victim-survivor patients, I suggest that groups have been particularly helpful in compensating for countertransference reactions. Whereas a therapist alone may feel unable to contain his or her patient's feelings or to provide a "holding environment" for them (Winnicott, 1965), the group as a unit is often able to do so. While particularly intense interactions evoked by trauma memories may prove overwhelming to some of those present, others invariably come forth with a variety of helpful reactions. Thus, the group functions as an ideal absorptive entity for abreaction and catharsis of emotions, especially negative ones, that might otherwise be experienced as uncontainable. Finally, the group modality offers a multiplicity of options for expressing, naming, verbalizing, and modulating feelings. It provides a safe place for exploring fantasies, for imagining, for taking on the roles of others, and for examining their significance for the identity of the participants. Finally, the group encourages and demonstrates mutual support and caring, which ultimately enhances self-care. All these considerations apply to therapists as well as to patients.

This training process assumes that the most meaningful way to tap into event countertransferences is to let them emerge, in a systematic way, from the particularities of the therapist's experience. She or he can thus learn to recognize her or his reactions in order to monitor, understand, and contain them, and to use them preventively and therapeutically.

There is an extraordinary richness to what can be learned in ongoing, prolonged, group-supervision processes and to the crystallization of countertransference through the tapestries of event countertransference and personal countertransference, the mutual impact of the differing adaptational styles of patients and therapists (Danieli, 1981a), the examination of mutual (counter) transferences among members played out in the group dynamics. One important instance of the last of these is the attempted expulsion of the supervisor—the person leading the exercise process, who thus becomes the symbolic agent of the trauma—by the group for exposing their vulnerabilities by encouraging them to confront—(re)experience—the trauma.

The exercise should not replace ongoing supervisory countertransference work. It does, however, provide an experiential, multidimensional framework for the trauma aspects of the patient's and therapist's lives.

The process also helps build awareness of the caregiver's vulnerability to being (vicariously) victimized by repeated exposure to trauma and trauma stories and to the toll countertransference reactions take on her or his intrapsychic, interpersonal, and family lives. Garbarino and his colleagues (1994) found that two out of forty southside Chicago caseworkers were absent from work at any given time owing to injuries sustained in the course of their work. Caregivers in Croatia showed burnout and vicarious traumatization by such reactions as forgetting the time of appointments and feeling happy when patients didn't come.

The exercise process makes poignantly clear the paramount necessity of carefully nurturing and regulating the self and ensuring the development of a self-protective, self-healing, and self-soothing way of being as a professional and as a full human being. Special effort is made to include in the exercise such soothing, supportive instructional language as "take all the time you need" and by paying caring, respectful attention to every element explored. The exercise incurs ambivalence as well. Claiming an inability to draw and a preference to do "only the words part" is an obvious example of resistance.

The composition of the workshop or seminar group may be unpredictable. One can be assured, however, that many of the psychotherapists present are themselves trauma victims or survivors and that their victimization either inspired and energized their choice of career and specialty or interacts with their patient's trauma as part of their countertransference matrix. Invariably there will be victims and perpetrators, such as a Cambodian boat girl and a Vietnam veteran turned psychotherapists who explore together the legacy of their mutually shared history, and Holocaust survivors and children of survivors and Germans. Group members invariably learn about cultures other than their own. They come to finish unfinished business with their patients and with themselves, to explore their wounds and heal them. They come to seek answers, to find forgiveness, compassion, understanding, and camaraderie. Mobilizing their creative energy, they allow themselves to be transformed as people, to become more authentic in their work and more actualized in their personal lives.

Some Principles of Self-Healing

The following principles are designed to help professionals recognize, contain, and heal event countertransferences.

1. To recognize your reactions:
    - Develop awareness of somatic signals of distress—a chart of warning signs of potential countertransference reactions (for example, sleeplessness, headaches, perspiration).
    - Try to find words to name and articulate your inner experiences and feelings. As Bettelheim (1984) commented, "What cannot be talked about can also not be put to rest; and if it is not, the wounds continue to fester from generation to generation" (166).
2. To contain your reactions:
    - Identify your personal level of comfort in order to build openness, tolerance, and readiness to hear anything.
    - Knowing that every emotion has a beginning, a middle, and an end, learn to attenuate your fear of being overwhelmed by its intensity and try to feel its full life cycle without resorting to defensive countertransference reactions.
3. To heal and grow:
    - Accept that nothing will ever be the same.
    - When you feel wounded, take time to diagnose accurately, soothe, and heal to make yourself emotionally fit to continue to work.
    - Seek consultation or further therapy for previously unexplored areas triggered by patients' stories.
    - Any of the affective reactions (including grief, mourning, rage) may

interact with your old, unworked-through experiences. You will thus be able to use your professional work purposefully for your own growth.

- Establish a network of people to create a holding environment (Winnicott, 1965) within which you can share your trauma-related work.
- Provide yourself with avocational avenues for creative and relaxing self-expression in order to regenerate energies.

Being kind to oneself and feeling free to have fun and feel joy are not frivolities in this field. Without them, one cannot fulfill one's professional obligations.

As I mentioned earlier, the therapists and researchers whom I asked to review the exercise training process described above nearly all responded with excitement to the principles of self-care. Some added that working with traumatized children made them appreciate their own and their children's lot more. Pointing out that overwhelmed caregivers cannot take a holiday or rest because of ongoing war, one therapist told me how important it was for her to go to professional meetings, where "I haven't learned much new, but I had two days to talk about my feelings and cry, and do it without guilt because I was doing something professional."

Although I had asked the therapists for suggestions on modifying the program for working with children, most of their comments focused on the level of training, sophistication, and experience implied by the exercise. To adapt it to community nonprofessional and volunteer workers, some supervisors suggested simplifying the exercise, perhaps by "cutting it into manageable pieces." Most of them cautioned that harm might result unless the process was led by a trained professional as part of a comprehensive long-term program that includes care and support (Danieli, 1994b; see also Black, Kaplan, and Hendriks, 1993, on the caregiver's need for support in working with child victims or witnesses, and Eth, 1992, for related ethical considerations).

Conclusion

Countertransference reactions are integral to our work—ubiquitous and expected. They are found among all professionals involved in caring for children in situations of war and community violence. These may be medical, nursing, and mental health caregivers, teachers, law-enforcement personnel, U.N. peacekeepers, soldiers, emergency or disaster workers, media, and clergy. Working through countertransference difficulties is pivotal to optimizing the training of professionals in the field of traumatic stress.

REFERENCES

Barocas, H. A., and Barocas, C. B. 1979. Wounds of the fathers: The next generation of Holocaust victims. *International Review of Psychoanalysis* 6:1–10.

Bettelheim, B. 1984. Afterword. In C. Vegh, *I didn't say goodbye*. R. Schwartz, trans. New York: E. P. Dutton.

Black, D., Kaplan, T., and Hendriks, J. H. 1993. Father kills mother: Effects on the children in the United Kingdom. In J. P. Wilson and B. Raphael, eds., *The international handbook of traumatic stress syndromes*, 551–559. New York: Plenum.

Boothby, N. 1994. Trauma and violence among refugee children. In A. J. Marsella, T. Bornemann, S. Ekblad, and J. Orley, eds., *Amidst peril and pain: The mental health and well-being of the world's refugees*, 239–259. Washington, D.C.: American Psychological Association.

Chodoff, P. 1980. Psychotherapy with the survivors. In J. Dimsdale, ed., *Survivors, Victims, and Perpetrators*, 205–218. Washington, D.C.: Hemisphere.

Danieli, Y. 1980. Countertransference in the treatment and study of Nazi Holocaust survivors and their children. *Victimology* 5(2–4): 355–367.

——. 1981a. Differing adaptational styles in families of survivors of the Nazi Holocaust: Some implications for treatment. *Children Today* 10(5):6–10, 34–35.

——. 1981b. On the achievement of integration in aging survivors of the Nazi Holocaust. *Journal of Geriatric Psychiatry* 14(2):191–210.

——. 1982a. Therapists' difficulties in treating survivors of the Nazi Holocaust and their children. Ph.D. diss., New York University, 1981. *University Microfilm International*, no. 949–904.

——. 1982b. Group Project for Holocaust Survivors and Their Children. Prepared for National Institute of Mental Health, Mental Health Services Branch, Washington, D.C. Contract no. 902424762.

——. 1984. Psychotherapists' participation in the conspiracy of silence about the Holocaust. *Psychoanalytic Psychology* 1(1):23–42.

——. 1985. The treatment and prevention of long-term effects and intergenerational transmission of victimization: A lesson from Holocaust survivors and their children. In C. R. Figley, ed., *Trauma and its wake*, 295–313. New York: Brunner/Mazel.

——. 1988a. Confronting the unimaginable: Psychotherapists' reactions to victims of the Nazi Holocaust. In J. P. Wilson, Z. Harel, and B. Kahana, eds., *Human adaptation to extreme stress*, 219–238. New York: Plenum.

——. 1988b. Treating survivors and children of survivors of the Nazi Holocaust. In F. M. Ochberg, ed., *Post-traumatic therapy and victims of violence*, 278–294. New York: Brunner/Mazel.

——. 1989a. Mourning in survivors and children of survivors of the Nazi Holocaust: The role of group and community modalities. In D. R. Dietrich, and P. C. Shabad, eds., *The problem of loss and mourning: Psychoanalytic perspectives*, 427–460. Madison, Conn.: International Universities Press.

——. 1989b. Countertransference and trauma: Vicarious victimization of the care giver. Workshop presented at the Critical Incident Conference, Federal Bureau of Investigation, Behavioral Science Instruction and Research Unit, Federal Bureau of Investigation Academy, Quantico, Va.

——. 1992. Preliminary reflections from a psychological perspective. In T. C. van Boven, C. Flinterman, F. Grunfeld, and I. Westendorp, eds., *The right to restitution, compensa-*

tion and rehabilitation for victims of gross violations of human rights and fundamental freedoms, 196–213. Netherlands Institute of Human Rights [Studie- en Informatiecentrum Mensenrechten], Special issue no. 12.

——. 1993. The diagnostic and therapeutic use of the multi-generational family tree in working with survivors and children of survivors of the Nazi Holocaust. In J. P. Wilson and B. Raphael, eds., *The international handbook of traumatic stress syndromes,* 889–898. New York: Plenum.

——. 1994a. Countertransference, trauma and training. In J. P. Wilson and J. Lindy, eds., *Countertransference in the treatment of PTSD,* 368–388. New York: Guilford.

——. 1994b. Resilience and hope. In G. Lejeune, ed., *Children worldwide,* 47–49. Geneva: International Catholic Child Bureau.

——. In preparation. In and out and in-between: Sharing and witnessing our patients' traumata.

Danieli, Y., and Krystal, J. H. 1989. *The initial report of the Presidential Task Force on Curriculum, Education, and Training of the Society for Traumatic Stress Studies.* Chicago: Society for Traumatic Stress Studies.

Dyregrov, A., and Mitchell, J. T. 1992. Work with traumatized children—psychological effects and coping strategies. *Journal of Traumatic Stress* 5(1):5–17.

Ekblad, S. 1993. Psychological adaptation of children while housed in a Swedish refugee camp: Aftermath of the collapse of Yugoslavia. *Stress Medicine* 9:159–166.

Eth, S. 1992. Ethical challenges in the treatment of traumatized refugees. *Journal of Traumatic Stress* 5(1):103–110.

Friedman, P. 1948. The road back for the DP's: Healing the psychological scars of Nazism. *Commentary* 6(6):502–510.

Furman, E. 1974. *A child's parent dies: Studies in childhood bereavement.* New Haven: Yale University Press.

Garbarino, J. 1993. Challenges we face in understanding children and war: A personal essay. *Child abuse and neglect* 17:787–793.

Garbarino, J., Kostelny, K., Dubrow, N., and Grady, J. 1994. Children in dangerous environments: Child maltreatment in the context of community violence. In D. Cicchetti and S. Toth, eds., *Child abuse, child development and social policy.* New York: Ablex.

Herman, J. L. 1992. *Trauma and recovery.* New York: Basic Books.

——. 1993. Father-daughter incest. In J. P. Wilson and B. Raphael, eds., *The international handbook of traumatic stress syndromes,* 593– 600. New York: Plenum.

Katzenelson, Y. 1980. The first ones. In *The song of the murdered Jewish people,* trans. and annot. Noah H. Rosenbloom, 37–40. Israel: Beit Lohamei Haghettaot—Ghetto Fighters' House. Hakibbutz Hameuchad Publishing House.

Keilson, H. 1992. *Sequential traumatization in children.* Jerusalem: Hebrew University; Magnes Press.

Kestenberg, J. S. 1985. Child survivors of the Holocaust: 40 years later. Reflections and commentary. *Journal of the American Academy of Child Psychiatry* 24:408–412.

Krell, R. 1985. Therapeutic value of documenting child survivors. *Journal of the American Academy of Child Psychiatry* 24: 397–400.

——. 1993. Child survivors of the Holocaust—strategies of adaptation. *Canadian Journal of Psychiatry* 38:384–389.

Krystal, H. 1981. Integration and self-healing in posttraumatic states. *Journal of Geriatric Psychiatry* 14(2):165–189.

Krystal, H., and Niederland, W. G. 1968. Clinical observation on the survivor syndrome. In H. Krystal, ed., *Massive psychic trauma.* New York: International Universities Press.

McFarlane, A. C. 1988. Relationship between psychiatric impairment and a natural disaster: The roles of distress. *Psychological Medicine* 18:129–139.

Nader, K. 1994. Countertransference in the treatment of acutely traumatized children. In J. P. Wilson and J. Lindy, eds., *Countertransference in the treatment of post-traumatic stress disorder,* 179–205. New York: Guilford.

Parson, E. R. 1994. Inner city children of trauma: Urban violence traumatic stress response syndrome (U-VTS) and therapists' responses. In J. P. Wilson and J. Lindy, eds., *Countertransference in the treatment of post-traumatic stress disorder,* 151–178. New York: Guilford.

Phillips, R. D. 1978. Impact of Nazi Holocaust on children of survivors. *American Journal of Psychotherapy* 32:370–378.

Rappaport, E. A. 1968. Beyond traumatic neurosis: A psychoanalytic study of late reactions to the concentration camp trauma. *International Journal of Psychoanalysis* 49:719–731.

Robinson, S., and Hemmendinger, J. 1982. Psychological adjustment 30 years later of people who were in Nazi concentration camps as children. In C. D. Spielberger, I. G. Sarason, and N. Milgram, eds., *Stress and anxiety,* vol. 8, 297–399. New York: McGraw-Hill/Hemisphere.

Straker, G., and Moosa, F. 1994. Interacting with trauma survivors in contexts of continuing trauma. *Journal of Traumatic Stress* 7(3):457–465.

Symonds, M. 1980. The "second injury" to victims. *Evaluation and Change* (special issue), 36–38.

Valent, P. 1994. *Child survivors: Adults living with childhood trauma.* Port Melbourne, Victoria: William Heinemann Australia.

Wiesel, E. 1960. *Night.* New York: Avon Books.

Williams, M. B., and Sommer, J. F., Jr. 1994. *Handbook of post-traumatic therapy.* Westport, Conn.: Greenwood/Praeger.

Wilson, J. P., and Lindy, J. 1994. *Countertransference in the treatment of PTSD.* New York: Guilford.

Winnicott, D. W. 1965. *The maturational processes and the facilitating environment.* London: Hogarth Press.

Wolfenstein, M. 1966. How is mourning possible? *Psychoanalytic Study of the Child* 21:93–123.

Wolfenstein, M., and Kliman, G., eds. *Children and the death of a president: Multi-disciplinary studies.* Garden City, N.Y.: Doubleday.

Yule, W., and Williams, R. M. 1990. Post-traumatic stress reactions in children. *Journal of Traumatic Stress* 3(2):279–295.

CHAPTER ELEVEN

Practical Approaches to Research with Children in Violent Settings

PETER S. JENSEN

Most of the previous chapters have focused on interventions with highly traumatized children and the problems attendant on attempting interventions. The authors of this chapter and the next consider how to collect more systematic and usable data in order to better understand the experiences and needs of children, to devise better programs, and to implement follow-up. An earlier review of research on children in war (Jensen and Shaw, 1993) helped to alert child mental health practitioners to the problems and research needs of this population. Here Peter S. Jensen provides a sophisticated methodological survey of possibilities for research. He addresses the chapter to clinicians as well as to researchers, offering guidelines on useful and feasible research that can be done even in difficult situations. Striking examples of such research have emerged from the Persian Gulf War; some of these are reported by Leavitt and Fox (1993; also see Laor et al., in press). In this chapter Jensen emphasizes the dialectic between interventions and research and attempts to bridge the gap between the stereotypes of "academic research" and ill-considered, hasty interventions.

Jensen also cautions us against "unproved premises" and unsupported generalizations, especially concerning the inevitability of scarring from war. He suggests that assertions made by authorities about children and violence may enter the consciousness of those affected and actually contribute to their sense of defect and hopelessness.

There has been no recent period in history when children and families have been spared the effects of war and violence. But the gruesome events of the past few years, heightened by the immediacy and visual impact of on-the-spot reporting, seem unparalleled in their senseless, willful destruction of human life, especially the lives of children. Public opinion and government initiatives are often shaped by such media accounts, but longer-term strategic planning by relief agencies designed to assist children and families in war-torn situations must rely on systematically developed knowledge of the effects of war and violence on children and well-designed, rigorously tested, efficacious interventions.

Without systematically developed research knowledge, efforts to protect children from the trauma of war may themselves have untoward effects that are perhaps even greater than the effects of the violence itself. A good example of well-intentioned but misguided public policy was the British effort in World War II to evacuate children from the cities and into the countryside, presumably to spare the children the deleterious psychological and physical effects of missile attacks on the cities. These evacuations usually separated children from their parents, and most of the available evidence suggests that these separations were probably more harmful for the development of children who were evacuated than were the psychological effects of the bombings on children who stayed with their parents (Straker and Thouless, 1940; Burt, 1940; Henshaw and Howarth, 1941; Jensen and Shaw, 1993).

Research knowledge is necessary to guide public policy concerning strategies to mitigate the effects of war and violence on children, but it is difficult to keep a scientific perspective amid terrible turmoil and loss of life. Arguing for research under such conditions may seem unrealistic in view of children's and families' immediate suffering. Maintaining scientific skepticism about the presumed effects of violence on children may seem to be an unsympathetic, unfeeling stance compared with that of the people who talk about its effects on children but have no data. Yet when I sounded just such a note of cautious skepticism in a recent review article, I received a letter from a mental health professional working with refugee children from Bosnia and Herzegovina who lamented the many inaccurate assumptions and characterizations of the effects of war on children:

> Our impression after seeing more than [a] thousand children and being very well informed about refugee children problems is that taking into account their experiences and present situation, [the] children are functioning incredibly well with relatively few symptoms and dysfunctions. . . . I think that the best characteristic of their mental health condition is given by some of their teachers: "Disturbances in our children are not more frequent than in other children. Deep, quiet sadness is present in our children."
>
> I appreciate [e]specially your paper because of the well-balanced overview concerning the psychological sequelae of war. . . . The opinion that the generation of war children is not "damned" does not mean that children exposed to war events and to the refugee situation do not suffer and do not need help. The problem is that suffering is not a diagnosis and [that] mental health workers addicted to [a] great diagnosis like PTSD do not pay sufficient attention to "just being unhappy and sad," and therefore so many children exposed to war events and refugee situation[s] in need do not receive help.
>
> Extremely pessimistic generalized long-term prognostic evaluation of the future development of war and refugee children stems from the uncritical repetition of some unproved premises about the fatal influences of child-

hood traumas on the later psychological health, from the overestimation of the role of mental health professions in helping people who have been exposed to chronic war-related adversities and intense traumatic events, and . . . most important, from emotional factors influencing the cognitive appraisal of mental health professionals. Sometimes also political motives condition the exaggeration of the prognostic estimation. Generalizations like "Generations of children will suffer all their life from the psychological sequelae of war . . . " are not only unscientific but also morally unfair toward children. They can influence in a negative way their self-image and raise anxiety in their parents.

The diversity of perspectives suggests the need for systematically obtained evidence to guide opinion and policy.

The scientist practitioner who works in war-torn situations and whose responsibility is to care for suffering children and families faces the dilemma of any clinician whose views are shaped only by those he or she sees and treats: it may be difficult to know whether the children for whom one provides care (whether in a school, clinic, hospital, or evacuation/refugee setting) are characteristic or atypical of the children who are not receiving such care (Caron and Rutter, 1991). While no one would argue the adverse effects of severe traumatic events on children, it is not always possible to determine the effects on children exposed to the lower levels of trauma and war that often characterize the larger population, or on those who do not seek out help. Nonetheless, the terrible effects of war and violence on some children mobilize strong feelings and calls to action for the larger population of children and families, and it is difficult to remain dispassionate in such discussions without feeling cold-hearted or at best pedantic.

Certainly, policy makers and clinical treatment teams need to know which types of intervention administered at which points are most likely to benefit specific children. While such questions are difficult to answer under extreme war-ravaged circumstances, research methods can be used to evaluate the possible benefits of programs that have been implemented and to determine whether effective use is being made of scarce resources. While one might argue that allocating resources for such a process in the midst of terrible conflict and suffering would be cruel, it would be unethical to deliver ineffective treatments under such circumstances. And while many clinicians feel that they know what is best for a given patient, a cursory review of the history of medicine should be sufficient to evoke clinical modesty from even the most ardent advocates of any particular program or intervention.

When research is made possible in war-torn or violent settings, researchers must be aware of the highly politicized context. While the findings of such research can be a valuable public health tool, they can be misunderstood or even explicitly misused for political purposes. This is not an argument against conducting research in these settings, but it is important that would-be investigators approach such research opportunities with appropriate caution.

Start-Up Considerations

Initial strategies to implement research in war-torn settings should involve an assessment of the current data needs of the clinicians. What information is needed to make clinical decisions concerning the children and families who are to receive specific interventions? How is this information to be collected, and what is the reliability of the procedures and methods used to obtain the information? To avoid overtaxing the current intervention system, research in such a setting ideally would focus first on the collection of the minimum data needed as part of the clinical process and for program implementation. It is critical that the data-gathering process and the specific measures used be reliable, valid, and clinically sensible. Although some measures may be psychometrically sound, they may not be appropriate to the clinical evaluation and treatment process, or they may be unacceptable to those receiving services or even to the treatment and evaluation teams.

Involvement of the Clinical Team

If the clinical team finds the assessment process or measures cumbersome or ill-advised, it is certain that the research will not progress even when it is mandated by administrative fiat. Clinicians and administrators operating under conditions of extreme human suffering may have little tolerance for externally imposed research efforts that are not clearly linked to benefiting persons "on the ground"—that is, the people who are in the midst of and most directly affected by the situation of armed conflict. They will often distrust and resent investigators who arrive on the scene to develop or implement research. In addition, outside persons themselves may feel somewhat apologetic for their seemingly trivial research questions, given the extent of the needs evident in the research population. For these reasons, it is critical that the researchers and those involved in the delivery of services work closely together to define the critical research questions, determine the most appropriate points of research access, and, to the extent possible, integrate the research into the ongoing system of care.

Investigators must work closely with the gatekeepers of the research population: those responsible for distributing resources, determining access to care, and, in many instances, even providing the actual care. Involvement of the gatekeepers is critical, not just because their reluctance to participate may make it impossible to conduct the research, but—more important from a scientific perspective—because such persons on the ground will have many clinical hunches and questions relevant to the population's needs and the effectiveness of the services provided. Sometimes, their questions will be informed by the practicalities of what can and cannot be accomplished in that setting. This "real world" perspective is needed to achieve and maintain a high degree of relevance to the research question.

At times, differences in opinion, approach, and prioritization of research questions may arise and lead to friction between the gatekeepers and the researchers. Finding ways to negotiate these differences is essential for an effective collaboration. The gatekeepers themselves frequently have research questions that they wish to address, yet they feel overwhelmed by their responsibilities to provide care to the needy population and so have been unable to mount a research effort. Understanding these issues and creating feasible interventions are critical to the success of the research effort, the ongoing commitment of the research participants, and the credibility of the data.

Sometimes a clinical team needs convincing. Team members may be uncertain of the value of the assessment procedures and may need to be helped to understand that the research approaches will increase the likelihood of improved assessments and effective treatments, can complement the clinical programs, may help create appropriate visibility for the program, and can provide deep satisfaction concerning one's contribution to scientific knowledge.

Program developers and implementers also may need to be reminded that ongoing evaluation is a basic part of program implementation. A good program evaluation (which is an appropriate form of research in these settings) will likely yield improvements in the quality of care and possibly in policy. Some clinicians may be wary of such efforts. These suspicions can often be allayed by involving the clinicians in the planning and by giving them concrete examples of other programs that have built research into their activity. For example, in studying the effects of military stressors and overseas deployment on children of military personnel (before access to children from the local hospital's pediatric and psychiatric clinical services was possible) I found it necessary and desirable to conduct a briefing for the hospital chief of staff and the heads of the pediatric, nursing, and psychiatric services—the gatekeepers. These briefings had several tangible, immediate results: First, several questions of interest and relevance to the project were suggested and consequently added to the study. Second, additional resources (office space and personnel) were supplied because the study was now seen as highly relevant to the missions of the hospital's clinical services and to the overall military command structure. Finally, a much higher degree of cooperation and support was evident throughout the study than would have been available had the study been "just another research project" competing with higher-priority tasks in the hospital and local military community.

Community Involvement

At times the gatekeepers are community leaders (for example, mayor, head of social services, superintendent of schools). Their involvement, as well as the involvement of other community members (parent groups, teachers and teacher organizations, and so on) ensures that the research is designed with sensitivity to the needs of the community and to cultural issues that may affect the choice of data-collection instruments, study design, and even basic hypotheses. Participatory research of this nature, although it is more difficult to develop, often reaps greater rewards in terms of community cooperation and eventual incorporation of research findings into systems policies. When research is developed with community support and involvement, it frequently will receive community logistical support in the form of personnel, money, supplies, research space, and access to critical information or sites in which to conduct the research. Such assistance will often make the difference between a highly successful research program and a research idea that never gets off the ground. For example, I developed what I supposed was a rather elegant study targeted for implementation in a school system. Unfortunately, the school system was consulted fairly late in the design process and did not approve the study's implementation. I learned from this experience to seek early consultation with community leaders, superintendents of schools, and others with decision-making responsibility.

Design Considerations
Correlational Studies

There are practical limitations on the kinds of research that can be done in war-torn or violent settings. For instance, control groups often are unavailable. Obviously, random assignment (for example, to a violent setting versus a non-violent one, or to an active treatment versus a waiting list) would be impossible and unethical. But these factors need not impede good research efforts. For example, randomly assigned control groups are not always needed. It is quite feasible, within certain research designs, to conduct a naturalistic study of the effects of violence, war-related variables, or specific interventions on child and adolescent outcomes. In this context there are many examples in the literature of investigators who examined the effects of the "dose" of trauma (for example, proximity to a disaster, witnessing versus hearing about violence) on the severity of the child's symptoms (Rutter, 1981; Chimienti, Nasr, and Khalifeh, 1989; McFarlane, 1987; Pynoos et al., 1987; Raviv and Klingman, 1983).

If one wishes to examine the effects of trauma on children, one strategy is to measure the extent, severity, and intensity of the trauma and examine its relationship to potential child outcomes. For example, Chimienti, Nasr, and Khalifeh found that children in Lebanon exposed to war conditions of shelling, destruction of home, death, and forced displacement were 1.7 times more likely to manifest regression, depression, and aggressive behaviors than those without such exposure. In the population of children being studied, it is likely that some will be exposed to higher levels of trauma than others. One can then, in a naturalistic design, demonstrate the relation between the presumed etiologic and outcome variables.

Similarly, one can also examine the presence of factors that seem to mitigate the nature of the trauma. For example, are there children who have a high level of exposure but who, for unclear reasons, have better outcomes than were predicted (see Elizur and Kaffman, 1983)? Assessing and measuring such children on a range of relevant variables will allow the investigative team to determine the factors that may mediate better outcomes. As these factors become better identified and understood, it may be possible to design new interventions that increase the presence of these protective factors. Important insights can be obtained through such quasi-experimental approaches (see Elizur and Kaffman, 1983; Lifschitz et al., 1977).

Sometimes novice researchers are concerned that the inability to use random assignment and true experimental methods (in which the variable of interest is actively manipulated by the investigator) effectively renders any meaningful research impossible. This is decidedly incorrect. Even rigorously designed experimental studies with random assignment always have flaws, and they provide only partial answers to complex questions. Other designs are needed to answer "real world" questions in situations of high generalizability and ecological validity. Quasi-experimental designs, in which investigators take advantage of naturally occurring experiments (for example, natural disasters, war, death of a parent) and naturally occurring subject-to-subject variation in variables of interest, are powerful methods through which to address many questions that cannot be examined through experimental methods. Most research on the causes and correlates of children's traumatic outcomes of necessity uses such approaches. (For more detailed discussion of these methods, see Rutter, 1981.)

When quasi-experimental designs are employed in studies of children and trauma, it is quite possible that a third, unknown variable mediates the presumed effects between the level of trauma exposure and traumatic outcomes. However, demonstrating this relationship is a good start. A sensible next step is determining which subgroups correlate most closely to these relations and exploring alternative explanations for these relations. Such a strategy has enormous potential to generate new research hypotheses. If the investigator can identify new variables that differentiate children with similar levels of trauma exposure but different outcomes, there may be a possibility of providing new evidence to inform public policy, shape preventive efforts, and design new intervention strategies, particularly if the variables presumed to differentiate good- and poor-outcome children are malleable or could be the focus of a strategic intervention. For example, if one determines that children who have lost a parent during war have better than expected outcomes if they have an affectionate, protective relationship with the remaining parent (for example, Lifschitz, 1975; Lifschitz et al., 1977), such information could be used to design and test prevention and treatment interventions for children who may lose or have lost a parent during war.

Intervention Studies

Even in studies conducted under difficult circumstances, it is critical that systematic efforts be made to determine the effect of the intervention. This process must begin with baseline and post-intervention assessments of the treated population, although demonstration of pre-post improvements alone is insufficient to establish that an intervention has been effective. If an intervention does not meet this condition, it is not likely that it will eventually prove to be effective under more controlled conditions.

Another research strategy involves the measurement of some aspect of the presumed therapeutic process (for example, quality, nature, number and length of sessions, intensity of the intervention) and examining its relation to children's outcomes. Finding such a relation may constitute another stepping-stone in scientific proof. For example, let us suppose that one develops and implements a school intervention for a population of children exposed to war. Examining children's outcomes, the investigator finds that at some schools children seemed to have benefited much more at follow-up than children in other schools, despite similar problem levels at the beginning of the intervention. Examining the characteristics of schools to find differences in how the intervention was delivered could yield new data about what are the effective ingredients in the intervention. For example, one might learn that in schools with better outcomes the parents of the children were informed about and encouraged to participate in the intervention. Only by the careful measurement of children's functioning before and after intervention, as well as the examination of intervening variables (for example, parent involvement), would such new knowledge become available. While this evidence alone would not establish parent participation as a necessary ingredient, it may stimulate additional, more systematically designed interventions in which this component is built in at the start.

Controlled Intervention Studies

If the resources are available when a new intervention is being tested, it is desirable to identify a population to serve as a control. This helps to show that the changes over time that occur to the subjects receiving the new intervention are probably the result of the intervention and not caused by the maturation of the subjects or another event. If the control population is similar in characteristics to the population receiving the new intervention but does not manifest the same changes, one can have greater confidence that the changes were indeed the result of the intervention. The problem is that the investigator chooses where to implement the intervention based not on random factors but on such factors as community characteristics, leadership, attitudes—and it may be these variables that are responsible for the differences in treatment outcomes in the two groups.

Choice of Measures

Given the difficulties of conducting research in such settings, it may be inappropriate to attempt to invent new tools of measurement if they are not absolutely necessary. Whenever possible, researchers should use instruments that have known psychometric characteristics. Frequently it is important to embed the data and research findings in points of comparison in the existing literature. This is possible only when one uses well the standardized tools used in the research literature. On the other hand, it is possible that the critical constructs one wants to measure—particularly those with immediate relevance to public policy issues—are not tapped by existing instruments. If so, one may need to proceed step by step, at first using appropriate but untested instruments that produce information that is credible and appears valid to knowledgeable persons. It may be necessary to supplement a new tool with other measures of known reliability and validity that are used by the larger research community. Care should be taken not to overburden the system or subjects. This strategy then offers the researchers and the public policy persons the best-fitting tools with which to measure the constructs that fit their respective needs for research information.

Multiple Informants

When evaluating interventions or outcomes in naturalistic settings, there is some danger that the independent and dependent variables—for example, the presumed etiologic variable (traumatic stress) and the variables of outcome interest (child behavior)—may become confounded, particularly in the case of children. Multiple information sources are necessary. Simply obtaining information from a single source is problematic. Commonly a halo effect takes place, such that the single-informant perspectives are likely to shape their responses on all kinds of questionnaires, even when there is no real relation among variables. For these reasons it is advisable to obtain data from multiple information sources—parents, children, teachers, clinicians, and so forth. Obtaining information concerning the independent variable(s) (for example, presumed risk factors or etiologic variables) from one source and information about the outcome variables from another data source provides some protection. In addition, obtaining information from multiple information sources also reflects the complexity of the child's world; multiple perspectives are often and usually needed to obtain a relatively complete understanding of the child's level of functioning and behavior, both within and across various settings.

Experimental Confounds

In conducting naturalistic studies, there is an ever-present danger of circular logic: that is, if one examines the data and uses them to inform and shape policy (including policies involved in the current service-delivery systems) the researcher runs the risk of shaping the data to support the research hypotheses. For example, if the investigator finds a relation between severity of trauma, childhood outcomes, and the nature of the service system interventions, and if the study team then changes the service system's policies and interventions as a result of these findings, subsequent findings are now shaped by the earlier impact of the data upon the service system policies. Subsequent findings and relationships in data gathered after that point may then reflect a type of circular logic rather than simple cause-effect between the independent and dependent variables.

Feasibility

It is critical that the researcher, gatekeeper, service system team be parsimonious in determining which data can reasonably and feasibly be obtained, which data are likely to be of the greatest importance to the ongoing service delivery needs, and which data could have the greatest impact on public policy. Obtaining too much information that cannot be reasonably and feasibly examined within the scope of the limited research capacities is counterproductive and will lead to discouragement of the research and clinical team. In addition, the quality of the data will suffer, because more variables must be tracked by the clinical and research team, monitored for completeness and correctness, and so forth. Too much data in the final analysis erodes the overall quality of the research and evaluation effort. This is one instance when less is more.

Quantitative versus Qualitative Data

There are a number of methodologic problems that clinical, research, and service system teams in violent and war-torn settings must consider in evaluating their efforts. Research using qualitative data emphasizes the validity of the information gathered but places less emphasis on the strict reliability of measurement, the reproducibility of the data, and the conditions under which they are gathered. Research using quantitative data, on the other hand, emphasizes the precision and accuracy of measurement and the reproducibility of the findings in other settings.

This choice of qualitative or quantitative approaches to research need not be an either-or; investigative teams must recognize the strengths and weaknesses of each. It often is useful to begin with relatively qualitative approaches, which initially impose less stringent requirements on a research team. Such approaches may have a great deal of ecological and cultural validity, because interesting research hypotheses may be generated through this strategy. More quantitative approaches, which emphasize the specific reliability of measures and the appropriateness of research designs, may be more reproducible within and across research settings. Such research may be reliable but invalid, however: negative or positive findings may be a result of the manner in which the research data had to be collected (for example, using less-than-perfect scales or interview measures) or of the constraints on the population during the course of the research implementation. For example, in research examining the effects on children of the absence of a soldier-parent because of wartime deployment, a reliable behavior problem checklist (completed by both teachers and parents) yielded no evidence of any emotional or behavioral problems in children. Only by obtaining data directly from the children did evidence emerge indicating elevated levels of child distress as a function of increased parental absence (Jensen, Martin, and Watanabe, in press).

For these reasons, the two approaches will often be blended: quantitative, presumably reliable and valid measures used and tested in other studies, so that important comparisons can be made, and measures that have immediate and obvious relevance to the demands and questions of a particular setting.

Multiple Measures

The use of multiple measures and multiple raters protects against some of the problems of any single data point. Conversely, researchers may be perplexed at the end of such studies, unsure of how to reconcile discrepant information obtained from multiple sources. While there is no single right answer or best approach to these questions, the standards and principles of parsimony of measurement (using as few measures as possible), reliability, validity, involvement of the clinical gatekeepers and service system team in the research, and emphasis on the quality and completeness of the data, without overwhelming the system, are critical.

Summary

Although there are many reality-based constraints on the research one can do in violent and war-torn situations (as is true of much clinical research on childhood and mental disorders), we suffer much more from a failure to apply research thinking to our work with every patient we serve. As clinicians responsible for delivering care to traumatized children and families, the most ethical and responsible position is to evaluate what we do as we do it. We must determine as much as possible the effectiveness of our interventions, clarify the populations for whom our interventions do (and do not) work, and use these data to inform policy, service system design, and specific treatments for children and families who are victims of violence and trauma.

REFERENCES

Burt, C. 1940. The incidence of neurotic symptoms among evacuated school children. *British Journal of Educational Psychology,* 10:8–15.
Caron, C., and Rutter, M. 1991. Comorbidity in child psychopathology: Concepts, issues and research strategies. *Journal of Child Psychology and Psychiatry* 32:1063–1080.
Chimienti, G., Nasr, J. A., and Khalifeh, I. 1989. Children's reactions to war-related stress: Affective symptoms and behavior problems. *Social Psychology and Psychiatric Epidemiology* 24:282–287.
Elizur, E., and Kaffman, M. 1983. Factors influencing the severity of childhood bereavement reactions. *American Journal of Orthopsychiatry* 53:668–676.

Henshaw, E. M., and Howarth, H. E. 1941. Observed effects of wartime conditions on children. *Mental Health* 2:93–101.

Jensen, P. S., Martin, D., Watanabe, H. In press. Children's response to parental separation during Operation Desert Storm. *Journal of the American Academy of Child and Adolescent Psychiatry.*

Jensen, P. S., Martin, D., and Watanabe, H. In press. Children's response to parental separation during Operation Desert Storm. *Journal of the American Academy of Child and Adolescent Psychiatry.*

Laor, N., Wolmer, L., Mayes, L. C., Golomb, A., Silverberg, D. S., Weizman, R., and Cohen, D. J. In press. Israeli preschoolers under the SCUDS: A developmental perspective on the "protective matrix" as a risk-modifying function. *Archives of General Psychiatry.*

Leavitt, L., and Fox, N., eds. 1993. *The psychological effects of war and violence on children.* Hillsdale, N.J.: Lawrence Erlbaum.

Lifschitz, M. 1975. Long-range effects of father's loss: The cognitive complexity of bereaved children and their school adjustment. *British Journal of Medical Psychology* 49:187–197.

Lifschitz, M., Berman, D., Galili, A., and Gilad, D. 1977. Bereaved children: The effects of mothers' perception and social system organization on their short range adjustment. *Journal of Child Psychiatry* 16:272–284.

McFarlane, A. C. 1987. Post-traumatic phenomena in a longitudinal study of children following a natural disaster. *Journal of the American Academy of Child and Adolescent Psychiatry* 26:764–769.

Pynoos, R., Frederick C., Nader, K., Arroyo, W., Steinberg, A., Spencer, E., Nuñez, F., and Fairbanks, L. 1987. Life threat and post-traumatic stress in school age children. *Archives of General Psychiatry* 44:1057–1063.

Raviv, A., and Klingman, A. 1983. Children under stress. In S. Breznitz, ed., *Stress in Israel,* 138–162. New York: Van Nostrand Reinhold.

Rutter, M. 1981. Epidemiological/longitudinal strategies and causal research in child psychiatry. *Journal of the American Academy of Child Psychiatry* 20:513–544.

Straker, A., and Thouless, R. H. 1940. Preliminary results of Cambridge survey of evacuated children. *British Journal of Educational Psychology* 10:97–113.

CHAPTER TWELVE

Assessing the Impact of War on Children

MONA MACKSOUD, J. LAWRENCE ABER,
AND ILENE COHN

The authors of this chapter bring together observations on child development and diagnosis with practical ways to assess the impact of violent situations on the individual child and on a community of children. In the previous chapter, Peter S. Jensen focused on methodology from the viewpoint of the researcher. Mona Macksoud, who has a Lebanese background, has worked in Lebanon, where she was able to build on her status as an insider and an outsider simultaneously, bringing clinical astuteness to a research situation (see her film documentary Childhood Lost *[1992]). In this chapter she and J. Lawrence Aber and Ilene Cohn, from the Columbia Project on Children and War, discuss their experience assessing children in Kuwait after the Iraqi invasion in 1990.*

Theirs is an approach that has been most helpful in gathering information that can be immediately useful. It demonstrates that evaluation need not represent further invasion but can in fact be therapeutic to the community being studied. It demonstrates the value of cumulative experience by investigators and the value of a clinically informed perspective. Children who revealed problems on the questionnaire could be identified and attended to by a social worker who was part of the research effort and could be contacted later on to ensure that assistance was provided.

Furthermore, the information gathered became the basis of a media campaign in Kuwait to inform the entire populace; it was a communitywide intervention drawing on the expertise of the few psychologists who performed the study. That study and other assessments by the group formed the foundation of excellent training manuals for parents, teachers, and clinicians. Symptoms that recur frequently and interventions that were found to be helpful have been generalized and presented as a brief handbook distributed by UNICEF *and used in other areas of the world. Although this chapter presents one example rather modestly, the*

the profound insights gleaned by this team from their assessments underlie much of the
work cited in this book and elsewhere. Here is an example of assessment that has worked
well for everyone—children, parents, teachers, clinicians, and researchers—in spite of all the
potential pitfalls described in the previous chapter.

Cross-national and cross-cultural studies of children in dangerous situations indicate that the objective features of the war-related experiences are only partial determinants of how children's mental health, educational, and even health outcomes are affected (Macksoud et al., 1993). The nature of war-related experiences differs enormously from child to child. For example, those who experience the occasional shelling of their community but who do not personally experience violence will differ from children who become separated from family members during flight or lose parents to unwitnessed acts of violence. These children in turn will differ from those who have been tortured or forcibly enlisted as combatants or obliged to witness the torture or death of a parent or other family member. Any research into these events must begin by clarifying the important distinction between type and degree of stressful and traumatic war-related experience.

The level of stress or trauma may be determined in part by the children's subjective understanding of the experience and in part by their level of cognitive development. For example, children who believe that they lost a parent "predictably" (for example, the father volunteered to fight in a holy war) are likely to experience his death differently from children who believe they lost a parent unpredictably (for example, to random violence spilling into their community). Similarly, youth who have achieved the cognitive ability to reason logically about abstract concepts (such as justice or nation) may interpret politically motivated violence differently from younger children. While we do not know how individual and developmental differences in appraisal processes—how children appraise stressful events—influence the effect of wartime experiences on children's development, research on children in other types of dangerous situations (for example, abusive or neglectful families) suggests a strong effect. We believe that these appraisal processes can be altered or enhanced through effective program strategies.

Ecologies

The ecologies of children's lives—parents, families, peer groups, schools, religious communities, and other community-based institutions—influence how war-related experiences affect children's developmental outcomes. The nature of their social ecologies prior to their exposure to armed conflict creates important individual differences in the children's developmental processes that in turn influence how war-related experiences affect their outcomes. Parents who are able to maintain a routine of daily caregiving in the face of armed conflict are more likely to buffer their young children against war-related stress and trauma. In turn, the larger family and community network may help or hinder parents' attempts to maintain the quality of care given to young children. Peer groups, families, and communities may influence how war-related experiences affect older children. For example, the sociodramatic play of preadolescents in peer groups may foster identification with older siblings, parents, kin, and neighbors engaged in war or may serve to direct their concerns to the nonviolent protection of families and loved ones.

Developmental Processes

The relation between war-related stress and trauma and subsequent child outcomes may be mediated by powerful developmental processes within the child.

Trust and security. Across a variety of cultures and socioeconomic classes, the predictability and sensitivity of parents' responses to their infants' cues appear to increase children's feelings of security and trust. The security of the early attachment bond predicts children's ability to adapt to future developmental tasks (for example, creating effective social relations with peers and nonparental adults) and psychosocial stressors (for example, separation from a parent).

Young children who have secure attachment relationships prior to their war-related experiences and who are able to remain with their parents or caretakers during war are less likely to develop negative behavioral symptomatology (for example, depression, anxiety, and aggression) than are children who do not have such a secure, trusting relationship and children who have lost the protection of their attachment figures during armed conflict.

Feelings of empowerment and competence. Just as security of attachment may mediate the effects of stress and trauma on the development of young children (infants, toddlers, preschoolers), thoughts and feelings of empowerment and competence may serve the same mediational role for older (school-age and adolescent) children. Children who believe that they can cope competently with stressful events are in fact more likely to cope well. Improved understanding of children's expectations and feelings of empowerment and competence, both prior to and as a result of war, would enhance our ability to predict how war stress and trauma affect children's outcomes.

Differences in attributional styles are also likely to influence how war-related stress and trauma affect outcomes for older children. Research with high-risk children indicates that those who spontaneously attribute the causes of negative events to internal factors ("It's me"), stable factors ("It's going to last forever"), and global factors ("It's going to affect everything I do") are more likely to become depressed in the face of new negative events. Clearly, a depressogenic attributional style may have a powerful effect on a child's ability to cope with stress and trauma. Although to an adult it may seem unimaginable that a child would blame himself or herself for a war-related negative event, some children do.

Identity, meaning, and purpose. As children reach adolescence and are capable of what Piaget refers to as formal operational thinking (the ability to reason logically about highly abstract concepts like personal and social values and future relationships), a whole new set of developmental processes emerges that may mediate the relation between war-related experiences and outcomes. Perhaps the most important process is identity formation. Some observers of youth in areas of armed conflict note that whether or not war negatively affects adolescents depends in part on the meaning the adolescents derive from their role in the conflict. Their ability to project a meaningful future for themselves is powerfully and intimately tied up with their role in the conflict. Despite the complexities of these issues, we believe that research into the emerging national-ethnic-religious identity of adolescents in areas of armed conflict will contribute enormously to a better understanding of how war-related experiences affect developmental outcomes.

Developmental Outcomes

Our decision to focus our studies on psychosocial developmental outcomes reflects our belief that these outcomes are effective predictors of adult functioning and also valuable targets for both rehabilitational and preventive interventions.

Across a variety of theoretical perspectives on childhood psychopathology, two major dimensions of children's problem behaviors have been identified. These are internalizing problems (turning against the self—for example, depression, social withdrawal) and externalizing problems (turning against others—for example, aggression, delinquency). While the frequency and precise organization and expression of internalizing and externalizing problems appear to be age-, gender-, and culture-specific, the basic dimensions themselves appear to have considerable validity across age, gender, and culture value. Because of their theoretical relevance to our framework, we focus on depression and aggression as mental health outcomes.

Recent research suggests that a third basic dimension of child psychopathology might be profitably distinguished from the first two, namely anxiety. Again, in light of its great theoretical and practical ability, it too is included in our studies.

A fourth and final aspect of negative mental health outcomes is the occurrence of post-traumatic stress disorder (PTSD) (see chapter 4). Called shell shock among adult combatants in the world wars, PTSD is now widely recognized as a result of a much broader range of trauma, as well as a characteristic of a broad range of developmental stages, including those of very young children.

In addition to mental health problems in children, war may foster the positive adaptation of children to their environments. Two key dimensions are children's prosocial behavior (for example, helping family members, friends, members of the community) and planful behavior (for example, the ability to regulate the self through time in order to pursue important and difficult goals).

Much less attention has been devoted to the measurement and cross-cultural meaning of these two constructs than to the negative outcomes, reflecting a profound bias toward illness and psychopathology in the current research on the effects of war. We evaluate the positive as well as negative outcomes because for some children, coping with war under supported, protected conditions may actually confer a comparative advantage, although perhaps at considerable personal cost.

Implications for Services

The theoretical framework that informs our research and intervention efforts is diagrammed in figure 12.1. The diagram incorporates two key assumptions of our approach. First, although war-related stress and trauma may directly influence children's psychosocial mental health and adaptational outcomes, we believe it is more likely that the effects of stress and trauma are mediated by the children's ecologies and by certain key developmental processes.

Second, all three major categories of influence—stress-trauma, ecologies, developmental processes—are viable targets for rehabilitation, intervention, and prevention efforts. When it is impossible (owing to the nature of the conflict) or undesirable (because removal from parents is riskier than exposure to war) to design programs and policies to reduce children's exposure to war-related stress and trauma, efforts can be mounted to work with children's ecologies to buffer the children from stress and trauma. Finally, efforts can be designed to enhance those developmental processes thought to protect children from the most serious effects of war.

Case Example: Helping the Children of Kuwait

One year after the liberation of Kuwait from Iraqi occupation we conducted a study in collaboration with a Kuwaiti child-care organization to investigate the effects of the occupation on the psychosocial development of children in Kuwait. The main objectives of the study were to document the atrocities of the occupation and to assist the Kuwaiti ministries of public health and education in the development of appropriate programs for the care of war-affected children.

Research Questions, Method, and Instruments

We were interested in answers to the following major questions:

1. How were Kuwaiti children's war experiences organized during the Iraqi occupation? In order to assess the effects of the war on children's development, it was crucial to first understand the typology of children's experiences during the Iraqi occupation.
2. What was the relation between Kuwaiti children's exposure to war and their psychological symptomatology and psychosocial adaptation? Did

Figure 12.1. Schema of Assessing Impact of War on Children

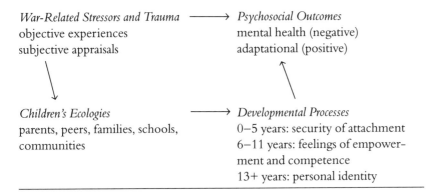

War-Related Stressors and Trauma ⟶ *Psychosocial Outcomes*
objective experiences   mental health (negative)
subjective appraisals   adaptational (positive)

Children's Ecologies ⟶ *Developmental Processes*
parents, peers, families, schools,   0–5 years: security of attachment
communities   6–11 years: feelings of empower-
                                                              ment and competence
                                                              13+ years: personal identity

       certain specific war experiences burden the development of the children while others furthered their coping skills?

3. Does knowledge of Kuwaiti children's social ecologies (for example, family and social network, family cohesion, community support) and developmental processes (for example, national identity) increase our ability to predict the symptomatology and adaptation of these children?

       In order to answer these questions we interviewed a sample of three hundred schoolchildren and their families from all the major geographical regions of Kuwait. The impressive infrastructure of the educational system in Kuwait had remained relatively intact during the war. We therefore decided to use the school system to select our sample and to disseminate our findings. The children we interviewed were selected from twenty governmental schools and were between the ages of eleven and sixteen. All the children had remained in Kuwait during the occupation. We trained several local psychologists and social workers in the administration of the measures and in conducting interviews with children and families. We made sure that the children and their families were well taken care of "clinically" during and after the interviews. In other words, we wanted our information-gathering procedure to be therapeutic as well. Each family was interviewed by a researcher and debriefed about the research interview by a social worker, who asked, "Was there anything upsetting to you in the interview?" and made a follow-up phone call the next week. The family was also given the telephone number of the social worker should they desire further contact.

       We developed or adapted the instruments (see appendix) assessing the constructs we were investigating—war exposure, mental health symptoms (for example, aggression, depression, anxiety, and PTSD), adaptational outcomes, family resources, and national identity—from existing measures and tested them for reliability and validity in several countries. (For a full description of the measures see Macksoud, 1992; Macksoud and Aber, in press; and Macksoud, Nazar, and

Aber, 1994.) In collaboration with our Kuwaiti colleagues, we adapted the instruments to the Kuwaiti context and tested them for cultural sensitivity.

Results

Our research helped us identify the organization of Kuwaiti children's war experiences during the occupation and the complex associations among histories of such experiences, children's social ecologies and developmental processes, and their psychosocial development. We found, for example, that some types of war experiences, such as watching media coverage of the atrocities committed by the Iraqi forces, being exposed to combat, and witnessing the torture of family members, were common occurrences for Kuwaiti children, while others, such as participation in the hostilities, displacement, and separation from parents, were rare occurrences.

The Iraqi occupation had affected the development of Kuwaiti children. Most children were negatively affected by the violence they had witnessed or personally experienced. But some children suffered more than others. Children who had been exposed to a greater number of war events or to specific types of war experiences (for example, witnessing the torture of family members or being detained, abused, or tortured by the Iraqi forces) suffered the most.

Moreover, important ecological and developmental factors mediated the effects of the war on the children's development. A strong family network and support from the community apparently buffered the impact of such war experiences as witnessing violence and participating in the hostilities. But there seemed to be an optimal level of family security. Children who had grown up in a relatively stable and problem-free family environment reacted much more strongly to the violence around them. We found that these children—unlike their peers from high-risk families, who were burdened by emotional and financial problems—were not accustomed to confronting conflict and stress and found themselves overwhelmed by the demands of the war.

Children who reported a strong sense of national identity, characterized by a romantic devotion to the state of Kuwait, also suffered more. On the positive side, the suffering made these children more altruistically inclined, as they became sensitive to the pain of others, condemned injustice, and protected the weak and vulnerable. Emotionally, however, they were left hurt, angry, and depressed. They had to confront their overidealized notion of home as a safe haven loved by all.

Implications for Intervention

There is no doubt in our minds that a follow-up study is needed to explore whether these developmental changes were transient situational adjustments or permanent ones. Also, it remains to be seen whether the Kuwaiti children's initial adjustments to the violence around them, which may be adaptive in the short term, will burden them in their long-term adaptation to a peaceful and non-violent situation in their country. However, the pressing need for action outweighed the importance of continuing research. Our findings offered some suggestions for action.

We saw how Kuwaiti children's war experiences were defined in terms of the number and types of experiences, and how each of these parameters of war exposure affected children. This research finding was used to help shape our intervention. We first targeted children most at risk for severe stress reactions or mental health symptoms—namely, those who had been exposed to a greater number of war events, those who had witnessed the torture of family members or friends, and those who had suffered directly from acts of violence, such as being intimidated, detained, abused, or tortured by the Iraqi forces.

The study also identified certain aspects of the children's ecologies that may have buffered them from the most damaging effects of war. A strong family network and community support during the crisis seem to lessen the impact of some war experiences. In light of the volatile political situation in the Gulf region, preventive efforts were mounted to sensitize Kuwaiti families to the importance of such aspects of family life during a crisis.

Last, our findings suggested that strong nationalistic sentiments had put some Kuwaiti children at risk for severe stress reactions and mental health symptoms following the Iraqi occupation but also had enhanced their adaptive behavior. It became crucial that, in addition to alleviating their immediate mental anguish, we try to prepare Kuwaiti children for the future. Educators were advised to help the children reassess their national identity, encouraging them not to overidealize their national belonging, to be more tolerant of other nationals, and to strengthen their altruistic sentiments. A strong sense of loyalty to the state, combined with a view of themselves as part of a larger world, would better prepare this generation of children for the future.

Psychosocial Programs

Using the insights gained from our study and from focus-group discussions with parents and teachers, we set out to develop two psychosocial programs to help the children of Kuwait.

School program: This program capitalized on the primary mental health care program that had existed in the schools before the war. The main objective of the program was to conduct brief in-service workshops to train school mental health workers (psychologists, social workers, and counselors) on how to intervene with children exhibiting problem behavior and severe stress reactions stemming from the war, and how to counsel teachers and parents in the care of their war-affected children at home and at school.

A "pyramid" procedure was used, whereby we trained a core group of mental health workers; they in turn trained a larger group who trained teachers and parents. The information used during the workshops was extracted from our findings and from a manual we compiled on helping children cope with the stresses of war (see Macksoud, 1993).

Media program: The media in Kuwait are a powerful tool in education and in shaping public opinion. Most families have easy access to daily newspapers, radio talk shows, and television programs. The goal of the media program we mounted was to empower Kuwaiti families by providing them with scientific information on how the occupation affected their children's development and by offering them guidelines on how to intervene with their children.

The first phase of the media program was aimed at shaping public opinion on the importance of attending to children's psychosocial needs after the war. In collaboration with our local colleagues, we prepared press releases and television and radio broadcasts to sensitize adults to children's postwar behaviors. In the second phase of the media program we produced television spots and radio broadcasts targeting parents and caretakers to educate them on how to manage their children's postwar problem behaviors in the home. The scripts for the television and radio educational programs reported our findings on the effects of violence on children's development and illustrated a right way and a wrong way to deal with specific problem behaviors exhibited by children following stressful experiences. In addition, each individual program included a short commentary from a local psychologist or social worker informing parents of the underlying causes of problem behaviors and of ways to handle these behaviors. The series ran for several months on local Kuwaiti television and radio stations.

Conclusion

It is clear that policy recommendations and psychosocial programs based on sound research methodology, sensitivity to local cultures, and the use of local resources are far more responsive and cost-effective than those which are rapidly constructed in response to a particular emergency. The psychosocial framework that we have developed can help identify the tools necessary to conduct culturally sensitive and valid studies on the effects of war on children, leading to the implementation of practical efforts on their behalf. This approach also offers the opportunity for collaborative action-research with local professionals in order to adapt the studies to the needs and priorities of those affected by each armed conflict.

REFERENCES

Macksoud, M. 1992. Assessing war trauma in children: A case study of Lebanese children. *Journal of Refugee Studies* 5(1):1–15.
——. 1993. *Helping children cope with the stresses of war: A manual for parents and teachers.* New York: UNICEF.

Macksoud, M., and Aber, J. L. In press. The war experiences and psychosocial development of children in Lebanon. *Child Development.*

Macksoud, M., Dyregrov, A., and Raundalen, M. 1993. Traumatic war experiences and their effects on children. In J. P. Wilson and B. Raphael, eds., *International handbook of traumatic stress syndromes.* New York: Plenum.

Macksoud, M., Nazar, F., and Aber, J. L. 1994. *The impact of the Iraqi occupation on the psychosocial development of children in Kuwait.* Washington, D.C.: Center for Contemporary Arab Studies, Georgetown University.

Appendix: Child Behavior Inventory From Kuwait Study

The CBI was adapted from a variety of widely used child behavioral scales. It was designed to assess children's behavioral symptoms in five domains: aggression, depression, anxiety, prosocial behavior, and playful behavior. Each domain is represented by a set of questions (or scale) about the child's behavior at the time, or six months prior to the assessment. The CBI exists in two versions: CBI-A and CBI-C. CBI-A is designed to be administered to parents or caretakers of children between the ages of five and sixteen, while CBI-C is designed to be administered directly to children between the ages of ten and sixteen. Both CBI-A and CBI-C can be administered either as a questionnaire or as a semi-structured interview. We strongly recommend the interview format, especially with children.

Questions	Answers				
	Don't Know 9	Never 0	Rarely 1	Sometimes 2	Always 3
1. Do you cry easily?	____	____	____	____	____
2. Do you get angry easily?	____	____	____	____	____
3. Are you jumpy?	____	____	____	____	____
4. Are you helpful to other children?	____	____	____	____	____
5. Do you take the lead in initiating activities?	____	____	____	____	____
6. Do you feel sad or unhappy?	____	____	____	____	____
7. Do you get easily irritable?	____	____	____	____	____

8. Are you frightened that something bad will happen to you? ____ ____ ____ ____ ____

9. Are you helpful to adults? ____ ____ ____ ____ ____

10. Do you plan and think ahead? ____ ____ ____ ____ ____

11. Do you worry about many things? ____ ____ ____ ____ ____

12. Are you verbally aggressive? ____ ____ ____ ____ ____

13. Are you scared of things or situations that don't usually scare other children? ____ ____ ____ ____ ____

14. Do you show care and concern for others? ____ ____ ____ ____ ____

15. Are you good at finding solutions to problems? ____ ____ ____ ____ ____

16. Do you feel unloved? ____ ____ ____ ____ ____

17. Are you physically aggressive to others? ____ ____ ____ ____ ____

18. Are you scared of new situations? ____ ____ ____ ____ ____

19. Do you feel sad or feel like crying when other people are suffering? ____ ____ ____ ____ ____

20. Are you sure of yourself in many situations? ____ ____ ____ ____ ____

21. Are you afraid of losing your family members through death or separation? ____ ____ ____ ____ ____

22. Do you destroy your own or other people's things? ____ ____ ____ ____ ____

23. Is it hard for you to concentrate on your schoolwork? ____ ____ ____ ____ ____

24. Do you try to comfort ____ ____ ____ ____ ____

and support others
who are suffering?

25. Do you keep on try- ⎯⎯ ⎯⎯ ⎯⎯ ⎯⎯ ⎯⎯
    ing when you face
    problems?

26. Do you feel tired? ⎯⎯ ⎯⎯ ⎯⎯ ⎯⎯ ⎯⎯

27. Do you disobey your ⎯⎯ ⎯⎯ ⎯⎯ ⎯⎯ ⎯⎯
    parents or teachers?

28. Is it necessary for you ⎯⎯ ⎯⎯ ⎯⎯ ⎯⎯ ⎯⎯
    to be with an older
    person to feel safe and
    secure?

29. Do you become upset ⎯⎯ ⎯⎯ ⎯⎯ ⎯⎯ ⎯⎯
    when injustice is com-
    mitted toward others?

30. Do you feel okay soon ⎯⎯ ⎯⎯ ⎯⎯ ⎯⎯ ⎯⎯
    after a stressful event?

31. Do you prefer being ⎯⎯ ⎯⎯ ⎯⎯ ⎯⎯ ⎯⎯
    alone rather than
    around friends or fam-
    ily?

32. Are you hot-tempered ⎯⎯ ⎯⎯ ⎯⎯ ⎯⎯ ⎯⎯
    or explosive?

33. Do you share things ⎯⎯ ⎯⎯ ⎯⎯ ⎯⎯ ⎯⎯
    (food, clothes, toys)
    with others?

34. Are you optimistic ⎯⎯ ⎯⎯ ⎯⎯ ⎯⎯ ⎯⎯
    about the future?

35. Do you feel lonely? ⎯⎯ ⎯⎯ ⎯⎯ ⎯⎯ ⎯⎯

36. Do you violate the ⎯⎯ ⎯⎯ ⎯⎯ ⎯⎯ ⎯⎯
    important rules of
    your community?

37. Do you help back or ⎯⎯ ⎯⎯ ⎯⎯ ⎯⎯ ⎯⎯
    are you friendly to
    people who have
    helped you or been
    friendly to you?

38. Do you stay calm un- ⎯⎯ ⎯⎯ ⎯⎯ ⎯⎯ ⎯⎯
    der stress?

39. Do you feel worthless? ⎯⎯ ⎯⎯ ⎯⎯ ⎯⎯ ⎯⎯

40. Do you blame others ⎯⎯ ⎯⎯ ⎯⎯ ⎯⎯ ⎯⎯
    for things that are your
    own fault?

41. Are you protective to-
    ward younger chil-
    dren?   _____   _____   _____   _____   _____

42. Do you feel helpless?   _____   _____   _____   _____   _____

43. Are you interested in   _____   _____   _____   _____   _____
    understanding the po-
    litical causes of war?

Contributors

J. Lawrence Aber, Ph.D.

J. Lawrence Aber is an associate professor of psychology and public health and the director of the National Center for Children in Poverty at Columbia University School of Public Health. At Columbia Aber has conducted both basic and applied research studies relevant to child and family policy. His basic research focuses on the social, emotional, behavioral, and cognitive development of children and youth at risk because of family and neighborhood poverty, exposure to violence, abuse and neglect, and parental psychopathology. His applied research focuses on rigorous process and outcome evaluations of innovative programs, comprehensive service programs, and violence prevention programs. He is the recipient of several awards for research on child and family development from national foundations.

Roberta J. Apfel, M.D., M.P.H.

Roberta J. Apfel is an associate clinical professor of psychiatry at the Cambridge Hospital, Harvard Medical School, and a member of the faculty at the Boston Psychoanalytic Institute. As codirector of the Children in War Project with Bennett Simon, she is conducting a longitudinal study of Israeli and Palestinian children. She is interested in studying the long-term effects of trauma and is coauthor of *To Do No Harm: DES and the Dilemmas of Modern Medicine* (Yale University Press, 1984) and *Madness and Loss of Motherhood: Sexuality, Reproduction, and Long-Term Mental Illness* (American Psychiatric Press, 1993). She is a practicing psychiatrist and psychoanalyst. She also works clinically with families with AIDS sufferers, and she is a contributor to Shelley Geballe, Janice Gruendel, and Warren Andiman, *Forgotten Children of the AIDS Epidemic* (Yale University Press, 1995).

William Arroyo, M.D.

William Arroyo is a clinical assistant professor of psychiatry and behavioral sciences in the Division of Child and Adolescent Psychiatry at the University of Southern California. He also serves as director of the Child / Adolescent Psychiatric Clinic at Los Angeles County–University of Southern California Medical Center. He has published in the areas of psychological trauma, refugee children, and mental health issues related to culture. He served as an adviser to the DSM IV Task Force. He has worked extensively with Central American refugees in the Los Angeles area. He volunteers on the staff of the Psychological Trauma Center, a nonprofit agency that provides services to schools whose students are affected by traumatic events. He has received awards for his work with refugees and earthquake victims.

Dan Bar-On, Ph.D.

Dan Bar-On is professor of psychology in the department of behavioral sciences at Ben-Gurion University of the Negev, Beer-Sheva, Israel. For the past decade he has been researching and writing about the descendants of Holocaust survivors and the descendants of Nazis. He is also involved in studies of psychosocial aspects of the Arab-Israeli conflict and possibilities of conflict resolution. His publications include *Legacy of Silence: Encounters with Children of the Third Reich* (1989) and *Fear and Hope: Three Generations of Holocaust Survivors' Families* (1995), both published by Harvard University Press.

Miriam Berkman, J.D., M.S.W.

Miriam Berkman is an assistant clinical professor in social work and is clinical coordinator of the Child Development–Community Policing Program at the Yale Child Study Center, Yale University School of Medicine. She is a contributor to Steven Marans et al., *The Police–Mental Health Partnership: A Community-Based Response to Urban Violence* (Yale University Press, 1995).

Neil Boothby, Ph.D.

Neil Boothby is professor of psychology at the Terry Sanford Institute of Public Policy Studies, Duke University, and director of the Hart Leadership Program. He has worked closely with Save the Children. Boothby cowrote, with Everett M. Ressler and Daniel J. Steinbock, *Unaccompanied Children* (Oxford University Press, 1988), and has worked in Cambodia, Mozambique, and Rwanda.

Donald Cohen, M.D.

Donald J. Cohen is the Irving Harris Professor of Child Psychiatry, Pediatrics, and Psychology and is director of the Child Study Center at Yale University School of Medicine. Cohen's research has focused on biological and psychological studies of children with serious neuropsychiatric disorders and on the interface between basic and clinical research and the shaping of social policy. He is president of the International Association of Child and Adolescent Psychiatry and Allied Professions, is a member of the Institute of Medicine of the National Academy of Sciences, and is a training and supervising psychoanalyst at the Western New England Institute for Psychoanalysis. He served on the National Commission on Children. His recent publications include *Developmental Psychopathology* (Wiley, 1995), with Dante Cichetti, and *Autism and Pervasive Developmental Disorder* (Wiley, 1996) with Fred Volkmar.

Ilene Cohn, J.D., M.A.

Ilene Cohn is an international human rights lawyer who was research director of the Project on Children and War at the Center for the Study of Human Rights, Columbia University, from 1988 until 1994. She is coauthor of *Child Soldiers: The Role of Children in Armed Conflicts* (Oxford University Press, 1994) and has published on children's rights in armed conflict situations. She has conducted field research on children's advocacy, child soldiers, unaccompanied and refugee children in Liberia, Mozambique, Malawi, Israel and the occupied territories, Sri Lanka, Croatia, El Salvador, Guatemala, and Brazil. She is a legal / human rights officer with the U.N. Human Rights Verification Mission in Guatemala.

Yael Danieli, Ph.D.

Yael Danieli is a clinical psychologist and traumatologist in private practice in New York City. She is cofounder and director of the Group Project for Holocaust Survivors and their Children, and is director of psychological services at the Center for Rehabilitation of Torture Victims. She is adjunct associate professor of medicine at Seton Hall University Graduate School of Medical Education. She also served as senior representative to the United Nations for the World Federation for Mental Health and chaired its Scientific Committee on the Mental Health Needs of Victims. She is consultant to the U.N. Crime Prevention and Criminal Justice Branch, the U.N. Centre for Human Rights, UNICEF, the U.S. National Institute of Mental Health, the Federal Bureau of Investigation, the Associated Press, and CNN. She cofounded the International Society for Traumatic Stress Studies, served as its president, and has remained its representative to the United Nations. She recently coedited *International Responses to Traumatic Stress,* published for the United Nations.

Spencer Eth, M.D.

Spencer Eth is a psychiatrist, child psychiatrist, and forensic psychiatrist based at the West Los Angeles VA Medical Center. He is an associate professor of clinical psychiatry at the University of California, Los Angeles, and the University of Southern California. He has written extensively on the reactions of children to interpersonal violence, and he has conducted funded research on innovative strategies for the treatment of combat-related post-traumatic stress disorder.

James Garbarino, Ph.D.

James Garbarino is the director of the Family Life Development Center and a professor of human development and family studies at Cornell University. His most recent books include *Raising Children in a Seriously Toxic Environment* (Jossey-Bass, 1995) and *Children in Danger* (Jossey-Bass, 1992). He is directing a study evaluating the effects of a violence prevention program aimed at children ("Let's Talk About Living in a World with Violence") and has served as an expert witness in youth violence cases and as a consultant for international programs dealing with children in war zones.

Michael B. Greene, Ph.D.

Michael B. Greene, a developmental psychologist, is the director of research and evaluation at the Hunter College Center on AIDS, Drugs, and Community Health and is adjunct assistant professor of public health at New York University. He served for more than ten years as the juvenile justice administrator in the New York City Mayor's Office, where he helped pioneer innovative programs for adolescent offenders and for youths exposed to chronic violence. He has lectured and consulted widely on the causes of youth violence and effective programmatic responses.

Peter S. Jensen, M.D.

Peter S. Jensen is chief of the Child and Adolescent Disorders Research Branch, National Institute of Mental Health. Recently he has turned his attention to problems of conducting systematic research on the impact of violence and armed conflict on children.

Kathleen Kostelny, Ph.D.

Kathleen Kostelny is senior research associate at the Erikson Institute for Advanced Study in Child Development, where she is director of the Project on Children and Violence. Her research on the psychological and developmental effects of violence on children has taken her to Cambodia, Mozambique, Nicaragua, Northern Ireland, and the West Bank and Gaza Strip, as well as to communities in the United States. She is coauthor (with James Garbarino) of *No Place To Be a Child: Growing up in a War Zone* (Free Press, 1991) and *Children in Danger: Coping with the Consequences of Community Violence* (Jossey-Bass, 1993).

Mona S. Macksoud, Ph.D.

Mona S. Macksoud is on the faculty of the School of Social Work at Columbia University and has a private clinical psychology practice. She has done extensive research on children and war in Africa, Central America, and the Middle East and has made a documentary film based on interviews with children in Lebanon, *Childhood Lost*.

Steven Marans, Ph.D.

Steven Marans is the Harris Assistant Professor of Child Psychoanalysis at the Child Study Center, Yale University School of Medicine, and is the coordinator of the Child Development–Community Policing Program, a collaborative effort of the Child Study Center and the New Haven Department of Police Service designed to address the needs of victims, witnesses, and perpetrators of community violence. He is an advanced candidate at the Western New England Institute of Psychoanalysis and is author of *The Police–Mental Health Partnership: A Community-Based Response to Urban Violence* (Yale University Press, 1995).

Bennett Simon, M.D.

Bennett Simon is clinical professor of psychiatry at the Cambridge Hospital, Harvard Medical School, and training and supervising analyst at the Boston Psychoanalytic Society and Institute. He was Sigmund Freud Professor of Psychoanalysis at the Hebrew University in Jerusalem (1989 – 1990), where he conducted, with Roberta Apfel, an international conference on children in war. With Roberta Apfel he has been following groups of Israeli and Palestinian children since the Persian Gulf War. He has supervised in the Victims of Violence Program at the Cambridge Hospital and is part of the Community Crisis Response Team.

Gillian Straker, Ph.D.

Gillian Straker is chair of and professor in the applied psychology department at the University of Witwatersrand, Johannesburg. She serves as the director of Clinical Training and Community Projects as well as coordinator for survivors of political repression. She is also a member of the board of directors of the European Association for Integrative Psychotherapy.

Karen Wahmanholm, M.D.

Karen Wahmanholm is an assistant professor of psychiatry at the University of Minnesota School of Medicine, and staff psychiatrist at the Minneapolis VA Medical Center. She has worked with refugee patients who have experienced combat or sexual trauma.

Joseph Westermeyer, M.D.

Joseph Westermeyer is professor and vice-chair of psychiatry and adjunct professor of anthropology at the University of Minnesota, Minneapolis, and chief of psychiatry at the Minneapolis VA Medical Center. He is adviser to the Mental Health Division, World Health Organization, and author of *Migration Psychiatry* (American Psychiatric Press, 1989) and numerous articles on adjustment and psychiatric disorders among refugees.

Index